CONTROLLING COLOURS

Function and Meaning of Colour in the British Iron Age

Marlies Hoecherl

ARCHAEOPRESS ARCHAEOLOGY

Archaeopress Publishing Ltd
Gordon House
276 Banbury Road
Oxford OX2 7ED

www.archaeopress.com

ISBN 978 1 78491 225 3
ISBN 978 1 78491 226 0 (e-Pdf)

© Archaeopress and M Hoecherl 2015

Cover illustration: Roos Carr Figurines. Photograph Ray Fuge
© Hull and East Riding Museum: Hull Museums

Printed in England by Oxuniprint, Oxford
This book is available direct from Archaeopress or from our website www.archaeopress.com

Contents

List of Figures

Acknowledgements

This book started life some years ago as a part time PhD Research with University of Cardiff. Combining archaeological research with my day job as a corporate lawyer is fraught with difficulty, and that I finally managed to publish it is largely due to the unfailing encouragement of Miranda Aldhouse-Green, an inspiring supervisor and friend, Ray Howells who made me change my mind and last but not least my Greek teacher Gustav Kramer who insists that he had nothing to do with it - I beg to differ.

I am grateful to numerous people for their help and support. In particular I would like to thank Adam Gwilt, Paula Gentil, Peter Northover, Melanie Giles, Alison Brookes, Paul Nicholson and Mary Davis for their time and valuable comments, Iain Calderwood and Beatriz Waters from the British Museum, Helen Burbage and Jenny Durant from Royal Albert Memorial Museum in Exeter, Maggie Wilson from National Museums Scotland, Nikki Braunton from Museum of London, Caroline Rhodes from Hull Museum, Bryan Williams from Dover Museum, Tim Pestell from Norwich Castle Museum and Art Gallery for their help with pictures and copyright, John Dobson and Simon Fineman of Timbmet for supplying me with wood, Ben Fergus-Grey for valuable insights into the effects of natural narcotics, Thomas Morawetz and Bernd Hertling for their continued interest in what I am up to, David Seligman and Duncan Macintosh for reading all of it, Dennis Kwong Thye Lee for the Lotus and above all my husband Ray Fuge for traipsing round museums and sites with me and taking great pictures.

Chapter 1

Introduction

'Colour is my day-long obsession, joy and torment'
(Claude Monet)

Some years ago I was told the true story of a little boy who asked his grandfather what the world was like 'when granddad was young and everything was black and white'. Having seen old black and white photographs of his grandparents, he assumed that colour did not exist when they were young.

This story made me realize that we perceive archaeological material in a similar way. We are so used to seeing monochrome photographs of artefacts that colour photographs come as a surprise. Even though colour photographs and illustrations in books have recently become more affordable due to advanced technology, a great number of archaeological publications still display black and white photography and illustrations. However, technology and the cost constraints of publishing houses are not the only reason why we have become conditioned to readily accept a monochrome view of archaeological material.

The hugely influential 18th century founder of German modern archaeology Johann Joachim Winckelmann saw beauty and aesthetics first and foremost in the line, form and harmony of an object. His obsession with '*edle Einfalt und stille Groesse*' (Winckelmann 1925: 81) led to a disregard of colour in favour of form which continues to this day. He would probably have been appalled to see the reconstruction of original paintings on Greek statues (Brinkmann and Wuensche 2004), since they display very little of the stillness and simplicity he was so fond of. The early and middle 19th century regarded bold colours as frivolous, feminine and unfashionable (Goethe 1840: 55, 329-330) and as a result colour is even now regarded as a side issue, although more recently it has become the focus of a number of studies in antiquity and prehistory (Cleland 2004: v). The importance of colour should not be underestimated. Our perception of the material world is shaped not only through form, but also through colour, and to examine one without at least having regard to the other may lead to a biased and perhaps even incorrect interpretation, as exemplified by Greek sculpture (Brinkmann and Wuensche 2004).

Aims and objectives

The aim of this work is to examine the function and meaning of colour in the context of the British Iron Age and to emphasise the importance of colour in the evaluation of archaeological data. I have concentrated my research on well documented material objects, such as metal weapons and horse gear, grave goods made out of metal, amber, glass or enamel, artefacts made out of stone such as chalk, and metal objects decorated with coral and enamel. I have not only examined the colours of the artefacts per se, but also colour associations suggested by the objects' biography, usage and contexts, in order to gain a better understanding of colour perception in Iron Age Britain, and to explore whether the deliberate use of certain colours may have had symbolic meaning. It is suggested that this will contribute to our insight into belief systems and social relationships within the context of the British Iron Age. I have given particular emphasis to the following objectives:

Stability and Transformation

The symbolic value of the consistent nature of certain colours, and underlying materials in contrast to materials whose biographies demonstrate colour changes, whether by manipulation or natural processes, have been examined within the context of origin, production and decoration of metal objects.

Light and Brilliance

I have explored the importance of light and brilliance in the context of materials such as metal and wood, and the manipulation of objects to enhance luminosity, e.g. polishing or simulating brilliance by using certain decorative patterns. My aim was to ascertain if such manipulation was used as a communicative tool or agent to express social relationships, but also to explore the metaphysical and symbolic aspects of such treatments.

Contrasting Colours, Colour patterns, Colour in Landscape

I have examined recurring colour patterns and contrasts within the material object per se, as well as the contrast between the object and its topographical, biographical and functional contexts including colours alluded to by, or related to, iconography. Linked to this I have also explored shamanic rituals and journeys, colour perception under the influence of hallucinogenic drugs and empirical evidence of colour perception of shamans during their rituals in order to strengthen the argument that Iron Age belief systems had shamanic elements.

Death, Life and Gender

I have studied the association of bodies and certain coloured objects with life, death, or life after death and the changes in colour occasioned by transference from a life to a death situation and beyond. In this context I have not only looked at the fluidity of boundaries between life and death, between this world and the Otherworld and various stages in between, but also preservation of life or giving life to material objects, and in particular associations of colour with bodily fluids. I have re-assessed gender specific materials in order to ascertain if certain colours echo such categorisation.

Body Decoration

I have concluded the research with a fresh assessment of evidence for body decoration, both in terms of materials and colours used and the reason for such decoration.

Methodology

In order to achieve the aims and objectives set out above I have used the following methodology:

Theoretical Aspects of Colour

It would not be appropriate to investigate colour in the context of Iron Age Britain without illustrating the limitations and inapplicability of our own colour perception and giving an insight into alternative colour perceptions, based both on archaeological research from other periods and ethnographical or anthropological sources. I have carried out a survey of research into colour and colour perception from the fields of psychology, philosophy, anthropology and colour theory, as well as recent theory on semantics, in order to provide the theoretical background required to attempt an interpretation of prehistoric colour perception.

Examination of Material Evidence and Collation of Data

I have re-examined well documented objects and sites of the British Iron Age in terms of their colour and colour associations, taking into account the context of their biography, location and use. The main sites, objects and human remains discussed are listed in Appendices 1, 2 and 3. As the symbolic meaning of certain colours may not be generic but circumstantial, each object or site has been treated on its own merits and where appropriate within its specific context.

Written Sources

I have examined colour symbolism in Classical Greek, Latin and early Irish and Welsh written sources which may assist in the interpretation of archaeological material or which hint at symbolic value of colours or colour perception.

Anthropological and Ethnological Comparisons

Colour symbolism has been the subject of various anthropological and ethnological studies. Apart from a critical assessment of some of these colour theories which claim to be universally applicable, I have also examined approaches to colour and colour symbolism in a variety of culture groups and used them as comparators. Of course such comparators can only ever be suggestive rather than conclusive, but nevertheless assist in understanding thought processes which may be of relevance. Cultures can be regarded as structural variants of each other especially if they share the same origin or cultural tradition. Even though is has been argued that analogies with more remote cultures are less powerful as they do not share ideological values (Diepeveen-Jansen 2001: 30), certain values and ideas transcended humanity and are universally applicable.

Experimental Archaeology

I have used the evidence gained from experimental archaeology especially in the field of metal working. I also carried out a certain number of experiments with different materials. Whilst replication experiments can never determine conclusively every detail of how something was made, they can provide insight into technology and are often the only basis of inference about prehistoric technologies. Even though they can only simulate activities of a past agent and not the past social agency (Brysbaert 2004: 13), together with contextualisation of the activities they prove a useful tool.

Difficulties with Methodology

As there are currently no comprehensive studies into the subject of colour in an Iron Age context, I have decided to use a wide approach and look at geographically and temporally diverse objects within Iron Age Britain, rather than concentrate on one particular area, site, or isolated aspect. I accept that this approach has certain flaws. Colour is a part of or applied to material objects and the study of colour is therefore the study of everything material, which would be a far too wide approach for the purposes of this research. I have therefore deliberately excluded detailed colour analysis of certain materials, such as pottery. The corpus of pottery from the British Iron Age is so vast that only a separate study of colour implications of pottery would do it justice. In addition, it is also as simplistic and incorrect to look at the whole of Britain as one homogenous region as it is to impose modern territorial descriptions such as Welsh Iron Age or Scottish Iron Age (Bevan 1999a: 14). It is similarly problematic to look at the whole period classified as Iron Age. Not only is the classification a modern concept (Wells 2001:35) which implies a definite differentiation from the Bronze Age and the Romano British period without allowing for overlaps or fluid transitions, but even within this classification the differences between the archaeology of the earlier and later Iron Age suggest changes in social constructs, belief systems and perceptions throughout the period.

I have refrained from relying too much on statistics in evaluating archaeological data. Statistics have only limited value because they usually lack individual context which in my view frequently provides answers, clues or at least suggestions which are instrumental in our understanding and interpretation of material artefacts. I have therefore opted for an exploration of themes on the basis of individual but well documented finds or sites. The use of individual case studies, as opposed to a survey, adds to difficulty, as the results of an analysis of an individual case study may not be universally applicable (Diinhoff 1997: 115). Certain objects and sites undoubtedly merit further and more detailed individual analysis than has been possible for the purposes of this research, but, as Bevan (1999a: 15) suggested, whilst only in-depth analysis and evaluation of parts will give meaningful insight, those parts must be seen as part of a whole. Despite the diversity displayed in British Iron Age artefacts, there are common themes which I have sought to identify and which, I hope, present a basis for further studies.

Contextual archaeology, to use the term introduced by Ian Hodder (1982: 217), has its own limitations. Certain conclusions can be drawn by merely examining a particular way in which material evidence is assembled in its context, but despite it being perhaps the most scientific and least subjective and interpretative approach to the subject of colours and their symbolic meaning we have to bear in mind that even contextualisation is a cultural construction. We superimpose our own context on 'how things are made' and it is incorrect to believe that meaning always follows context. However, whilst context may not necessarily reveal meaning, probing into contextual circumstances can expand our ideas as to what we mean by the concept of context. A contextual approach as opposed to formalistic assessment can widen the interpretative scope, as has been demonstrated by contextual approaches to prehistoric rock art (Conckey 1997: 361–362). However, care must be taken not to impose preconceived general rules for possible meaning or intent (Marshack 1981: 190–191). The use of red ochre in Palaeolithic and Mesolithic contexts for example, could have had symbolic value or it could have been a ritual body decoration to mark rank, status, age or sex. It could even have been both, as one does not necessarily preclude the other. On the other hand ochre was at that time already a deeply rooted symbolic

construct, but it seems to have attained different meanings and significance for the culture groups who used it in a variety of circumstances (Hovers *et al.* 2003: 510). Hodder (1989a: 69) likens the process of interpreting context to interpreting writing. Interpretation of the written text itself is meaningless if it is taken outside its reading.

In order to assess possible symbolic meaning, it is therefore necessary to go beyond mere contextualisation and observation. By using a hermeneutic or 'emic'[1] approach, and by interpreting material evidence and its contextual associations with the help of colour psychology, anthropology, literary as well as linguistic sources, and interpretation of art in its widest sense (which has been largely ignored by post-processual archaeologists (Haselgrove and Moore 2007: 3)), we might not obtain definite answers or conclusions beyond doubt, but at least suggestions, which in turn may allow us to look at archaeological evidence from a new perspective and ask new questions (Melas 1989: 139, 153; Symonds 1999: 114–115).

Each of these methods of interpretation has of course its own flaws and I just want to briefly outline some of them. Firstly, we cannot presume that the available archaeological evidence for the Iron Age period in Britain is representative. Not only are we faced with a deficiency of preserved organic material, but even inorganic objects are likely to be selective. In addition, many objects lack context and archaeological site reports often ignore any colour or colour association.

In terms of written evidence, we do have very few primary written sources dealing with the British Iron Age. The few which exist may be biased, temporally remote or based on hearsay and their reliability is therefore questionable. It is doubtful if any classical sources concerning the Gauls can be used as evidence for the British Iron Age. In addition, translation often offers interpretation which in itself may already be biased. Early Welsh and Irish vernacular literature is temporally so far remote that any attempt to use it as evidence for prehistoric times can only be suggestive rather than conclusive, although it contains many references to pre-Christian mythology and paganism (Green 1993: 10; Green 1999: 54).

Using anthropological or ethnological analogies can lead to an interpretation which is based on the observer's or the other culture group's paradigms (Bruner 1993: 3).[2]

---

[1] The terms 'emic' and 'etic' are used in linguistics and have been applied by Melas (1989: 139) to anthropological study. Etic approach is to acquire knowledge through observation whereas emic approach means determination within a style of reasoning or insight. The emic approach is external rather than internal and empathy and implication are prevalent in this approach.

[2] Anthropologists tend to compare culture groups by reference to the closeness or strangeness to their own cultural background. The

Symbolic classifications can be manifold (Turner 1969: 41) and material culture can only be really understood within the implications of particular social practices (Barrett 1990: 179). As Joanna Brueck (1999: 327) argued, the assumption of practices being governed by universal laws of behaviour must be questioned and familiarity does not necessarily allow explanation.

Conclusion

In the light of the issues and problems outlined above, it would be easy to be defeatist, but in the words of Goethe:

'It is useless to attempt to express the nature of a thing abstractedly. Effects we can perceive, and a complete history of those effects would, in fact, sufficiently define the nature of the thing itself. We should try in vain to describe a man's character, but let his acts be collected and an idea of the character will be presented to us' (Goethe 1840: xxxvii).

Adopting the approach outlined above can be likened to one of the mirror balls which used to hang from the ceilings in every 1970s discotheque. Each part of this study is a little shiny facet which provides a limited and isolated glimpse at the function and meaning of colour. But all the facets looked at together might just provide sufficient material to see the outline of a shape.

anthropologist Spiro argued that cultures, which can be explained and interpreted by reference to our own cannot be that strange. If they cannot be explained, then either their culture is strange or, if we believe contemporary anthropology, our own world is strange (Spiro 1990: 59).

Chapter 2

Literature Review

The systematic study of colour is a relatively new concept within the context of archaeology and prehistory. Although there have been recent attempts to interpret colours on material objects, these have been focused mainly on the Stone Age and Bronze Age periods. Due to the technological advancement during the Iron Age, its material objects present us with a greater variety of colours and hues than earlier periods, yet colour and especially its symbolic importance have so far been largely ignored in Iron Age archaeology, although some attempts of interpretation have been made in the fields of anthropology, folklore and linguistics.

Archaeology

A number of scholars have examined the composition and crafting of certain materials from the Iron Age and discussed the resulting colours and colour contrasts, such as Mansel Spratling (1972), in respect of bronze and coloured enamel, Barber (1991) and Banck-Burgess (1999) in respect of fabrics and dyes of the Hallstatt period, Cunliffe (1979) and Moscati (1991) on polymaterialism, Dungworth (1997) in relation to copper, Guido (1978) in respect of glass beads, Champion (1995) in respect of jewellery or Miles *et al.* (2003) in respect of the white horse of Uffington. However, these studies contained no significant attempts at a symbolic interpretation of colour other than fairly cursory assumptions such as the possible apotropaic connotations of the colour red (Champion 1995: 415).

More recent trends to explore archaeological objects not just per se, but within the wider contexts of inter alia interaction within landscape and social relationships, biographies of objects, synaesthetics and the interaction between materiality and meaning, have occasionally led to the subject of colour as signifier. Miranda Aldhouse-Green discussed the dichromatic cosmology presented by Lucan's description of a sacred grove near Marseille, the colour transformation of organic material such as wood caused by decay, the enhancement of the colour of wood by carving or polishing, and the symbolism attached to such transformation (Aldhouse-Green 2004: 9-11, Aldhouse-Green 2004a: 87-107). She also briefly touched on the possible symbolism of colour transformation of metal in the process of iron or bronze working (Aldhouse-Green 2004a, 107-112) as a further aspect of the wider symbolism of ironworking which has been discussed inter alia by Hingley (1997). John Creighton (2000: 38-40) presented the fascinating theory that the yellow colour in Iron Age coins was more important than the value of the metal content on the basis that the yellow colour seems to have been preserved, whilst the gold content in the alloys used for coinage fluctuated.

In 2001 a working party of eminent Iron Age archaeologists set out in their agenda for 21st century Iron Age research that decoration and colour along with other headings, such as identity, food and feasting, rubbish deposition etc., should form part of a holistic and contextual exploration of archaeological material (Champion et al. 2001). Since then colour has started to feature in a number of publications on British Iron Age artefacts. Fitzpatrick discussed the red decoration on Iron Age shields and swords, associating it with aggression (Fitzpatrick 2007: 344-345), Giles examined the agency of Iron Age decorative art and likened the red decoration on metalwork to symbolic bodily fluids (Giles 2008: 72-74), and Gwilt and Davis looked at the alloy composition and decoration of the Severn Sisters hoards, taking into account not only the technical composition, but also briefly touched on the symbolism of red decoration as possibly masculine and the potential shift of meaning by the usage of brass instead of bronze (Davis and Gwilt 2008: 159-161).

More detailed studies have been carried out, as mentioned above, in respect of earlier periods, and whilst it cannot be readily assumed that any symbolic connotations of colours made the transition from earlier periods into the Iron Age, they still require examination in relation to a possible application to later periods. It would not be appropriate for this paper to cover the entire discussion of colour symbolism in respect of earlier periods and I will therefore outline just some of the recent theories.

One recurring theme appears to be the symbolism of red, black and white as bodily fluids. The use of ochre in funerary rites as a signifier of blood can be found in the Palaeolithic, the Mesolithic and the Neolithic periods throughout Europe (Jones and McGregor 2002; Boriç 2002). Andrew Jones also suggested that the use of coloured stones in Scottish Neolithic tombs relates to such body symbolism (Jones 1999). However, this approach is not without flaws as will be discussed below.

The interrelation between stone colour, light and seasonality and associated cosmological symbolism has been highlighted in relation to Irish passage graves, the Clava Cairns and the Recumbent Stone Circles of Aberdeenshire (Jones and McGregor 2002). Whilst stone circles and passage graves are of course features of earlier periods, the concept of colour and seasonality should not be ignored in the Iron Age. Similarly, some suggestions and hypotheses, whilst argued from the perspective of the Bronze Age, may still be valuable in assessing colour symbolism in the Iron Age. Examples are Andrew Jones' suggestions that objects made from materials such as jet or amber and their respective colours are landscape specific (Jones 2002: 163), that the colour of amber and gold must not be neglected, even though these materials are generally interpreted as valuable because they are exotic (Jones 2002: 159), and that the colour of material may not be as important as the social relations mediated by it (Jones 2002: 166). Stephen Keates explored the red colour and luminosity of copper in copper age artefacts, and suggested connotations of liminality, embodying power, heat and fertility and Otherworldly presence (Keates 2002: 117). He suggested that copper played an important role in developing the 'the leitmotif of luminosity as a signifier of Otherworldly presences which was to have an enduring significance in European Prehistory' (Keates 2002: 110). Gavin MacGregor's studies in relation to recumbent stone circles raises the notion that colour may be interrelated with texture and that the temporal or spatial aspects of colour should not be overlooked (MacGregor 2002).

Alison Sheridan and Mary Davis argued that jet was substituted with other similarly black coloured materials in Bronze Age Wales (Sheridan and Davis 1998). This concept of colour being sufficiently separate from materiality, to the extent that material can be substituted, echoes the findings of Creighton in relation to alloys discussed above and may indicate a continuation of colour perception from Bronze to Iron Age which requires further exploration.

Classical archaeologists Brinkmann and Wuensche have attempted for over two decades to reconstruct the colour of painting on Greek sculptures (Brinkmann 2004; Wuensche 2004) and whilst the results are striking, yet again no attempt at interpretation of the semantic quality of colour has been made. Born (2004) argued that despite technological difficulties to assess the original colour and patina of bronze, some hints of different colours on lips and eyes on Hellenistic or Roman bronze statues and statuettes and the fact that iconographic representation in the Roman and Hellenistic world was usually naturalistic, led him to the assumption that polychrome effects were achieved through gilding, patination or painting. Wuensche (2004a) furthers this argument by citing Pliny and Plutarch as sources for the usage of different alloys to achieve different coloration as demonstrated by the statue of a boxer in the National Museum of Rome where coloured inlays were used for blood and a different alloy resulting in darker bronze was used to show bruising under the eye. The retention of the luminosity and golden colour of bronze would have been achieved by the application of Bitumen thinned with oil, a solution which according to Wuensche is used even today to protect iron (Wuensche 2004a: 142). Although naturalistic representation of colour would have been less likely within the British Iron Age, we cannot rule out that British craftsmen had the technological knowledge to achieve polychrome bronze artefacts.

Anthropology

The hermeneutic approach used by archaeologists such as Jones, MacGregor, Cooney, Keates *et al.* draws heavily on anthropological and ethnological colour theories. Victor Turner's theory that the colour triad red, black and white represents abstract moral or cosmological statements based on bodily fluids (i.e. red for blood, white for milk, semen or bones and black for faeces) and human environments (Darvill 2002: 74, 85; Scarre 2002: 237; Turner 1967: 60-91) is now widely used in archaeological contexts. Whilst the empiric experience of bodily fluids is universal and can therefore not be ignored, Turner's approach alone would be too limited as it does not take into account contextual circumstances, the polysemantic aspects of colours or the fact that certain colour associations may be limited to individual communities or even individuals within such communities (Boriç 2002; Darvill 2002: 83; Jones and McGregor 2002).

Equally flawed is the anthropological study on colour carried out by Berlin and Kay (Berlin and Kay 1969; Loebner 2002: 163-165) who studied the terminology for basic colours in over one hundred languages and deduced from their studies an evolution of basic colour terminology in various stages, which according to Loebner derives from the nature of human colour perception. Stage I languages have terms for black and white which juxtapose light and warm colours with dark and cool colours. Stage II languages recognise red as a third colour, associating black with cool colours, red with warm colours and white with light colours (Loebner 2002: 166). The next evolutionary stages are the addition of blues and greens, and further colours are added as colour perception progresses.

Whilst Berlin and Kay are cited in most anthropological colour studies and the results of their studies have undoubtedly contributed to a better understanding of semantics of colour, they have been heavily criticised by some scholars. For example, D'Andrade (1990: 69) argues that the Berlin and Kay system, which is based solely on nomenclature, relies on the presumption that differences in linguistic terms mirror differences of perception and mnemonics, but questions the validity of this presumption on the basis of comparative linguistic studies. He demonstrates his argument by the usage of the term 'blue green' in modern America where it describes a language related closeness of hues as opposed to the Tarahumara tribe in Northern Mexico where a like term in their language referred to an actual hue without any reference to a closeness of hues (D'Andrade 1990: 71). In terms of prehistory, the Berlin and Kay studies are therefore also of very limited use.

Chapman (2002) suggested as an alternative the study of relationships between social practices and associated colours. He differentiates between so-called environmentally salient colours such as yellow or gold for sun, blue for sky or the sea, black for night or earth, green for vegetation, red for blood and white for bone, and salient object colours which are colours associated with materials such as gold, stones and certain animal and marine materials (Chapman 2002: 55-61). The problem with this differentiation lies in the fact that there may be an overlap of colours having environmentally salient meaning and being a salient object colour, which casts serious doubt on its validity.

Other scholars such as Firth dismiss the notion of colour studies without reference to linguistics due to insufficiency (1992: 25). Scarre (2002: 230, 239) adds to this argument that we do not only need knowledge of colour terms to ascertain colour semantics, but we have to examine colours also in the context of other sensual experiences such as texture, sound and smell. Whilst this approach may well be extremely useful in terms of anthropological studies of contemporary communities, it is of course very difficult to apply such a multi sensory approach to prehistoric periods without resorting to an element of guesswork. Having said that, it must surely be of merit to examine any multi- sensory contexts of material evidence where it can be ascertained.

Another aspect of anthropology which concerns itself with both colour symbolism and British prehistory, although not necessarily connecting the two fields, is the study of shamanism. Scholars such as Eliade are convinced that Iron Age British and Irish communities were shamanistic, based on evidence from early Irish mythology (Eliade 1989: 382), and even suggest that certain aspects of shamanism are universally applicable. In terms of colour he suggests for example similarities between multicoloured ribbons tied to trees among the Buryat of Mongolia, which may represent different stages of heaven but also have connotations of different branches of shamanism such as white and black shamanism (Eliade 1989: 117), to the ladder to heaven in mithraic mysteries where the different metals of the rungs, i.e. lead, tin, bronze, iron, another alloy, silver and gold represent Saturn, Venus, Jupiter, Mercury, Mars, the moon and the sun (Eliade 1989: 121-122; Turcan 1996: 235).

Eliade argued that luminosity as representation of divinity is a concept which can be found in shamanic societies throughout the world. In some Pygmy tribes quartz stones represent celestial spirits (Eliade 1989: 125), Australian aborigines believe that by symbolically cutting open and stuffing a shaman with quartz, i.e. solidified light, he becomes a supernatural being (Eliade 1989: 138-139) and in European folklore the crystal or glass mountains represent a celestial ascent (Eliade 1989: 139). This ascent can also be symbolized by a rainbow, a bridge, the shamanic drum (Eliade 1989: 135) or the shamanic flight on a white horse. This is often metaphorically represented by a sacrifice of the animal (Eliade 1989: 191-192), the shaman sitting on white mare skin or the burning of white horsehair (Eliade 1989: 469). Whilst Eliade does not presume the white horse to be a universal aspect of shamanism, it may nevertheless be relevant for communities who relied heavily on horses and in whose iconography horses are of paramount importance. Similarly the idea of the tree of life or sky pillar (Eliade 1989: 261), which scholars such as Bryony Coles accept to be a feature of shamanism in Germanic myth (Coles 1998), the importance of the smith and metallurgy magic (Eliade 1989: 473), the black and white dualism for chthonic and celestial spirits or divinities and accordingly coloured sacrifices or clothing of shamans (Eliade 1989: 188-189) could all be relevant for Iron Age British communities.

Archaeologists such as Miranda Aldhouse-Green (2001; 2004; 2004a; Aldhouse-Green and Aldhouse-Green 2005) and Bryony Coles (1998), and Celto-linguists such as Birkhan (1997) and Ó hÓgáin (1999) have embraced the idea of shamanism in Iron Age Europe, yet Eliade's approach of a general shamanic theory has been heavily criticized by fellow anthropologists. Francfort (2001) sees it as a vague and at best only phenomenological concept, where fragments of belief systems are taken out of their contexts and collated into the prehistory without validation. Bahn (2001) goes as far as likening Eliade in his approach and reliability of sources, or rather lack thereof, to the discredited writer Carlos Castaneda. He also argues that trance does not equal shamanism and that we do not have any means to determine the state of consciousness of prehistoric humans, prove the use of hallucinogenic drugs in prehistory or differentiate shamanic imagery from non-shamanic imagery.

This kind of criticism appears to be concerned with aspects such as terminology or the perceived vagueness of hermeneutics and misses the arguments put forward by those archaeologists or folklorists who explore shamanism. If the definition of a shaman is not interpreted in the strict sense of a Siberian practitioner of shamanic ritual, but is widened to include persons who seek altered stages of consciousness and ecstasy through either mind altering drugs or other means, then the argument of trance not equalling shamanism falls away. Moreover, whilst similar phenomena do not necessarily imply similar belief systems, they can still hint at a solution which can be substantiated or at least furthered by other evidence. Perhaps Robert Wallis, who explored shamanism in European pre-history and neo-shamanism as an alternative archaeology and who is by no means supportive of any uncritical use of the word shaman in the context of British Iron Age (Wallis 2003: 139), has the correct solution when he suggests that we should 'embrace a diversity of interpretative narratives which contribute to an ongoing debate rather than promote a monolithic and judgmental view in which academic standpoints are privileged over other, alternative provisions' (Wallis 2003: 11-12). It remains to be seen, however, whether the so-called Celtic neo-shamanism explored in his studies can contribute in any way to the understanding of colour symbolism.

Folklore and Linguistics

A perhaps not quite so open minded, but nevertheless multidisciplinary stance can be found in the attempts of interpreting Iron Age colour symbolism by folklorists and Celtic philologists. The question whether folklore or early Irish and Welsh vernacular can be used in the interpretation of Iron Age archaeology has been addressed elsewhere. In terms of specific references to colour Darvill argues that Welsh 19th century autumn rites involving white pebbles may indicate a continuation of pre-historic rituals involving not only seasonal, solar or lunar connotations but also associations with water (Darvill 2002: 84-85). Ó hÓgáin believes that recent Irish traditions, such as using concoctions of yellow dandelion to cure jaundice or not wearing green clothes to avoid withering away may have their origins in the Irish Mesolithic (Ó hÓgáin 1999: 4).

Ó hÓgáin further strongly believes that Irish and Welsh myth can shed life on belief systems of the Irish Iron Age, Bronze Age and even earlier periods. He explored colour symbolism such as white and black dualism as representing life and death, day and night, or this world and the Otherworld. He also explored the use of the colour red as a symbol of death, war and ecstasy, and the colour white as a symbol of wisdom. He based his arguments not only on the colour descriptions found in early Irish and Welsh narratives, but perhaps more importantly on the nomenclature of divine beings or supernatural heroes, such as the Irish hero Fionn (literally translated as 'white') or the lord of the dead Donn whose name means 'black', which must predate Christianity in Ireland and Wales and are therefore likely to have originated in the Iron Age or even earlier periods.

Sioned Davies (1997: 126) examined the colour white from a linguistic angle and concluded that the Welsh word '*canwelw*' meaning pale white and used to describe Rhiannon's horse in the *Mabinogi*, indicates supernatural connotations. She believes that white had special meaning because like black it was an uncommon colour. One could argue, that white is actually far less common,

as true black can be encountered in substances such as coal, jet or chert. Even the darkness of a moonless night or still water can appear black. Mary Condres (1989: 177) suggested that white may have been a symbol of life itself. She demonstrates this with the example of an Irish custom lasting into the 12th century AD to baptize children with milk rather than water, which was based on the belief that milk was transmitting spirit.

None of these scholars, however, make any references to Iron Age archaeology, unlike the Austrian scholar Birkhan, who suggests that the cognomina of Gaulish divinities such as Matres Coccae, Mars Rudiobus or Rosmerta refer to prehistoric rites of rubbing coloured substances such as blood, ochre or fat onto the sculptures of such gods. His argument is based on the Celtic word '*smert*' within Rosmerta which refers to rubbing and to the fact that some Iron Age heads featured insertions for pouring libations (Birkhan 1997).

However, whilst this theory merits further investigation, he has not followed it up with a closer examination of archaeological material. Furthermore the meaning of '*smert*' which can also be found in the cognomen Smertrius for the god Mars, has also been translated as a 'provision of abundance' (Green 1992a: 193) and the connotations to the colour red found in Matres Coccae or Mars Rudiobus may not refer to the literal redness of these divinities but refer to certain aspects of their divine power which may be symbolized by the colour red (Polomé 1997; Sterckx 1997: 838-840).

Conclusion

Colour studies in British Iron Age archaeology tend to be narrow, ancillary and generally focused on aspects of workmanship and material rather than agency or meaning. Whilst studies concerning earlier periods have a much more interpretative stance, they, like anthropological, folklore and linguistic studies can only provide ideas and suggestions. The approach used in those studies, however, provides certain templates which can be applied to an exploration of colour in the Iron Age. As Fitzpatrick (2007: 340) recently pointed out, Celtic art is perceived to be a highly specialized and arcane field which appears to be divorced from mainstream archaeology. He suggests that new ways must be found to deal with art in order to overcome this seemingly elitist approach. Some progress has been made in integrating art into mainstream archaeology as part of a more holistic approach to Iron Age archaeology (Garrow et al. (ed.) 2008). There is no reason why the same approach cannot be applied to colour.

Chapter 3

Theoretical Aspects of Colour

We are constantly surrounded by colour and use it, consciously or unconsciously, for the definition, identification and differentiation of material objects. Colour is of equal importance to shape as a tool for communication, evaluation and signalling. We take it for granted, yet have little understanding of what colour actually is or does. Some philosophers actually deny the existence of colour altogether and argue that colour is not a physical reality but merely a subjective conception of the world (Stroud 2000: 15). Our modern Western perception and interpretation of colour is very narrow and is perhaps more of a hindrance than help in understanding colour in prehistory. As an example how our own paradigms can lead to a biased interpretation, I want to set out a number of assumptions which I have encountered during discussions with non-archaeologists on the subject matter of this research:

Assumptions on Colour

We don't have any paintings from the Iron Age, so how can we know anything about colours?

Most people immediately think of either paints, paintings or coloured fabrics when they hear the term 'colour'. It is, however, important to look at colour in a much wider sense and to take into account innate colour of materials, brilliance, luminosity and colour changes. These aspects of colour will be discussed below in further detail.

People used the materials that were available to them, and only a limited number of colours were available. How can there be colour symbolism?

Even if only a limited number of materials and colours were available, this does not preclude symbolism. Anthropological data from societies such as the Ndembu tribe in Central Africa which has similar technology to Iron Age Britain demonstrate sophisticated and often complicated symbolic constructs in relation to colour (Turner 1967: 59-91). Furthermore, we cannot assume a separation of function and ritual or a separation between function and art. Everyday objects may be imbued with deep symbolic meaning and aesthetic qualities. The markings and colour of cattle is highly important to cattle keeping Nilotic tribes such as the Dinka or the Bodi of Southern Ethiopia. The perception of the Dinka's visual world is shaped through the perception of colour configuration on cattle (Coote 1992: 256-257). The Bodi manipulate the colour and patterns through breeding programs, associate such patterns with social and group identity and use cattle with certain colour configurations for certain rituals (Sharples 2008: 203-204).

Colour is closely connected to fashion

Fashion is usually associated with clothing or hairstyles, but more importantly, it is frequently perceived as something frivolous and meaningless. However, even in the narrow sense of fashionable clothing, fashion is still a way of communication which is closely linked to culture and social constructs. Fashion has its use in social integration or differentiation and is a means of communication of identity and a symbolic code, which unlike language or writing continues to shift and change frequently (Davis 1992: 4-5; Wiessner 1989: 62). Colour is an important part of this highly symbolic communication tool and even if we cannot assume any knowledge of Iron Age fashion in the modern sense of the word, we can explore the effect of colour and potential symbolic meaning on Iron Age material.

The use of colour is primarily a question of aesthetics

In our own fashion and style obsessed world we associate the term aesthetics with home decoration, popular culture (Coote 1992: 246) and objects that are beautiful to look at. However, anthropology uses a variety of definitions resulting in Murphy's summary of aesthetics as 'a rubric term with no simple universally acceptable definition' (Murphy 1992: 181). The term certainly deals with the agency of objects within their cultural context (Coote and Shelton 1992: 8-9) and a visual identification of form, shape, colour, sheen, pattern and proportion of such objects (Coote 1992: 248). It may even have a correlation with the underlying ethics of a particular culture (Gell 1992: 41), but whilst there is invariably an aesthetical notion in every culture, it is not a particularly helpful tool in the context of deducing function and symbolism of colours in an Iron Age context. We are not only unable to properly define the term itself, but we are also unable to deduce the aesthetic judgements of a society whose values are outside the parameter of our knowledge (Shelton 1992: 229).

Colour Theories

It would be futile to attempt an interpretation of the symbolic value of colour without a basic understanding of colour and its effects. Yet, as will be demonstrated, all attempts to explain its nature have so far only raised further issues and questions, which in turn impact on the perception, function and cultural significance of colour.

The phenomenon of colour has fascinated philosophers, scientists and artists throughout history. The first known colour theorist was Alcmaeon of Croton who wrote in the early fifth century BC about the antithesis of black and white. Later in the same century Empedocles connected black and white and primary colour terms to elements such as fire, water air and earth. He also related colour and elements to temperature such as the sun being white and hot, and rain being dark and cold. He was the first known writer to discuss light and darkness as having an impact on the way material objects present themselves. He discussed the technique of 'σκιαγραφία', drawing with shading and highlights, with which painters can achieve a three dimensional aspect. Democritus furthered the idea of four simple primary colours, namely white, black, red and a further colour which he termed 'χλωροσ', by proposing that all other colours derive from mixing these primary colours (Gage 1993: 12; Ierodiakonou 2004: 92-94).

In the fourth century Plato (Timaeus 76d-68d) not only listed a number of chromatic hues, but also introduced the idea of dilation and contraction of the rays sent out by the eye. Whilst his ideas have since been proven to be scientifically unsound, he nevertheless made important progress in as much as he dealt with colour not only in terms of hues, but also impact of light and vision. His theories were further developed by Aristotle who emphasised the modification of colours depending on light and concluded that colour should not be studied by blending pigments but rather by investigating the rays reflected from colours (Aristotle De Anima 2.7; Gage 1993: 14). Aristotle's ideas about colour formed the basis for all colour theories until Isaac Newton's Opticks, published in 1704. Newton denied the existence of only a few specific primary colours, but argued that all the rays of refracted light were primary. He qualified Aristotle's view that pure light is colourless and requires materiality to create colours by demonstrating that light could be bent by a prism to produce a whole spectrum of colour, although unlike many of his followers he did not believe that rays of light themselves are coloured. Newton also introduced the idea of a circular table of colour relationship and the notion of complementary colours (Gage 1993: 168-171; Judd 1970: vii; Kuehni 2005: 138).

Whilst Newton deliberately concentrated on objective and quantitative scientific experimentation and excluded subjective aspects of colour vision, e.g. colours seen in dreams or as the result of striking the eye (Gage 1993: 191; Kuehni 2005: 138), Johann Wolfgang von Goethe's *Farbenlehre*, published in 1810 was meant to be a comprehensive study of all aspects of colour

and colour perception, concerned perhaps more with the phenomenon of colour rather than a scientific explanation per se. He dealt with numerous aspects of colour ranging from effects of light and darkness, objective and subjective colour vision including colour blindness, imagined colour and after-images of colour, nomenclature of colours, chemical and physical effects, evanescence and permanence of colour and manufacture of colour to the relationship of colours with other colours. He also explored the relationships between colours and the fields of mathematics or music, and the moral, aesthetical and symbolic aspects of colour. Whilst most of the scientific explanations of Goethe's theory are now no longer accepted and indeed found little support from scientists even in his day, his philosophical comments were welcomed and further explored by philosophers such as Schopenhauer whose own work 'On vision and Colours', published in 1961, remains largely ignored and did not add significantly to Goethe's work. Goethe also greatly influenced artists such as Turner and Runge (Gage 1993: 209; Kuehni 2005: 156-158) and his experiments, albeit often simple and not sufficiently explored from a scientific point of view, remain valid. None of the later colour theories have been as influential or comprehensive as Goethe's work.

In the nineteenth century Albert Munsell went to the other extreme and took a very narrow approach to colour by devising a system referred to by him as colour tree or colour sphere. It is a systematic chart not only of hues, but also of the quality by which colours are distinguished from another, of the value or the degree of lightness or darkness of a colour, and finally of chroma, or strength and weakness of colour. He also discussed harmonies and balance of colour (Birren (ed.) 1969). The Munsell charts are used to this day for colour charting and for archaeological analysis of soil, and formed the basis for Berlin and Kay's anthropological studies on colour (Berlin and Kay 1969) which have been referred to in chapter 2, but the system itself is merely a descriptive tool rather than an analytical theory.

The twentieth century impressionist movement *Der Blaue Reiter* led by the painters Wassily Kandinsky and Franz Marc added yet another dimension. They explored spirituality in art and in particular in colours, introducing the notions of gender, metaphysics, psychology and extreme relativity of colour sensations into colour theory. Their writings influenced the Bauhaus group of which Kandinsky was also a member, but had no long lasting effects. Later in the twentieth century the empiricists, led by Josef Albers, spurned any form of colour theory and embraced instead a spontaneous approach based on pure empiric experience (Gage 1993: 207-209, 265; Kuehni 2005: 159).

The above is only a brief overview of the most important and innovative colour theories and largely ignores secondary colour theories such as interaction between colour and sound or separate studies on chemical composition of pigments. Whilst it is conceded that it is only of limited use in relation to an assessment of colour perception within the British Iron Age and it is by no means comprehensive, it nevertheless gives an insight not only into the development of understanding of colour, but also the multitude of approaches which have and can be taken when looking at colour, as well as the difficulties and limitations of each of these approaches. Also, despite the geographical and cultural remoteness of classical Greek writers on the subject, the temporal overlap and the exchange of ideas which follows invariably as a result of trading, leads to the suggestion that some of these theories may have been known in Iron Age Britain. They may reflect an understanding of colour which may not have been dissimilar to that inherent in British Iron Age communities and could therefore be used, albeit with caution, as a means of interpretation of the material culture of the British Iron Age.

Definition of Colour

Despite the wealth of colour theories colour remains still a phenomenon which resists definition. As has been demonstrated above, there is not even a single universally applicable approach to colour (Cleland 2004: 5). By way of example, the Oxford Dictionary defines colour as:

1. the sensation produced by rays of light of different wavelengths, a particular variety of this;
2. the use of all colours, not only black and white (…);
3. a ruddiness of complexion (…);
4. the pigmentation of the skin, especially if dark;
5. pigment, paint, or dye;
6. the flag of a ship'.

Whilst this definition is not particularly satisfying, even taken as a whole, it nevertheless presents us with a variety of angles from which colour can be explored. The first part of the definition is concerned with the physical causes of colour, the second deals with aspects of perception and use of colours, i.e. the plural of the term rather than the singular, the third and fourth definition are examples of specific uses of the term in the English language, the fifth definition deals with sources of colorants and practical aspects of applying colour, and the last definition uses colour as a signifier. These aspects can be divided into two categories, namely the cause of colour and the effect of colour.

Physics and Psychology

It goes beyond the scope of this book to give a detailed account of the underlying physical aspects of colour, but some aspects of the scientific approach to colour should not be ignored. Firstly, it is important to note that even on a scientific level the phenomenon of colour cannot yet be adequately explained. A relatively recent attempt by the scientist Karl Nassau (1983) shows fifteen scientific causes of colour, which, as Nassau himself admitted, may not be comprehensive, and which range from physical optics to the effects of electrons in the chemistry of materials causing absorption or emission of light at certain wavebands. It is interesting to note, however, that the one element which pervades all these identified causes of colour is light (Kuehni 2005: 3).

Secondly, looking at the effect of colour on human beings, scientists can not yet explain the neurological colour vision process (Kuehni 2005: 17). Although the physiological experience of colour is universally shared by human beings because we use the same neurophysiologic organs and our colour vision is processed through three types of light sensitive cells, or cones in the eye, the interpretation of the physical experience by the brain and the level of consciousness of vision is subjective and can vary enormously (Jones and MacGregor 2002a: 14; Kuehni 1983: 27-39; Kuehni 2005: 18). External factors such as fatigue, stimulation and diversity of visual interests can also influence the mere physiological aspect of colour vision and thus individualise the experience of colour vision (Verity 1967: 110-111). The perception of colour terms is also subjective. The same colour can be described by some people as green, by others as blue. In addition colour blindness and certain illnesses can have an influence on the subjective perception of colour. In my own experience, fever can cause material objects to appear in a reddish hue.

Various attempts of offering a universally applicable understanding of colour and its effects have been made in the field of colour psychology. Sigmund Freud's associations between certain colours and bodily functions such as blood, faeces and semen (Freud 1999) are echoed in Victor Turner's anthropological studies of the Ndembu initiation rituals (Turner 1967: 89). However, followers of Jung's theories spurned Freud's theory as too simplistic, even though Jung did not deny the psychological effect of colour on human behaviour (Jung 1992). Whilst more recent attempts to explain the psychological response to colour remain inconclusive, the human response to the experience of colour can be expressed in simple terms as a scale of six levels (Holtzschue 2002: 41), i.e. personal relationship with colour; influence of fashion style and trend; cultural influences and mannerisms; conscious symbolism and association; collective unconscious association and biological reaction to a colour stimulus. The first four levels are not universally applicable as they require at least some knowledge of either the individual or the individual's cultural background. However, the last two levels are neither consciously learned nor the result of isolated individual experience, but are either based on a common physiological reaction or common human experience (Holtzschue 2002: 41).

Examples of commonly shared human experience influencing symbolical associations with colour are the associations between red and blood, white and milk, bone or semen, black and earth, faeces or night, green and vegetation, yellow and the sun, and blue and sky or water which can be found in culture groups throughout the world (Favre and November 1979: 24) and which allow us to make certain assumptions of the symbolic meaning of colours in respect of prehistoric culture groups of whose belief systems and semantics we have insufficient or no knowledge.

Equally, the physiological reaction to colour may allow us to draw conclusions about the function of colour within such culture groups. It is a scientifically proven fact that red wavelengths stimulate hormones and blood pressure and blue wavelengths lower blood pressure and create a calming effect, thus inciting or reducing aggressive behaviour and changing moods (Holtzschue 2002: 36-38). Even without the benefit of scientific proof, such physical reactions would be apparent in any community through empiric evidence which may be passed on. Repeated experience and utilisation may then ultimately result in symbolic meaning for certain colours. One example would be the use of the colour blue in healing. As already stated exposure to blue light eases high blood pressure and is believed to sooth inflammation (Holtzschue 2002: 38; Pavey *et al.* 1980: 46-47). It is therefore conceivable that a repeated and successful use of blue substances for the purpose of healing may lead to that colour having a symbolic healing and protection value.

Perception of Colour

Basic Colour Terms

Going beyond the mere physical and physiological aspects of colour vision and colour experience, the process of interpretation of the information received by the human brain in terms of colour presents us with further difficulties. The modern approach to colour in Western societies is mainly one of chromatic hues or more precisely, linguistic basic colour terms such as black, white, red, blue etc. This approach is fraught with difficulty as basic colour terms do not deal with other aspects of colour such as saturation and value which may be just as important as hue (Gillis 2004: 56). The term red, for example, covers a huge spectrum of colours as demonstrated by reference to colour charts such as the Munsell chart. The limitation of the hue based approach throws some doubt on the validity of the anthropological studies about the evolution of colour perception carried out by Berlin and Kay (see chapter 2). A further criticism of the Berlin and Kay studies is the concentration on the evolution of linguistic colour terms only. The absence

of a precise colour term does not mean the absence of cognition (Jones and McGregor 2002a: 7) and can always be overcome by a choice of descriptive adjectives. Care should be taken not to confuse the two but rather explore the interrelation between them. Even in terms of merely linguistic evolution, outside influences cannot be overlooked. In his research on Ancient Egyptian colour terms Warburton (2004: 129) has come to the conclusion that some terms may have been borrowed from other cultures and used alongside specifically Egyptian words, but that the use and evolution of these terms depended on a variety of circumstances such as the objects described, the intercultural contacts prevalent at the time, the development of a complex division of colour ranges and the need of a vocabulary for Egypt's literary classes.

Two further issues arise out of the limitations of a mere linguistic approach to colour perception. Firstly, the colour terms themselves evolve and the present meaning of a certain basic colour term may be different to its historical meaning. The colour blue was used in the 19th century to describe diverse materials such as milk, flint or the leaves of numerous plants such as ivy, none of which may necessarily be perceived as blue by today's standard of perception (Ziderman 2004: 41). Even today we use the term blue in terminology of animal breeds such as the Burmese Blue cat or the Irish Blue Staffordshire dog, the colour of both of which would be perceived as grey. Clarke (2004: 138) goes even further in proposing that in the development of classical Greek colour terms have been de-contextualised but may have had initially wider meaning, not only describing colour but also perhaps a sense of movement or an association of references. This is of course not only restricted to Greek colour terms. The Latin word *rubor* is not only a reference to a reddish colour, but is primarily translated as blush. It has therefore connotations of shame and embarrassment, but also a rush of blood and would not fit easily into an abstract colour chart (Bradley 2004: 120).

Secondly, the translation of colour terms from different languages into basic English colour terms cannot be taken for granted. Both the studies by Berlin and Kay and the Munsell arrays have attracted criticism for their use of English terms (Clarke M. 2004). For example the ancient Greek colour term 'χλωροσ' can mean both green and red. It is conceivable that the term was not meant to express a hue as such but had connotations with aspects of fecundity and vitality which depending on context can be interpreted as red or green (Clarke 2004: 134-135).

Whilst these observations have of course no direct impact on the exploration of British Iron Age colour perception due to the absence of indigenous written sources any reference to classical, early Irish or Welsh literature or indeed anthropological studies from other culture groups must be viewed in the light of these limitations.

Innate or Applied Colour

Colour and material are closely connected and should not be explored in isolation. There is numerous archaeological and historical evidence of the correlation and interaction between material texture and innate colour such as MacGregor's studies on the deliberate choice of grey and pink stones in Scottish recumbent stone circles (Lynch 1998: 66; MacGregor 2002: 146, 156). In terms of linguistics the Latin expressions *Creta anularia* and *Caeruleum Aegyptium* refer to both the material or underlying pigment and the resulting colour. *Creta anularia* is a mixture of chalk and white mica which was used for both painting and make up (Davidovits 2004: 18). *Caeruleum Aegyptium* was not only a term for a specific bluish hue but referred to the artificially manufactured blue pigment (Davidovits 2004: 18-21). Another form of interaction between colour and material in antiquity is suggested by Nosh (2004: 32, 37), who concluded that certain Greek Linear B terms may not only indicate a colour but also the quality of a certain material. She suggests that the term *e-ru-ta-ra* indicates a very specific red cloth or red hides, whereas the term *ka-na-ko e-ru-ta-ra* refers to the safflower florets which were used as a dye substance. The term *pu-ru-wa* on the other hand refers to a natural red brown wool colour. Duigan (2004: 78) supports the view that colour in ancient Greece may have been seen as a particular coloured substance or coloured artefact. He believes that colour terms were connected to and can often be explained in terms of functional use of a material object.

In the context of materiality and innate colour the aspects of value and imitation should not be ignored. The question must be asked whether it is the underlying material, its colour or a mixture of both which give value to an object. There is evidence from Bronze Age Britain that the more readily available but similarly black shale was used in substitution for jet beads in funerary contexts (Sheridan and Davis 1998). It would be interesting to explore whether this substitution only applies in a funerary context. If so, it may well be that it is an attempt to fool the witless dead (Duigan 2004: 81-82), a concept referred to in Homer's Odyssey and discussed later in this chapter. It is also suggested that sometimes less valuable colorants substituted those of a higher value such as lapis lazuli in Ancient Egyptian paintings, yet still achieved the same colour, whereas in other cases an obvious variation of colour to the norm may have been the result of the painter using readily available minerals and dyes (Eremin *et al.* 2004: 5). Another example of colour substitution is the use of madder and ingotin instead of the more valuable real murex purple during the Roman occupation of Jordan (Shamir 2004: 51). This indicates not only a complex relationship between material and colour but also possible shifts of the attachment of value from material to colour or from colour to material, depending on factors such as availability and social contexts, and further introduces the notions of illusion and visual deception. It is therefore not only imperative to explore the relationship between materiality and innate colour (MacGregor 2002: 144), but also the deliberate application of colour to objects, whether by way of painting, dyeing or covering with coloured material and the underlying reasons for it, whether dictated by necessity, or deliberate statement or attempt at deceit.

There are a number of references to the deliberately ambiguous and deceitful use of colour in Greek written sources. In the Odyssey Athena makes Penelope more alluring and highly unusual in the context of the Southern Mediterranean, by making her skin whiter than ivory (Homer Odyssey 18.195); in the myth of Pandora, Zeus receives a gift of white bones of ox which are disguised in shining fat, but then returns as a gift Pandora, who although made of earth appeared radiant as she was dressed in shining clothes (Hesiod Theogony 572-601). Duigan (2004: 81–82) believes that the deliberate application of colour such as gilding or painting inferior materials, thereby endowing the material object with 'Χαρισ', is a manipulative exercise of power which can seduce or mislead a stronger opponent. Duigan also notes that the use of jewellery and alabastra which is made out of clay but intended to resemble gold, in Greek funerary practices exemplify the use of deceitful colour. He suggests that the reason for this deliberate deception is the view expressed by Homer (Odyssey 10.493), that the dead are witless and cannot distinguish between objects of real value and coloured copies. However, it is also possible that any differentiation in a funerary context becomes meaningless as the colour may have represented the essence or spirit of the object which was intended for use in the Otherworld and materiality therefore ceased to have any further meaning.

Application of colour, however, should not only be regarded as a means of deception, but it can also mean enhancement and decoration which in itself could be linked to ritualistic significance (Firth 1992: 27) and, especially if colour is combined with iconography, a powerful means of communication. In terms of ritual application of colour consideration must be given to whether the application of colour involved interaction with or was dependent on an audience, such as oral recitation requires listeners (Finnegan 1992: 93), and whether the application or the result had greater importance.

Spatial and Temporal Qualities of Colour

In addition to the interrelation between colour and material in isolation the temporal and spatial qualities of colour and its context must also be considered. The recent tendency in archaeology to examine the biographies of material objects, e.g. Aldhouse-Green (2004; 2004a) must also include a 'biography of colour' (Jones 2002), i.e. an examination of the process of change of colours of material objects during the process of manufacture, the process of colour application by painting or decoration with other material, the changes in colour resulting from manipulation or natural processes such as oxidisation or fading and the relationship between such colours and colour changes and social contexts (Tilley 1999: 264), both in terms of process and usage. This must also encompass the interaction between colour and surface or texture of material, the notion of a ceremonial application of colour as opposed to a mere mechanical process, and the change of colour resulting from deliberate inaction, i.e. the conscious decision to allow colours to fade or become dull, which may suggest ritual significance (Cooney 2002: 95; Owoc 2002: 128).

In terms of spatial qualities we must take into consideration not only the attribution of colour to inherent colours of flora, fauna and minerals (Jones and MacGregor 2002a: 10) or the deliberate import of exotic colours, but also the interaction between the colour of a given object and its surrounding landscape and related objects, the deliberate juxtaposition of colours on the same object or, bringing into play yet another temporal aspect, the variation of such colours depending on the light of the time of day or year.

Luminosity and Brilliance

A further significant aspect of colour perception is luminosity, brilliance and iridescence. The fascination with shiny objects, adornments or materials such as silk, mirrors, shiny metal or iridescent shells and feathers is known from a whole range of societies (Keates 2002: 119) and luminosity may be valued higher than hue. It has been suggested that the importance of brightness and shininess of colours outweighed hue in the Mycenaean Bronze Age and this may have been the reason for a limited range of basic colour terms. Hue may have been determined by adjectives and association, but symbolic value may have been given by luminosity (Gillis 2004: 58–59). Duigan (2004: 80) agrees that luminous materials such as gold or brightly dyed textiles, whilst being expensive and therefore a signifier of material value, would also have enhanced the visual quality of artefacts. In the Odyssey and Iliad divine or semi-divine objects or characters are frequently described in terms of sheen and brilliance.

Further examples for the importance of brilliance from Greek and Pre-Roman Italian cultures are the associations between amber, a material which was highly valued because of its brilliance, glow, transparency, yellow colour and magnifying properties, and sun, fertility, rebirth and protection (Causey 2004: 74) and secondly the use of the Greek terms γλαυκοσ and γλαυκοπισ which have associations with the bluish green colour of the sea

or olive leaves. According to Deacy and Villing (2004: 84–88) the terms were not restricted to mere hues. Their argument is that γλαυκοπισ, especially when used as a description of the goddess Athena, has a far wider and ambivalent meaning.[3] It refers both to the flashing and potentially threatening gaze of Athena's blue eyes and her divine status expressed by the brightness of her eyes, but it has also associations with the olive tree, a symbol of peace and yet also a means of arousing fear, and the owl, an animal which is generally, although not exclusively, nocturnal. The term is therefore not so much used to describe a colour, but a degree of brightness with a wealth of ambivalent associations befitting a goddess of both war and learning, who is paradoxically at the same time terrifying and nurturing and concerned with occupations atypical for her gender.

It is not only the reflective quality and iridescence in certain objects and the interaction between light and dark (Scarre 2002: 237), which create luminosity and brilliance, but also the use of vibrant colours and colour patterning. The deliberate juxtaposition of two or more colours, which was well known throughout the Mediterranean World although we do not know its symbolic meaning (Eaverly 2004: 55), or even hatching and criss-crossing can create a sense of movement and agency which can be likened to that of reflective luminosity (Jones and MacGregor 2002a: 14-15).

Symbolism and Symbolic Value of Colour

It is not sufficient to ask the question whether colour in Iron Age Britain may have been perceived as hue or in terms of luminosity or saturation; we also need to ascertain what meaning these categories may have had (Duigan 2004: 78). In order to assess the symbolism associated with certain colours, it is necessary to explore the principles of symbolism as a whole. Symbolic values can be found in most societies, but different emphasis may be given to symbolic interpretation. For example, it is probably safe to assume that certain symbolic principles such as life and death, or male and female are common to most societies, although not necessarily perceived as opposites (Hodder 1982: 215; Hodge and Kress 1988: 64-73). There can also be distinctions within these symbolic principles such as a differentiation between the recently deceased and the long dead (Fowler 2004: 79-100).

Goethe differentiated in his colour theory between symbolical colour, i.e. where the meaning of the colour coincides with the natural effect of the colour on the human mind, and allegorical colour, where values must

---

[3] Blakolmer (2004: 62) argued that in the Aegean Bronze Age colour terms do not necessarily correspond to definite hues but are determined by reference to aesthetics, sensibility and intellectual attitude towards their environment. Lustre and luminoscity, heteromorphics, irregularrity and movement are important categories in such determination.

first be communicated to be understood (Goethe 1840: 915-916), which broadly corresponds to the notions of unconscious and conscious colour symbolism, i.e. symbolism learned by indoctrination (Holtzschue 2002: 41), as referred to above.

The founder fathers of the discipline of semiotics, Saussure and Peirce had different understandings of the term symbol. The more structuralist Saussure believed that a symbol was never arbitrary and, like Goethe, he inferred at least a certain degree of natural connection between the signifier, i.e. the form or vehicle in which the sign is transmitted and the signified concept. Peirce, who came from a more positivistic and behaviourist background, referred to symbols as signs interpreted according to rules or habitual connections but without the need for a natural connection. He distinguished between symbols where the relationship between the sign and the concept behind must be learned, iconic signs and indexation. Iconic signs have qualities resembling those of the object or concept they wish to represent such as a painting or a sound effect. Indexical signs are those where the signifier is not at all arbitrary but directly connected by way of cause-effect chains to the signified, such as smoke as a sign of fire, footprints, measuring instruments or personal trademarks (Chandler 2002: 18-42; Hodge and Kress 1988: 17-27). Both approaches have been criticized and expanded but still form the basis for the subject of semiotics and as such cannot be dismissed. Much of the criticism and modification of their theories is based on linguistics, but some further studies and thoughts apply to the use of colour as signifier.

Peirce's separation of signifiers into symbols, icons and indices presupposed a clear differentiation, but in reality none of them are mutually exclusive (Chandler 2002: 43). The same signifier can be ambivalent or even polyvalent. With reference to Greek classical poetry Founoulakis established that in Bion's epitaph on Adonis the colour red can stand simultaneously for a rose, desire, but also flowing blood and death (Founoulakis 2004: 110-115). A similarly multivalent web of colour associations suggesting notions of gender, power shifts, transitions and associated imagery can also be found in Catullus' long poems (Clarke 2004: 122).

The study of semiotics is primarily concerned with language and colour or non verbal signs are attributed a lesser degree of importance. However, some studies into the significance of colours have been made. Roman Jacobson argued that primary colours have meanings analogous to certain vowels. For example, the colour red equals the vowel 'a', meaning high energy, whereas blue equals the vowel 'o' or 'u' and means low energy. Colour can have gender specific connotations, but the relationships between certain colours and gender can vary in different culture groups. However, it could be argued that the degree of luminosity or brightness of colour as

a signifier of constraint or energy could be universally applicable (Hodge and Kress 1988: 104-107).

In exploring the symbolic meaning of colours it should be remembered that the medium itself, i.e. the colour or coloured object, is not neutral, but may have its own rules of structure. Umberto Eco went as far as proposing that the medium itself may have isolated cultural significance (Chandler 2002: 52-54; Eco 1976: 267).

Symbols need to be analysed both in terms of their spatial or sequential relationships with other symbols or objects, but also in terms of underlying paradigms and concepts. Spatial positioning for example can infer modifications of meaning in terms of importance, dominance or marginality (Chandler 2002: 79-98). An example of a sequential relationship would be the use of colour in Mycenaean paintings as a symbol for the social status of the depicted persons, which may only have worked in association with certain iconography (Muskett 2004: 71).

Furthermore, symbols and signs should be analysed not only structurally, but also within their historical and social frames. By way of example the colour blue in the English language had historically sometimes negative connotations such as the associations of blue gowns in Scotland with licensed beggars, the term 'blue belly' signifying a protestant dissenter, or the term 'blue day' meaning a day on which something bad happened (Ziderman 2004: 41), none of which are still in use, although the expression 'having the blues' which has negative connotations is still used. The symbolism of royalty associated with the colour purple in antiquity may have been a cultural influence of the classical Greek and Roman world but may not have been significant in the Bronze Age (Nosch 2004: 37).

The social aspects of semantics, which were largely ignored by Saussure and Pierce (Chandler 2002: 213) introduce a number of further issues. Whilst it is conceivable that certain symbols are internal and particular to one person only and not understood or even intended to be understood by others, for a social use of semantics both the transmitter of a symbol and the receiver of the symbol must be acquainted with it (Gillis 2004: 56).

Once the structure of a symbol is understood, it can of course be used modified. The phrase 'making the familiar strange and the strange familiar', first coined by the German Romantic poet Novalis in his Aphorismen und Fragmente (1798: 20) is widely used in modern media, but by no means a modern idea. The use of irony, which is one example of using signs not in their literal sense but signifying the opposite, is well known in Latin and Greek rhetoric. However, examples of subversive use of the familiar can also be found in iconography, such as the use of certain imagery in Roman occupied Gaul to subvert the acceptance of Roman imperialism as suggested by Aldhouse-Green (2004: 29-30). The reversion of the familiar during certain rituals and at certain, perhaps sacred times is a phenomenon which can be found in numerous cultures. Examples are cross dressing during carnivals or during funerary rites, or the role reversing during a wedding ceremony where the man places a ring, symbolising a vagina, on a brides' finger, symbolising the phallus (Hodder 1982: 200; Hodge and Kress 1988: 73-78). The recognition of such subversion, however, presupposes the knowledge of the literal or familiar, which may not always be possible.

Conclusion

Where does this leave us in terms of exploring colours in the British Iron Age? Apart from the fact that we cannot yet scientifically explain the cause or effect of colour and do not possess a comprehensive colour theory, due to the absence of indigenous written sources and lack of knowledge of the language spoken in Iron Age Britain, we have no knowledge of the underlying paradigm of cognition and conscious symbolism of Iron Age culture. The recognition of any abstract concepts which may be represented by mere physical signs is difficult (D'Andrade 1990: 68). We do not know if British Iron Age culture groups had any conscious theories on colour, whether or not their cognition of colour was perceived in terms of hue, luminosity or saturation and whether or not colour terms and thus perception had wider associations such as agency or fertility. We do not even have a comprehensive or accurate picture of the colours extant in British Iron Age society due to the scarcity and under representation of material objects, but also due to the changes in colour of material objects over time, due to chemical processes. Even if contextual evidence allows us to draw conclusions as to a literal interpretation of colours, we need to bear in mind that such literal interpretation may not be sufficient. This should, however, not discourage the exploration of colour in the context of the Iron Age, but merely serve as a reminder of the limitations we are faced with.

Chapter 4

Colour and Creation – Colour Implications in Metalworking

'Their armour was of bronze, and their houses of bronze, and of bronze were their implements: there was no black iron. These were destroyed by their own hands and passed to the dank house of chill Hades, and left no name: terrible though they were, black Death seized them, and they left the bright light of the sun'

(Hesiod Works and Days: 2.140–155)

Introduction

The anthropologist Alfred Gell introduced the notion of 'The technology of enchantment and the enchantment of technology' in his essay on the relationship between art, technical processes and the effect and power of such processes (Gell 1992). Colour can play an important part in such processes. The manipulation and technology in metalwork lends itself as an ideal object of research as the processes involved almost always result in colour changes. In the following parts of this chapter I will consider each stage of the metal making process in turn and assess its colour implication. In addition to the colours of the underlying ore and the resulting metal, I will also look at the contextual colours of mining, smelting and forging, which may well have had their own symbolic significance, whether in their own right or as part of a broader cosmological or sociological context.

Mining and Metal Extraction

The main difficulty in researching mining and metal extraction in the British Iron Age is the lack of archaeological evidence for mining. There are two different ways of mining, namely open cast mining and underground mining. It is safe to assume that underground mining technology was known in the British Iron Age, as it has been in existence since at least the Bronze Age. The copper mines at Great Orme in North Wales, for example, provide evidence of possibly extensive underground mining during the early to middle Bronze Age (Ottaway 1994: 72; James 1990: 4). There is no evidence that the underground mining activity at Great Orme or at other British mines which had been worked during the early and middle Bronze Age, e.g. the copper mines at Parys Mountain or the silver and lead mines at Nantyreira and Copa Hill in Wales (James 1990: 4; Timberlake 1990: 21; Timberlake 1990a: 27), continued during the late Bronze Age and the Iron Age. There is, however, implied evidence and support from classical written sources that underground mining, possibly even on an extensive scale, may have taken place in Britain during the Iron Age.

Unlike iron ore, which can be extracted easily through opencast mining, the production of significant quantities

of copper, silver and gold requires underground mining (Pleiner 2000: 87). Whilst Britain has considerable copper resources, it is nevertheless difficult to distinguish between artefacts made of native copper and those made of smelted and traded copper (Craddock 1995: 95). Pliny mentions in his Natural History (4.104) that tin was found on the island of Mictis near Britain, and Strabo (Geography 4.5,2) states that Britain produces gold, silver and iron, but neither mention copper. We have evidence that tin was exported during the Iron Age from Cornwall (Cunliffe 1991: 460) and we can assume that Britain must have produced sufficient quantities of gold and silver to export them or at least bring them to the attention of classical writers. It is therefore likely that underground mining technology was used to mine these materials. Copper may have been imported to Britain, or perhaps it was mined locally but not exported and therefore it may have been ignored by classical writers.

Recognising Metal – Colours as Indicators

Colour plays a significant role in mineral prospecting as in the absence of chemical analysis the colour of minerals is a key identifier of the existence of ore, both in terms of finding a new bed, new mineral veins or surface ore in an area which is already known to contain the desired resources (Miller 2009: 147–149). It is interesting to note that the colour of the ore on the surface or even in the mine is often very different from the colour of dressed ore or the resulting metal. For example iron ore, which is more frequently found on the surface than copper ore (Ottaway 1994: 20) and would have been available in the British Iron Age in considerable amounts in areas such as the Weald, [4] the Forest of Dean or Yorkshire (Pleiner 2000: 40, 92), would have appeared mostly in the form of limonites. Limonites are of a yellowish brownish colour with rusty coloured streaks. According to Pliny, ores containing silver or lead would have been recognized by their red or ashen colour and these would also have been indicators of other minerals such as quicksilver or antimony (Natural History 33.95). Copper ore found underground is red in colour, but above ground it usually

---

[4] Iron was also mentioned by Caesar in his De Bello Gallico (5.12) as being found near coastal areas.

oxidises to form green or blue copper minerals such as malachite and azurite (Craddock 1995: 28). Prospectors[5] would therefore not have looked for red, but for blue or green as indicator of underlying red copper ore.

Gold is the only mineral which would have been easily recognizable by its permanent golden colour. Pliny describes in his Natural History (33.67) the processes of obtaining surface gold either by sifting the gold residue found in rivers or searching for golden sparkles in the earth which indicate a surface vein.

Underground Mining

Without going into extensive detail of the process of underground mining, it is worth looking at Pliny's description of a gold mine to visualise the contextual impact of colour in mines and underground shafts of the Iron Age period. Pliny tells us that miners worked in the galleries of shafts by lamplight and did not see the daylight for many months (Natural History 33.67-71). He describes the process of fire setting, i.e. the breaking of and extracting the mineral in shafts or galleries by means of fire. Evidence of the use of fire setting has been found inter alia in a Bronze Age context at Great Orme (Timberlake 1990b: 52). The colour implications would have been manifold. Initially, the miners would have had to dig shafts and tunnels, thus entering the darkness of the very bowels of the earth. It is conceivable that the act of digging may have had chthonic associations, akin to the symbolic connotations of the Danbury pits, which will be looked at in further detail in chapter 9. Perhaps the functional aspect of mining was combined with the symbolic or ritual function of a journey into the Underworld. Then the dark tunnels would have been artificially lit by fire, thereby revealing the colour of the mineral veins or the rock. Fire setting was an immensely dangerous procedure which would have required the use of substantial quantities of black charcoal or wood (Lewis 1990: 7). Again, specialist knowledge would have been required to obtain the right temperature of the fire by gauging the colour of the fire. The resulting breaking of the stone would have been a frightening and apparently magical spectacle and it would have ultimately revealed further mineral colours. Also, evidence from excavations of Bronze Age mines and experimental archaeology shows that the immense heat would have led to a reddening of the exposed rock such as limestone due to oxidation of the iron oxide contained in it and a black sooty residue would have coated walls and ceilings (Lewis 1990: 7). The specialist fire setter may have been perceived as a powerful person with the magical powers and knowledge to control and manipulate the colours of fire, minerals and rock. As will

be discussed later in this chapter, smiths are often likened to shamans. Perhaps fire setters played a similar role. The journey into the bowels of the earth and the dangers associated with it may have been seen as a shamanic journey into a dangerous spirit realm and the material procured during such a journey may have been imbued with special sacred status. To give an analogy from an anthropological source, in Pre-Columbian America, the sacredness of objects such as shells or pearls was derived from their procurement. Diving into lakes was likened to a shamanic journey from which the diver returned with sacred matter (Saunders 1999: 247).

Blue Men – Colour Changes on Metalworkers

Colour changes would have been visible on the miners themselves, if they had spent months underground as described by Pliny. Not only would the work in underground mines have led to the exposed skin being ingrained with dirt, soot, and mineral traces, but underneath the grime the miners' skin would have been extremely pale due to lack of exposure to the sun. It is also possible that working in copper mines might have led to hair, fingernails and toenails of the miners being green or blue due to exposure to oxidised ores. William O' Brien (2004: 576) cites the story of an encounter between a Joseph O'Connor and a certain Cooty Cournane, an Irish shanachie or storyteller. Cooty tells O'Conner that his grandfather used to know the Blue Men or Fir Groma, who were miners drafted in from Cornwall to work the copper mine in Ross Island. Their name derived from their blue hair and fingernails, a result of working in the copper mines. European folklore is abound with supernatural beings connected to mining activity, such as the English pukkas or pooks, the Cornish knockers and the German kobolds[6] (Topping and Lynott 2005: 183-185), all of which strengthen the argument that mines are dangerous places and linked to spirits and Otherworldly beings, but these supernatural beings are often distinguished by their fanciful colouring. It may well be that the origin of such characters lies in the strange colouring of copper miners.

Such appearance would have set the miners visually apart from other members of Iron Age communities, although this does not necessarily imply differences in social standing or rank. In order to explore the possibility of such impact on skin colour and any social connotations it is necessary to explore further the possibility of a large scale mining industry in the British Iron Age. Opencast mining could have been carried out by one or a few people as well as large groups and they would not have had any distinct skin or hair coloration as a result of their work. Shallow opencast iron mining leaves hardly any trace in the archaeological record, for it is scarce and evidence is disproportionate to the archaeological records for smelting or forging. It is therefore difficult (if not

---

[5] The term prospector is used here merely to describe somebody looking for minerals but does not imply any commercial profiteering.

[6] The name derives from Greek 'kóbalos' meaning joker, but also little miner (Topping and Lynott 2005: 183).

impossible) to ascertain how many people were involved in the process. Pleiner (2000: 87) believes that iron ores would have been collected geographically close to the smelting place. He argues on the basis of ethnographic parallels that there would have been specialised iron making groups, perhaps extended families, who would have extracted the ore, dressed it, made the charcoal and constructed the furnaces for smelting and then returned to their community with iron in the form of blooms. He also believes that the mining, dressing and smelting process would have been seasonal (Pleiner 2000: 104). Pleiner's arguments can only be speculative and may be true for smaller scale iron production. However, it must be taken into account that iron was exported from Britain, as stated above and iron currency bars were used for trade. There were three centres of large scale iron production in Iron Age Britain, namely the Weald, the Forest of Dean and the Jurassic Ridge of middle Britain, although iron ore is common throughout the British Isles and blacksmithing was far more generalised than mining or smelting (Ehrenreich 1999: 218- 219). It is therefore at least conceivable that some large scale iron ore mining activities, albeit probably shallow opencast mining, were carried out during the Iron Age. Irrespective of how many people were involved in the process, it is undoubtedly the case that opencast prospectors and miners would have had specialist knowledge and an important part of their specialism would have consisted of the recognition of minerals and ore using colour as identifying guide.

In terms of prehistoric underground mining there is presently insufficient archaeological evidence to determine the scale of such processes. A shaft or tunnel, if such form of mining was indeed used during the British Iron Age, could have been dug by a large number of people in a relatively short time and large quantities of ore could have been extracted relatively quickly. This kind of mining might have required a system whereby labour would have been divided into the hard physical work of digging and carrying, which might have been carried out by ordinary men, women and children, perhaps even prisoners, without any specialist skills, as opposed to the management of the mining process, the prospecting and the pyrotechnical technology such as fire setting, all of which would have required specialist knowledge. In this hypothetical system a large amount of people would have been taken out of their community to carry out the hard non skilled labour, and ancillary industries such as the supply of food would have been required. On the other hand, underground mines could also have been dug and worked by small groups of people over a long period of time, perhaps seasonally, and the process could have been similar to that of small scale opencast mining. If we were to accept the hypothesis of extensive copper mining it is possible that the specialists might have been perceived as people who would create, manipulate or control colour by means of technology, but might not themselves have been affected by it, whereas the non specialist labourers would have had no control over colours but would have been coloured in the process. This poses the question whether the external signs of colour on the skin might have led to a recognition and differentiation of specialists and non specialists within the context of mining.

Whilst early Irish and Welsh myth frequently features blacksmiths and the work of the blacksmith, whose symbolic values will be examined in detail later in this chapter, there appears to be very little mention of miners or mining (Scott 1990: 176). Perhaps the activity of mining as opposed to that of blacksmithing was a secretive one which was not seen by many people and the result of such work was not immediately recognised, whereas the results of the blacksmith's labour would be known. Perhaps those who performed the mining process were outside society and only linked to communities via the blacksmith. On the other hand, the old Irish word for mining or quarrying ore 'oc buain mianna' has interesting connotations as 'buain' can stand for cutting, striking, reaping and harvesting (Scott 1990:177). This not only suggests that mining activity may have been perceived as akin to agricultural activities, which also involve digging the earth and specialist knowledge which often centres around the recognition of certain colours, but it may also strengthen the argument that mining, like agriculture, may have been a seasonal activity.

Ore Dressing

We have very little knowledge about prehistoric ore dressing. The oldest and simplest but very inefficient and time consuming way of dressing (i.e. concentrating) ore such as copper oxides or limonite is hand picking (Bick 1990: 76; Ottaway 1994: 16). The more advanced method of crushing ore and separating it by gravity or with the help of water was known prior to the third century BC in Greece (Bick 1990: 76) and is also referred to by Pliny in his Natural History (33,76), but in Britain there is as yet no archaeological evidence for such procedures. Watercourses or leats found in mining areas such as Copa Hill in Wales may not necessarily have been connected to mining and are in any event difficult to date (Bick 1990: 78). Whichever method was used, colour is again a very important factor for the identification of the concentrated ore.

The crushed and separated oxidised copper ore may have been the preferred ore due to ease of process and availability. It could be smelted without any further operation, whereas sulphide copper ore and probably iron ore required a further step of preparation prior to the smelting process. In order to convert the sulphide contained in the ore into oxide, dry the ore out and thereby release oxygen, the ore must first be roasted. This involves the setting up of a roasting pit or hearth. There is little evidence of roasting pits from the British

Iron Age, but Tylecote (1986a: 155-156) describes two types, both dating from Roman times. Due to the quality of Pre-Roman British metalwork and the associated high standard of technology it is likely that the process of ore roasting would have been known. One circular roasting hearth, located at Great Chasterton and measuring two metres in diameter was lined with yellowish clay, in which black charcoal and yellowish or brownish or blue ore, depending on the material, would have been laid and roasted. The other type, found at a site in Bardown Sussex, featured a stone lined trench of two metres length and 30cm width, closed at one end. The stones were lined with clay and the trench would have been filled with ore and charcoal or possibly wood (Tylecote 1986a:155-156). It is probable that this process would have been repeated a number of times (Ottaway 1994: 101; 105). The roasting of the ore would have resulted in a reddening of both the ore and the clay lining.

Smelting

The next step in the process of obtaining metal from ore is smelting. Again, the archaeological evidence for smelting in the British Iron Age is scant. It is often difficult to differentiate between smelting furnaces and melting or forging furnaces, and dating is frequently inconclusive (Tylecote 1986a: 156). In the absence of hard archaeological data we have to rely on experiments carried out by metallurgists such as Peter Northover or Ronald Tylecote.

The smelting process differs for different metals and I will examine in turn the most widely used metals, i.e. iron, gold, copper and copper alloys.

Iron

The more advanced furnaces such as slag tapping furnaces and developed bowl furnaces were widely used by the Romans (Tylecote 1986a: 210; 1986a: 157) but there is evidence that they were used in the late Pre-Roman Iron Age in Britain (Bayley et al. 2008: 43; Craddock 1995: 260; Paynter 2007: 209; Tylecote 1986a: 136). The simplest form of smelting furnace which would have been used during the Pre-Roman Iron Age in Britain is the bowl furnace, a hole in the ground or rock, lined with clay and filled with a mixture of ore and fuel, such as charcoal or peat.[7] This may have been topped with a dome shaped clay structure. Air would have been blown into the furnace with the help of a tuyere. The slag would have collected into the sunken hearth or pit (Crew 1991: 22-25; Paynter 2007: 202; Tylecote 1986a: 210). The more advanced tapping furnaces would have had a

ground level hearth and the red slag would have flowed out through an opening in the furnace wall, whilst still hot (Miller 2009: 53; Paynter 2007: 202).

Iron differs from the other metals discussed in this chapter in respect of its melting point. Unless the temperature of the furnace rises to 1600 – 1800 degrees (temperatures which can only be achieved with modern technology) only the slag melts during the process, but not the iron itself. In simple bowl furnaces the slag begins to melt at a temperature of 1200° Celsius and drains off either to one side or the bottom of the bowl or into a separate slag pit. In its liquid form the slag looks blood red but it takes on a blackish bluish colour during the cooling process. The resulting iron bloom remains solid in the furnace and is of a blackish colour. It is interesting to note that in the process any liquidity and heat equates with a reddish colour, suggesting a connection between heat and movement with the colour red, and inertia with the colour black.

Gold and Copper

Gold was probably simply smelted in crucibles. Pliny describes this process in his Natural History (33.71). He states that the crucibles for smelting gold were made out of a white earth resembling clay, which according to him is the only substance which can stand the required heat during the smelting process. Pliny also mentions that this process may have been repeated. Gold of course does not alter its colour during the smelting process, but simply becomes liquid and can be drained. Whilst clay would have been a perfectly adequate material for smelting gold, it is interesting that Pliny specifically mentions a white material. The combination of gold and white is echoed in his account of white clad druids harvesting mistletoe (which in itself is a combination of golden leaves and white berries) with golden sickles.

It is not certain whether copper was smelted in furnaces or simply in crucibles. Experimental archaeology backed up with some archaeological data from sites in Jordan has shown that small quantities of copper calcites, broken into small pieces could have been smelted in little smelting crucibles, made of clay and heated with pulverised charcoal and the resulting red liquid copper could then have been used for founding (Craddock 1995: 126-143; Miller 2009: 154; Ottaway 1994: 18, 28, 94; Tylecote 1986a: 19). Evidence from sites such as Gussage All Saints, Dorset and Weelsby Avenue in Grimsby, Yorkshire suggest that three cornered round bottomed crucibles were in use during the Iron Age (Foster 1995: 55).

For the production of larger quantities of copper a furnace would have been required. Tylecote (1986a: 195) shows a possible model of a complicated shaft copper smelting furnace, but simple bowl furnaces are perhaps more likely for the British Iron Age, although in analogy with iron

---

[7] There is no evidence in Britain of the so-called Catalan type of bowl furnace in which ore and charcoal was layered (Tylecote 1980: 210, 1986a: 131). Deliberate deposition of layers of reddish ore and black charcoal would have been perhaps visually more striking than the mere filling in with a mixture of these materials.

smelting technology advanced furnaces with separate tap holes and clay moulds may have been used during the later Iron Age. In a clay lined bowl furnace filled with a mixture of charcoal and copper ore, the copper would have melted at a temperature of 1084° Celsius, similar to the temperature required for melting gold, whereas the slag would have melted at a temperature of 1150° Celsius and, due to its higher density, the copper would have separated from the slag and collected at the bottom of the bowl. After the cooling process the black slag would have been broken away from the reddish copper ingot. The smelting process might have been repeated a number of times to increase the purity and thus quality of the metal. Pliny states in his Natural History (34.96) that the metal in Gaul was smelted between stones which had been heated red hot, but that it was only smelted once, and thus of inferior quality.

Alloys

The context of copper and gold smelting lends itself to a discussion of the technology of alloying. Only a limited number of metals, such as gold, silver, platinum, copper, antimony and to a lesser extend iron are available in pure native form. Other metals, e.g. silver, copper, lead, iron or mercury can be made pure by furnace technology (Northover 1998: 113). A number of alloying metals such as tin, arsenic or antimony occur naturally in copper ore and gold often contains certain quantities of silver. During the smelting process, the combination of these metals results in the creation of natural alloys. Chemical analysis shows that the addition of alloying metals such as arsenic, antimony or tin in the smelting process was by no means always accidental, but often a deliberate process, although the exact technological process is not yet clear (Ottaway 1994: 133-140).

Peter Northover (1998: 113) lamented the fact that in the past too much emphasis in prehistoric metallurgy had been placed on metal extraction, trade and utilitarian aspects of metal. Not enough work has been carried out to appreciate the full spectrum of alloying skills and alloying metals. Luckily this seems to be changing with more advanced methods of analysis, but chemical analysis of metal alloy artefacts is still relatively sparse. Even though we do not have a comprehensive picture of geographical or temporal development and distribution of alloys, we may still gain some insight into a number of colour implications with the data currently to hand.

The technology of alloying gold was already known during the Bronze Age. Gold often has a natural silver content which makes it appear whiter in colour. The deliberate addition of copper gives the metal a warmer, more yellow colour. Different mixes of silver, lead and copper added to gold during smelting result in a variety of colours ranging from greenish yellow to reddish gold (Ottaway 1994: 24; Tylecote 1986a: 2-4). During the early Bronze Age the copper content in gold was significantly lower than during the later Bronze Age and the Iron Age (Ottaway 1994: 25). There could be a mere technological explanation for this tendency towards an increased copper content in gold. Natural gold with a high silver content of 20% or more is fairly white in colour and too hard to be hammered into thin plates. A more yellowish colour, i.e. gold with a higher copper content, would therefore have been a visual indication for the smelter or smith that the gold was of a more malleable quality and metal workers might have tried to achieve this colour to make the metal more workable.

This explanation, however, does not justify the higher tendency towards a warmer, yellow gold in Britain and Germany than elsewhere (Ottaway 1994: 25). Whilst the quality, workability and strength of the metal would undoubtedly have been important to the metalworkers, the colour itself may have played a significant role (Wheeler and Maddin 1980: 104, 105). Whether this may have been purely aesthetic or perhaps symbolic will be discussed further below and in chapter 8.

The addition of tin or arsenic to copper creates alloys of varying colour and quality. Arsenic content in copper decolorizes the resulting metal and makes it appear more golden or silver, depending on the quantity (Charles 1980: 169), but it also makes it harder and more suitable for cold working than pure copper (Charles 1980: 170). If the arsenic content is between four and six percent and the surface is arsenic enriched, the resulting alloy has a silver appearance which tarnishes to gold (Northover 1989: 115). Arsenic alloys were replaced by bronze during the Bronze Age, an alloy created by the addition of tin to copper, resulting in colours ranging from nearly white to dark brown to reddish or yellowish golden, depending on the tin content and other alloying agents such as nickel, antimony or arsenic, which may have been naturally occurring in the ore or deliberately added.

One of the reasons why tin may have been used as alloying agent is the lower melting point of the combination of tin and copper, which makes the smelting and founding process easier (Ottaway 1994: 138). We do not have sufficient evidence to ascertain whether tin was added to liquid copper, or smelted with the copper thereby reducing the melting point, although metallurgists such as Barbara Ottaway believe that Iron Age metalworkers would have been aware of this fact and utilised it (Ottaway 1994: 139).

The preference for tin rather than antimony as alloying agent may have been due to the fact that antimony makes the copper hard, but brittle (Charles 1980: 171). But Charles (1980: 177-178) also believes that the garlicky smell of arsenic alloys and the damage to health caused by arsenic may have been contributing factors. He believes that the image of the crippled Greek god Hephaistos may be a reflection of the health problems of the miners and smiths working with materials such as arsenic.

Tylecote, however, who experimented with arsenic alloys, believes that the health risks were negligible and that the arsenic content of an arsenic copper alloy could have been lowered by oxidative cold working, which makes the metal more malleable, but also leaves a white residue on the smith's tool and white smoke in the air (McKerrell and Tylecote 1972: 212); an interesting correlation between the malleability of the metal and colour imagery, suggesting more malleability and softness connected with and perhaps perceived to have been caused by the escape of white material.

During the Pre-Roman Iron Age a bronze containing up to 25% tin, often modified with other metals such as arsenic was used for coinage. This high tin alloy would have been nearly white in appearance, and a similar alloy had been used during the Bronze Age for votive or representative function (Northover 1998: 115). Apart from the earlier stated technological advantage, another reason for the use of tin as alloying agent may have been the wider colour spectrum which could thus be achieved. It is also possible that tin itself was perceived to be a valuable and perhaps even magical material, as argued by Gillis in relation to the use of tin in the Aegean Bronze Age. When heated to a temperature just below its melting point at 232° Celsius tin foil oxidises to a golden colour (Gillis 1999: 142-144).

There is archaeological evidence of brass, a gold coloured copper zinc alloy, from Iron Age Britain, e.g. one of the upper discs on a shield found as part of the Tal-y-llyn hoard (Savory 1964: 450, 464-465) or the La Tène II sword from Syon Reach, Isleworth which has a brass foil stamp showing an animal, possibly a deer with antlers (Craddock et al. 2004: 340). It is generally believed that brass had been imported, perhaps from as far away as Anatolia in the form of a coin and may have been believed to have been gold (Craddock et al. 2004: 344).

Dungworth (1996: 410-411) argued that copper alloying had changed little between the Bronze and Iron Age and that the use of brass began around the beginning of the first century AD. He believes that the conquest had scarce impact on metallurgy, yet the use of good quality brass artefacts decorated with geometrical motifs in the Seven Sisters hoard, which appear to have been made locally and are of a British Iron Age style and form, show that Roman technology clearly had impact on native metalworking (Davis and Gwilt 2008: 161). These artefacts will be discussed in further detail in chapter 7.

Further Processing of Metal

After the smelting process was completed gold, copper and copper alloys were melted in crucibles, and then cast into ingots or artefacts with the help of moulds, which may have been made out of stone, clay or metal. These metals are also soft and ductile enough to be worked on by a smith when slightly reheated or annealed. They could also have been cold worked. Gold, for example, can be hammered into thin sheets without annealing (O'Faolain 2004: 76; Ottaway 1994: 114-123; Wheeler and Maddin 1980: 104). Unlike blacksmiths, copper or gold smiths did not require repeated reheating of the material for their craft. Indeed, cold working of metal increases the strength of the material. The colour of the metals would not have changed significantly during these processes. There are further processes such as tinning or gilding which are used increasingly in the Late Iron Age and in the Romano-British period and which have an effect on the colour of the object. Examples are a silver trumpet brooch with gilded scroll work dating from the first half of the first century AD (Boon 1975: 41- 43) and the tinned plaques on the Tal-y-llyn shield, which has been dated to the first century BC or the first century AD (Savory 1964: 464-465). There appears to be also increased patination activity during the Roman-British period (Northover: personal comment). Such processes may be due to the influence of Roman technology (Corder and Hawkes 1940: 349-350) and merit further investigation but for the purposes of this chapter it should be noted that all these processes have the effect of either changing the colour of the underlying metal or creating a polychrome effect. In either case, they are creative and transformative processes.

The process of forging iron is entirely different and blacksmiths would have had quite different skill sets from those of gold and copper smiths. The blacksmith would have required a forge with a sufficiently hot fire to heat and reheat the iron bloom in order to hammer it into the required shape. He would have had to constantly monitor the size, colour and sound of the fire to ensure the required level of heat, and control it by adding fuel as and when needed. The anthropologist Keller, who took an apprenticeship as a blacksmith, stated that it would have taken some time to gain the expertise to control fire to such a level and keep it permanently in mind whilst working the iron (Keller and Keller 1996: 139).

During the forging process the iron itself constantly changes colour through repeated heating, and again, the smith must recognise the correct colour and work without any delays (Scott and Eggert 2009: 9). If two pieces of iron are to be welded together the colour of the iron must be pale yellow and wet looking. In order to change the shape of the iron, the colour must be a bright orange, and for planishing a low red or black is sufficient (Keller and Keller 1996: 46-47). Generally, the hotter and whiter the metal, the softer it is. As in the process of smelting, there is a correlation between colour, heat and movement. The time of heating and cooling is also important for the process and the metal must be alternatively heated, forged and reheated, a process which Keller describes as rhythmic and episodic (Keller and Keller 1996: 48). This rhythmic process is echoed in the colour changes of the process. The black of charcoal and iron bloom changes to the red and ultimately white of the glowing fire and the forged iron, and then back to the blackness of the cooled iron. Goethe's description of his experience of looking at a glowing mass of iron on an anvil adds a further colour dimension (Goethe 1840: 19). During his experiment he turned away from the red hot iron and looked into a black coal shed. A large red image floated before his eyes. When he then turned from the coal shed to a light coloured surface the image appeared half red and half green depending on the background. Undoubtedly, blacksmiths who constantly look at the fire in their hearth and glowing iron would experience similar colour imagery.

Steel was certainly produced during the Iron Age, but the chemical reaction leading to the process, i.e. the carbonisation of iron was of course not known. In order to produce steel the iron object would have had to have been in prolonged contact with charcoal and the white hot colour of the iron during this process may have been perceived as a purification of iron (Aristotle Meteorologica 4.6), making it harder, less likely to rust and less brittle (Wheeler and Maddin 1980: 116). The process of quenching was known to Homer, who describes it in the Odyssey. Odysseus and his men blind the Cyclops Polyphemus with a red hot olive wood stake. Homer likens the effect of driving the stake into the Cyclop's eye to the hissing sound heard when a smith plunges an axe into cold water to strengthen the iron (Odyssey 9.390). Quenching has no effect on iron but hardens carbonised steel (Muhly 1980: 52; Wheeler and Maddin 1980: 124) which would suggest that during Homer's time there was no real notion of the difference between iron and steel. It is unclear whether British Iron Age blacksmiths would have known the effect of quenching. Not enough examination for evidence of quenching on Pre-Roman Iron Age tools has been carried out, but Tylecote states that even during the Roman period quenching was not much in use. Quenching steel with a high carbon level or at the wrong temperature can make it brittle. An easier method to harden steel with high phosphorus content is to harden it by cold hammering (Tylecote 1986a: 145). Whichever method was used, the resulting metal would have had a different, more bluish colour and appear more lustreous than iron.

A further colour association in relation to steel making might have come from the use of bone in the carbonizing process. There is evidence from the Scandinavian Iron age, backed up by experimental archaeology that crushed bones may have been used in order to make steel. Crushed animal or human bones would have been placed in a metal container which in turn would have been placed with the opening facing the earth. A fire would have been lit for several hours to burn the white bones to a dull grey-black colour. Bone and charcoal would then have been crushed into a powder and poured into a metal box containing a piece of iron. The sealed box would then have been placed into a small smelting furnace. Experiments have shown that after six hours at 900° Celsius iron turns into steel (Gansum 2004: 42-43).

Further Biographies of Metal

The function of metal artefacts, their iconography and any correlation with colour, as well as manipulation of the finished products and their ultimate deposition, whether ritualistic or otherwise, will be dealt with elsewhere. For the purposes of this chapter I want to briefly allude to the topics of corrosion and oxidation. Gold takes a special place, as it not only retains its colour, but it does not corrode. Silver is more corrosion resistant than lesser metals, but its surface tarnishes and looses its lustre unless polished. Copper and bronze, if left unpolished, untreated and exposed, oxidise to a greenish or bluish colour and will ultimately corrode, but will last considerably longer than iron and steel. Steel retains its lustre longer than iron, but both rust relatively quickly to a reddish colour and then corrode (Selwyn 2004).

Discussion

Apart from the colour implications of the process of metal making, we have to ask the question whether the colour of metal, both in terms of processing and the finished metal had any significance over and above the technological aspects; in other words whether there was a hierarchy of metals. In the Western world we assume that gold is the metal with the highest value, but this is not universally the case. In West Mexico copper was the only metal in use from 600 AD to about 1200 AD even though tin, gold and silver were readily available (Gillis 1999: 140).

We know from classical sources that there was a perception of a hierarchy of metals in Mediterranean culture groups. Hesiod describes in his work Works and Days (109-201) the ages of men in terms of metallic colour. During the golden age men lived in a blissful state ignorant of hard labour, disease, sorrow or death. The following age, the silver age, produced men who were without sense. Then came the age of bronze with fierce men and finally the iron age which was peopled with cruel and unscrupulous men. Ovid retells the myth in his Metamorphoses (1.89-150) and closes this myth of origin with the story of Deukalion and his wife Phyrra, the survivors of Zeus' rage against the men of the iron age and how they were instructed by the goddess Themis to throw the bones of their mother behind them. They correctly interpreted this as stones, the bones of the earth mother goddess, and thus they created men and women of stone, a race whose lives were filled with hard labour (Ovid Metamorphoses 1.313-415). Apart from the golden age each one of these ages ends due to degeneration. A similar imagery features in the teachings of Zarathustra. A tree with four branches, one gold, one silver, one steel and one iron alloy (*sic*)[8] represents the ages of men (Zand-i Vohuman Yasht, chapter 1*)*. This suggests perhaps an Indo-Germanic belief system which may have been introduced alongside metal technology to the west.

The Persians thought of iron as an instrument of torture and the ancient Hebrews regarded iron as an impure metal (Pleiner: 2000, 20) perhaps recognising it as an alloy. A distinction of the value of metals is also prevalent in classical Roman sources. Cicero describes the iron age in his de natura deorum, 2.154-158 as an age where men dared to forge iron swords; whilst in the golden age no harm was done to oxen, in the iron age men eat the meat of the oxen who plough the field. Cicero regards the use of iron as violence both against the earth and animals. Pliny in his Natural History (34.138) calls iron the worst and best apparatus in life. It is used to plough, plant, trim vines, build houses and quarry rocks, but it is also used for slaughter and war.

We do not know whether a similar belief in a hierarchy of various metals existed in Iron Age Britain. It is the case that certain metals were used for certain objects and in certain circumstances and we can therefore imply that a different value, whether socio-economic or symbolic, was attributed to different metals. The connection between certain metals and iconography or symbolic quality will be explored in greater detail in chapter 8.

Some scholars believe that a differentiation of value has technological reasons. According to Locher (1998: 4) the discovery and processing of small quantities of silver and gold required far less pain and labour than the production of iron, especially given the terrible conditions in deep mines. His argument is flawed, however, as the smelting of small quantities of copper does not require more labour than gold. Also, iron ore could have been found and processed in small quantities with relatively little added work. Equally, the conditions in underground gold and silver mines as described by Pliny (Natural History 33.71; 33.95) and Diodorus Siculus (Library of History 3.12-13; 5.38) would not have been any better than in iron or copper mines.

Another technological argument for a hierarchy of value could of course be the sequence of discovery of metal. The argument presented inter alia by Ottaway (1994: 20) that the switch from bronze to iron was due to the fact that iron ore is far more frequently found, is not conclusive for Iron Age Britain. In the British Isles copper ore is mostly found in Ireland, Wales and the Western part

of England, whereas iron ore is more concentrated in eastern and middle parts of England (Tylecote 1986a: 11-12). Iron working had been known for a number of centuries in Europe before iron production really took off (Needham 1990: 136). This may have been due to the fact that it would have taken some time to acquire the drastically different skills involved in smelting and forging iron, but it could also be due to a gradual shift of production centres and therefore perhaps power, in line with the geographical areas supplying the iron ore. However, iron did not replace bronze. Indeed, if iron had been introduced due to a shortage of availability of bronze, as has been claimed (e.g. Ottaway 1994: 105), why did bronze continue to play a major role especially in ritual contexts, and why were large quantities of bronze deposited during the iron age, ritual or otherwise (Needham 1990: 137)?

Another argument for the differentiation of value in metal is the quality of the material. However, this argument is also inconclusive. Gold is very soft and useless for tools, yet used for prestige objects. Whilst admittedly iron can be brittle and is in many ways inferior to bronze, if it is carbonized it is certainly of a superior quality to bronze.

In some cultures the purity of metal is the most important aspect. The brahmanical texts of ancient India tell us that copper was seen as the most pure base metal and superior to copper alloys. These were considered as polluted, even though they represented a technical advancement and their technical quality was superior to that of copper. The reason for this belief in the superiority of copper is purely metaphysical. The Brahmans are likened to fire which is echoed in the reddish colour of copper. The metaphysical origin of copper was seen as the casting off of the brilliant embryo of Siva by the deity Ganga, during which process any impure elements became tin and lead. For this reason copper was used for rituals to the exclusion of alloys in India up until the 19th century (Lahiri 1995: 118-121).

Could it be then the colour, rather than the quality of the metal which attributed value? Hesiod first compared the inferior black and grey colour of iron in comparison to gold silver and bronze in his Works and Days. The spectrum of colour of different metals is beautifully demonstrated by a work of modern artist Carl Andre, 32 Bar Square Fugue on 4 Ancient Metals (Figure 11a). The mere colour of metal in isolation is, though, perhaps not sufficient. Pliny remarks that the colour of gold is not as bright as that of silver, which he likens to daylight, but that gold is the preferred metal due to its purity, the fact that it does not loose substance in fire and that it does not rust (Natural History 33.58-59). It is interesting that Pliny, who lived in the warm climate of the Mediterranean where light is much brighter, prefers the colder colour of silver to gold, whereas, as noted above, there was a tendency in Germany and Britain

---

[8] Whilst iron is an element, the translation of the term as 'iron alloy' probably indicates the impurity of the metal.

towards warmer colours, perhaps due to lack of warmth and light, particular in winter.

Wheeler and Maddin (1980: 99) think that value was determined not only by colour but also by lustre. The lustre in gold remains constant, whereas silver, bronze and iron tarnish at varying speeds. Wertime (1980: 5) argued that iron seemed to be a common material, associated with charcoal and the requirement of repeated forging. I would go further and argue that colour and luminosity are a substantial part of the valuation process, but that they are intrinsically correlated to perceived purity, lifespan and human interference or pollution of the material, and in this context the colour changes during the biography of metal also play an important role. Colour has undoubtedly aesthetic values, but these are merely a part of a wider cosmology of metalworking.

Looking at possible anthropological parallels, the South American Inca associated gold with the sun, the ruling Inca and masculinity (Bauer and Stanish 2002: 14), metalworkers in west Mexico prior to the Spanish conquest were primarily interested in the sound and colour of metal and, as is demonstrable by the percentage of alloying agents used, sacrificed mechanical quality and optimal design for the sake of colour and sound. Golden and silvery colours were valued higher than reddish metals on purely metaphysical grounds. The production of shimmering golden and silvery metallic colours meant the recreation of the sacred and divine in material objects. The possession of such of shimmering objects imbued with the divine spirit gave the kings and nobles a link to divinity. Gold and silver were perceived to be associated with the sun and moon as shown by linguistic parallels,[9] and gold and silver also validated the divine authority of the nobility. The reflective and shimmering quality of gold and to a lesser extent silver is a reminder of the sacred garden of the Aztec paradise, which is filled with divine fire and where the light of the sun reflects from flower petals and iridescent feathers of birds. The quality of the sound of metal is also metaphysically interlinked with the making of shimmering metals. In Nauhatl mythology sound can create colour (Hosler 1995: 100-113).

To my knowledge no work has been carried out in relation to the synaesthetic aspects of metal in the British Iron Age, but it would be interesting to find out whether there is a similar link between metal and sound. It is conceivable, though, that there was a perceived link between luminosity and iridescence of metal and supernatural power. It has been argued that a link between brilliant material and spiritual brilliance (whether this is interpreted as ancestral spiritual power or perhaps as symbolic representation of the sun, moon

or a rainbow deity) operates cross-culturally (Keates 2002: 119; Morphy 1992: 202; Saunders 1999: 245). I will explore brilliance and luminosity in further detail in chapter 6, but on the assumption that there is such a link, it would make sense that gold which does not corrode and keeps its lustre, may have been regarded as imbued with more sacred power and would have had an entirely different status than bronze or iron. Both these metals loose their lustre, but also require far more technology and manipulation to bring out and maintain a shiny surface. This leads to several further questions: How were copper or iron ore perceived as they, unlike gold, are not shiny or iridescent, and what meaning, if any may have been attributed to colour changes during the metalworking process? Were metals or metallic objects which change their colour, seen as organic and what role did the metal worker play in this process?

In his Natural History, Pliny states that iron was 'punished' by rusting (33.141). The process of punishment not only implies that iron is given the status of a being which can experience punishment, but also that it has acted in a certain way which requires punishment. He further writes that 'nothing in the world is more mortal than that which is most hostile to mortality'. The material has become imbued with personality or at least some kind of mortality, hence life.[10] It is also interesting that red rust with its association of blood which precedes corrosion, i.e. the death of the material, is seen as punishment. Whilst this metaphor is of course derived from a Roman context and may not have had any parallels in the British Iron Age, it is still worth considering whether metals were perceived as organic.

There are numerous anthropological examples of a connection between metalworking and fertility. For the Karagwe tribe in Uganda the furnace represents female genitalia whereas the smelters and the bellows represent male sexuality. The whole process of iron smelting is a ritual, requiring ritual knowledge and creating a source of power. The smelters live in a state of pollution and danger, both metaphysically as they mediate between natural and cultural worlds, but also in a real sense due to the danger of furnace technology. The king is associated with the symbolism of the smith, perceived to be a less dangerous occupation than that of the smelter. In order for the king to control and harness the spiritual power of the smelters, the smelting clans are governed by women, thereby emasculating the smelter's power (Reid and MacLean 1995: 144-161). The Ga'anda in Nigeria used two types of ore, 'male' and 'female', which had to be combined in order to produce the required metal and which were distinguished by colour (Herbert 1993: 39; Ottaway 1994: 217), and in Cameroon iron

---

[9] In Nauhatl the literal translation for gold is yellow divine excretion of the sun deity (Hosler 1995: 106).

[10] In the above stated passage of the Odyssey, Homer uses the word 'screaming' in the context of the sound made by steel during the quenching process, thus also treating the metal object as animated or living.

making is associated with pregnancy and childbirth. The symbolism of fertility and childbirth is easily explained by the imagery of the furnace. The insertion of the tuyeres and the blowing of bellows are akin to sexual acts, e.g. the smith penetrates the female and womb-like furnace and fertilizes it. The mixing of materials creates a symbolic 'child' in the form of a bloom. In South West Ethiopia the local term for tuyere is the same as the male sexual organ, and the furnace is referred to as womb. The removal of the bloom is referred to as the woman giving birth. Similar associations with sexuality and procreation are made by the Fur in Dafur, the Fipa of Tanzania, the Ekonda in Zaire and some communities in Nepal   (Haaland 2004: 3-11; Herbert 1993: 58-65). The associations between the red liquid slag draining away and either menstrual blood or blood flow during the birthing process only further such metaphors. The resulting material is seen by the Oromo in Ethiopia, Kenya and Somalia as dead. Married women wear iron bracelets on the upper right arm as the marriage act itself is seen as a symbolic death following the husband's spilling of the wife's virginal blood, although through this death children, i.e. life is created (Kassam and Megersa 1989: 29).

A further association between metalworking and creation has already been referred to above in the use of bones for the making of steel in Iron Age Scandinavia. These associations may not just be metaphors but, as Melanie Giles has argued, the transformative processes might have been perceived as actual births (Giles 2007: 402). Steel weapons might have been 'born' from the bones of deceased warriors in a transformation that included black iron, the whiteness of bone and the red of fire.

The imagery of giving birth to metal does not quite work for the production of copper and copper alloys. But there are other connections between the metal working process and fertility or life giving which allude to a different imagery and cosmology. Ottaway (1994: 220-221) cites numerous examples from African tribes which treated the making of metal as a seasonal activity. There is no consistency as to which season smelting or forging is carried out. The Bai-la in Rhodesia smelt in spring time whereas the Embu in Kenia must not carry out this process at any time other than the 'black time', the time when the rivers have dried up. This may of course have purely technical reasons, such as the fact that the iron ores can only be collected on dried up river beds, or it may be linked to the availability of fuel. Temperature also has an impact on the hardness of metal (Ottaway 1994: 122). This was certainly known to Pliny who wrote that copper and bronze fuse better in very cold weather (Natural History 34.96). It is possible that metal production and smithing took place only during certain times of the year in the British Iron Age, which in turn may have meant that other metalworking activities, such as mining and forging were also seasonal.

Beyond the mere technical explanations for seasonality the colour associations explored earlier in the process of copper production present interesting analogies with the processing of agricultural products and seasonality. The frequently green copper ore has to be extracted or 'harvested' from the earth and it is then processed and transformed into a new reddish substance with the help of fire, similar to the process of cooking or baking. Ultimately the metal object looses its lustre and oxidises. The colour of the verdigris is similar to that of the mould on rotten fruit or vegetables. Rotten fruit or vegetables would have been placed in a midden or composted in some way. Perhaps the ritual deposition of bronze or copper items would have been perceived in a similar way. This does not mean that the objects so discarded would have been regarded as rubbish or worthless. Our concept of rubbish is relatively modern and in many societies all products or objects would have had value, whether socio-economic or symbolic. Slag, for example is often associated with either faecal matter or menstrual blood, but it is also used as a healing compound in some societies (Lahiri 1995: 129; Pliny Natural History 33.105). In several Greek temples scrap metal was offered as a votive gift (Blakely-Westover 1999: 88)

As any gardener will confirm, the composting of rotten vegetables and fruit will lead to a fertile soil and this would have been known in largely agricultural communities. It is possible that the deposition of bronze was meant to encourage the growth of copper ore or to enrich the soil. Further associations can also be made between copper and blood. During the melting process copper becomes a red liquid, akin to live blood and, unlike iron which could not have been melted with the technology available, copper and copper alloys could be recycled, a process during which the metal would have turned again into a bloodlike substance. Blood, as will be discussed in further detail in chapter 7 is a very ambiguous fluid, as it can represent both life and death. The analogy with blood, coupled with the fact that bronze has an ambiguous quality (i.e. it is not consistent and can become duller and darker if unpolished or untreated) may be the reason why bronze and copper often have similarly ambiguous qualities or threshold symbolism in classical sources and early Welsh and Irish myth. Hesiod described the western Mediterranean as entrance to an Underworld, a place 'where night and day draw near and greet each other as they pass the great threshold of bronze' (Ó hÓgáin 1999: 55; Hesiod Theogonia 745-750). In the Odyssey the palace of king Alcinous, who as a descendant of the god Poseidon is semi-divine, has a threshold and floor of bronze (7.90; 13. 4). Interestingly Odysseus' arrival at Alcinous' palace marks a turning point in his destiny and the symbolism of bronze may indicate this.

In Irish myth Conchobar, who is not only a king but a supernatural hero, resides in a room guarded by screens of copper (Kinsella 1970: 6). Bronze is also mentioned in circumstances where a liminal area is entered into. In Irish myth Connla travels over the ocean from a supernatural island in a little boat of bronze with gilt oars. Finally bronze seems to be also linked to acts of magic. In book 4.504-527 of the Aeneid, Dido cuts magic poisonous herbs with a bronze knife, perhaps indicating that bronze rather than iron was to be used for magic rites as it crosses the boundary into the supernatural world. Pliny tells of the ritual of harvesting a plant called selago, which was used as a charm against evil. The plant had to be gathered by the harvester being dressed in white and he was not allowed to use iron implements (Pliny Natural History 24.103). Pliny does not tell us what the material of the implement should be, but there seems to have been a taboo against iron which is reminiscent of fairies' fear of iron in Irish tradition (Birkhan 1997: 38) or Tacitus' description of the worship of the German goddess Nerthus in a secret grove during which ritual all iron must be locked away (Tacitus Germania 40).

If we assume that the process of metal making had associations with fertility and perhaps even the creation of life, the metalworkers and smiths would have been perceived as very powerful people. The role of the smith in prehistoric metalworking has been discussed by a number of scholars (e.g. Budd and Taylor 1995; Charles 1980: 178-180; Hingley 1997; Ottaway 1994: 221-227; Pleiner 2000: 104) but literature seems to give divergent pictures. Sometimes the smith is seen as an itinerant worker, at other times as part of the community, albeit on its fringe, some perceive him as a magician or shaman and there are also discussions on centres of metal production with emphasis on the economic value of the metalworker, although the underlying assumptions in these works are probably more apt for 19th century miners.

It is misleading to talk of the smith per se when discussing metalwork. Firstly, it is likely that there was a differentiation between blacksmiths and copper or goldsmiths. Secondly, mining, smelting and forging may all have been carried out by different specialists and they may all have had a different status in their respective communities. For purely physical reasons it is unlikely that the whole process of metal making would have been carried out by one single person. Radomir Pleiner (2000: 104) argues that based on ethnographic parallels mining may have been a specialised group activity, perhaps based on extended family units. Members of this group, perhaps even a family, would extract and, if required, roast ore, prepare the charcoal, construct furnaces, smelt ore and then return to their community with iron in the form of blooms which could then be forged by the blacksmith.

Budd and Taylor (1995) concur that the process of metal making, even smithing, could have been carried out by family groups and that there is no reason why women could not have been involved. They argue that metal making should not be seen as necessarily male driven, but perhaps as a task carried out by a number of specialists who shared their skills. Whether the process was carried out by a team of specialists each of whom was responsible for one of the various stages of metal making or by groups working together, it required specialist knowledge and a high degree of skill which would have been passed on by some kind of lengthy apprenticeship. Bronze and gold workers would have had to learn the skill of adding alloying agents in order to achieve the correct consistency (Charles 1980: 179) and all metal workers would have had to have a high level of pyrotechnical knowledge. Fire is perhaps the most important aspect of metallurgy as it is essential to transform ore into metal and to forge metal. The colour of the fire as well as its sound would have been the only indicator for the metalworker to judge its temperature. Not only would it have taken some time to gain the requisite knowledge to work with fire, it is also a dangerous element and the metalworker would have been in constant danger.

It is also important to keep in mind that technology and ritual should not be treated separately. With the help of fire the metalworker would have achieved a process of transformation and ultimately creation and without our modern knowledge of chemical transactions the changing colour of the fire, as well as the transformation of the ore into metal and the associated colour changes would have been perceived to be extraordinary if not magical. Budd and Taylor (1995: 139) argue that in non literate societies complex procedures such as the technical and chemical processes involved in metal making are seen as ritual or even magical and hence myth and folklore often perceive the smith as a magical persona. The Anglo-Saxon Wayland and the early Irish Goibnhiu are but two examples of supernatural or semi-divine smiths. In Siberian tradition the smith was seen as the shaman's elder brother (Vitebsky 1995:104) and the connection is easy to understand. Both are involved in transformation, both are in dangerous positions and both deal with the supernatural (Aldhouse-Green and Aldhouse-Green 2005: 131-132), but unlike the smith, the shaman is not a creator and thus inferior. In European legends and folklore the smith is a twilight figure and a shape shifter, often with secret knowledge related to the transformative nature of their work (Haaland 2004: 14; Rhys 1990: 294). In order to achieve the transformation, the metalworker would have had to have the power to harness supernatural forces (Giles 2007: 407).

Both the shaman and the smith are connected to healing or protective powers. In early Irish myth the druid smith Olc Aiche places five protective circles around Cormac (Aldhouse-Green and Aldhouse-Green 2005: 132; Scott 1990: 186). The protection of those circles against wounding, drowning, fire, enchantment and evil is reminiscent of Pliny's account of the healing power of various metals. In his Natural History he states that gold is an amulet for wounded people and is protective against poisonous charms (33.84), copper and copper slag can be used as eye salves (33.107) silver slag has healing properties (33.105) and iron protects against nightmares and noxious drugs (34.151). As alluded to elsewhere iron in this context may have been perceived as protection against the supernatural. Even in respect of healing properties which may or may not be connected to the smith or metalworker as producer of such materials, there seems to be a differentiation between the various metals, gold being perhaps the most powerful.

There is also a certain ritual aspect to the blacksmith's work. Not only is the constant heating and reheating rhythmic and episodic like a repetitive dance (Keller and Keller 1996: 48), this rhythmic dance is echoed by the colours the blacksmith works with, turning from black to red to white hot and back to red and black. The blacksmith's work is also visionary. Unlike the bronze or copper workers who operate with casting methods such as *cire perdue*, the blacksmith has to visualise the object he is going to produce whilst making it, seeing it with his inner eye. As Keller observed (1996: 140), if the smith works away from his usual environment, e.g. in bright sunlight, his perception of colours will be different and the resulting quality of his work may vary considerably. In order to produce high quality materials it is therefore important for the blacksmith to operate in the same place and using the forge and tools he is accustomed to. This would contradict the view of the blacksmith as an itinerant worker which has been proposed inter alia by Budd and Taylor (1995: 140). They suggested that the blacksmith provided a range of liminal and magical services to sedentary communities who would keep the smith both physically and metaphorically on the outskirts of the community to avoid contamination with pollution. This is contrasted with the role of the bronze or copper smith, who may have been part of the community, perhaps even formed part of the elite or leadership. Sandra Blakely Westover (1999: 89) argued convincingly that the view of the smith as itinerant in Greek myth does not reflect factual circumstances but rather the symbolical view of the smith by society as a man apart, an embodiment of liminality. This may be for reasons of the physical danger of fire and perhaps the element of pollution associated with the smith's work, it may be due to the different colour of the metal worker's skin, but it could also be the fear of the smith's magic, his power to change matter and colour, to create and to interfere with and play with powers which are generally controlled by divine forces.

Conclusion

Each metal seemed to have played a very specific role in Iron Age Britain and there may have been a certain perceived hierarchy of metals. Gold may have belonged to the supernatural sphere whereas iron, which was 'born' in this world, was used for mundane and earthbound tasks or in warfare. Copper and copper alloys on the other hand had ambiguity, creating links and moving between this world and the Otherworld. The process of metalworking may well have been linked to the symbolism of fertility, creation and regeneration. Metal may have been seen to be alive or at least imbued with life. Each stage of metalworking involved some form of either recognition of colour or transformation evidenced by changes in colour, not only of the metal, but also the immediate environment, such as the fire necessary for the transformation process or the metalworkers themselves. The changes in colour were an outward signifier of the transformative process which may have been perceived to be an act of magic. The person carrying out such acts would have seemed to have had magical powers. Gold was the only metal which did not alter much in colour and may have been perceived to be something immortal or divine. However, the deliberate addition of red (perhaps magical) copper which started during the late Bronze Age and continued during the Iron Age (Hawkes and Clarke 1963: 208; Ottaway 1994: 25) and which resulted in a more reddish colour of gold may have been perceived to be a powerful act of human intervention with something belonging to the realm of the supernatural.

Chapter 5

A Whiter Shade of Pale – Chalk in the British Iron Age

Our mother is the Earth,
and I may judge the stones of earth are bones
that we should cast behind us as we go.

(Ovid Metamorphoses 1.381-395)

Introduction

The large regions of white chalk land in the British landscape appear to have had certain significance to British Iron Age people. Areas such as Wessex, the chalk hills of Kent, the wolds in Yorkshire and the Berkshire Downs have not only revealed a wealth of archaeological material from the Iron Age period, but the landscape itself and the relationships between the landscape and the people inhabiting it may have had symbolic meaning (Gosden and Lock 2007: 291). Hill forts such as Danebury seem to have integrated the brilliant white colour of the chalk into their very their design (Cunliffe 2003: 47-49). In the East ridings of Yorkshire there seems to have been a clear divide between the chalky hills as landscapes for the dead and the dark moors as landscapes for the living (Fenton-Thomas 2003: 135) and the significance of the chalk landscape for burials will be discussed in details in chapter 9. However, chalk was also used for the creation of artefacts and monuments. In this chapter I want to explore the relevance of white chalk in archaeological remains which are made out of this material, but are on opposite sides of the spectrum: The monumental Uffington White Horse from Oxfordshire and a group of little chalk figurines from Yorkshire.

The Uffington White Horse

One of the most striking examples of colour within the British Iron Age landscape is the White Horse of Uffington (Figure 11b), so far the only one of the numerous white horses carved into hillsides in Britain which has been proven to be of genuine antiquity. Even though its origins probably date to the late Bronze Age (Miles, Palmer *et al*. 2003: 78), it is of interest for the Iron Age period for several reasons. Firstly, the iconography of the horse resembles the abstract horse depictions on Iron Age coins (Green 1992: 154). Secondly, the very fact that it still exists in a form which differs only slightly from the original Bronze Age design is an indication that it must have been periodically renewed or 'scoured' throughout its existence and archaeological evidence suggests activity in the surrounding landscape of White Horse Hill including the hill fort at Uffington Castle throughout the Iron Age (Gosden and Lock 2007: 284). The horse

and its surrounding landscape may be an example of Richard Hingley's suggestion of 'otherwordly' Bronze Age features or materials which connected Iron Age people to their past and their landscape (Hingley 2009).

Even now the striking features and location of the Uffington white horse affect and inspire us. David Miles and Simon Palmer wrote of the memorable experience during their excavation work at the site of seeing the horse 'bathed in sunlight above a sea of mist' (Miles and Palmer 1995: 373), New Age druids use the horse for their rituals, local business people and the community use it as a logo (Miles, Palmer et al.2003: 267, 268), New Age jewellers use the design for alternative jewellery, and the horse even features in fictional literature such as Terry Pratchett's children's book 'a Hatful of Sky' and Rosemary Sutcliffe's 'Sun Horse, Moon Horse'. A number of attempts have been made in the past to interpret the symbolism of the horse. Barry Cunliffe (1995: 58) suggested that it may have been a territorial marker of the tribal identity of the Atrebates, necessitated by the density of the population. Whilst this symbolism should not be dismissed, it does however, not take into account the evidence of ritual activity discovered during archaeological excavations in the surrounding area (Miles, Palmer et al. 2003: 121, 124-125; Miles and Palmer 1995: 377). David Miles and Simon Palmer (Miles, Palmer et al. 2003: 78) attribute special status to the horse as a liminal being on the boundary between domesticated and wild animals, between culture and nature. The fact that the horse is not ridden, nor saddled or bridled, but runs freely and untamed, enhances the imagery of a semi-wild being.

Even though the white chalk of the hill figure is one of its key elements, no significant attempts have been made to investigate the significance of the colour or bring it into any interpretation of the horse's symbolic value. In order to explore the potential symbolic meaning of the white colour it is necessary to examine the horse within the context of its landscape and its biography. The horse is depicted with its head in a southwesterly direction on an escarpment between dragon hill, two round mounds or barrows, one long barrow and higher up and further southwest, Uffington Castle. Dragon Hill is a chalk mound which may or may not be artificially shaped (Miles, Palmer *et al.* 2003: 36). It has been used in the past for chalk quarrying and may have been used as a burial mound or for ritual activity (Miles, Palmer *et al.* 2003: 37). Excavations on the barrows indicate construction and use for burials during the Neolithic or Bronze Age (Miles, Palmer *et al.* 2003: 54) and re-use for burial during the late Roman period. Uffington Castle is a hill fort constructed in the early Iron Age. No signs of continuing activity have been found for the period from the Middle Iron Age until the Roman Period, but it was probably re-used in the fourth and fifth century AD. Although excavations have been limited, it has been suggested that the hill fort was a ceremonial centre used for ritual involving perhaps seasonal activities and the proximity of the horse suggests mutual influence, significance and meaning (Miles, Palmer *et al.* 2003: 124).

A number of factors strengthen the argument of a symbolic and perhaps ritual meaning of the horse within the context of the landscape and its colour is a material element of such interpretation. Despite being a static figure, the horse is depicted in full running movement and its abstract appearance enhances the impression of energy, swiftness and sense of movement, thus appearing to move geographically up the hill away from Dragon Hill towards the burial mounds, a place of the death and the Hill fort, a place where ritual activities, i.e. interactions between the material and the spiritual world may have taken place. This sense of movement is visually enhanced by the use of the striking white colour. If regularly scoured the chalky white colour makes the horse into a brilliant and permanent feature against the background of the ever changing colours of the surrounding landscape, both in terms of the changing light of day and night, but also in terms of seasonal colour changes. The horse therefore appears to transcendent not only the landscape and the boundaries between the material and the spiritual world, but also the boundaries between day and night, the seasons of the year and therefore time itself. The only time when the horse may not have been as visible would be during winter, when the hill may have been covered in snow. Winter may have been associated with death, thus giving the re-emergence of the horse in springtime connotations of re-birth. The interpretation of the white horse as a winter horse or a horse transgressing the boundaries of time, life and death adds a further dimension to the horse's status as liminal animal on the boundary between culture and nature.

A further reason for the use of white colour which would contribute to this boundary symbolism may be that white horses may have been perceived as special, perhaps not only because of their rarity and the immediate attraction of the colour,[11] but also because true greys, as

---

[11] Even today people tend to place bets on white horses for no reason other than that the colour stands out and appeals (pers.comment Ed Clifford, retired bookmaker).

white horses are generally called, have black skin, thus alluding again to the polarity and diachronism of day and night, life and death and this world and the Otherworld, all combined in one being.

Turning then to the biography of the horse a number of observations can be made which appear to be at first glance contradictory, but may provide some further insight into underlying symbolic and perhaps ritual meaning. The figure of the horse may have been initially cut into chalk, but the subsequent 'scouring', involved the addition of successive layers of puddled chalk and hill wash (Miles, Palmer et al. 2003: 77). The horse was thus cut into the underlying and permanent material of the chalk, suggesting perhaps associations with an ancestral white landscape. Even though it was created by humans, it was and remains therefore a part of the landscape in a very material and real sense. The chalk may have had connotations with skeletal bone, possibly death and the iconography of the horse may actually hint at its skeletal structure rather than represent a fully fleshed horse. Paradoxically, the creamy consistence of white chalk puddle, which must have been added on a regular basis to maintain the figure, brings to mind milk and semen, both bodily fluids which have connotations of fertility and life giving (Turner 1967: 89). Pliny connects chalk and milk in his Natural History (37.162) in the description of the substance 'galactitis' which has been interpreted as chalk. According to Pliny it has a milky smear and flavour when rubbed between fingers and ensures that wet nurses have plenty of milk. It is interesting to note that up to the 12th century in Ireland children were baptized with milk rather than water, in the belief that milk was transmitting spirit and life (Condren 1989: 177).

The scouring or 'whitening' of the horse would have meant a social, controlled and recurring activity of perhaps an entire community or perhaps just selected persons of certain status, all involved in a process which was at the same time creative and manipulative. Yet it also re-affirmed, honoured and enhanced an existing, permanent and perhaps ancestral structure as well as existing values and, being a team effort, created a sense of community spirit. The deliberate deposition of hill wash and chalk puddle, which as stated above may have had symbolic associations with milk, introduces material from a different geographical location, perhaps dragon hill, the shape of which may even have symbolized a breast. This imagery is evocative of the so-called paps of Anu in Ireland, a site where landscape is intrinsically linked with the fertility goddess Anu.

At the same time the 'making white' of the horse also meant a deliberate process of enhancement and renewal, a manipulation of the landscape which was both creative and conservative and which may have given a sense of interaction and communication with and possibly even empowerment and influence over landscape, nature, fertility, life and death.

If the horse was meant to be a means of communication from the people who scoured it, it would have been a communication to someone either geographically or temporally removed from it, as its shape is only recognizable from afar, and indeed best from above. Even though the landscape and the gradients of the hill may have changed since the Iron Age, it may even then have been intended to be seen from above, perhaps by supernatural forces or beings who reside in the sky, the colour of which sometimes echoes that of the horse. The position of the horse is deliberately distancing the communicators from the perceived receiver of the communication, thus creating a social definition for the communicators.

Links between white horses, landscape, death and afterlife can be found in Irish mythology, Norse mythology, Sanskrit cults and Irish history and folklore.[12] The ritual sacrifice of a white mare, 'asvadedha', is cited in two hymns of the Rigveda and thus appears to have been practiced in early Indian antiquity (MacDonell 1968: 109). It is according to Hartmann (2001: 45-47) interlinked to the Sanskrit term for world tree, asvattha which in itself contains the word for horse 'asva'. The horse had symbolic connotations with or represented the sun, pulling the chariots of the gods, but it was also associated with death and afterlife and was therefore an integral part of the Sanskrit cosmology (Hartmann 2001: 47; MacDonell 1968: 109). Similarities to this cosmology can be found in the Norse myth of 'Yddgrassil Askr', the tree on which the god Odin was sacrificed. Although the myth does not mention a horse as such, the word 'Yggdrassil' is composed of the words 'Yggr', another name for Odin, and 'drassil', meaning horse (Hartmann 2001: 45-60). Solar or seasonal connotations of horses are found in Irish myth and Gaulish myth such as the description of a Gaulish sun god as Apotemarus, meaning great horse or the Irish god Dadhdha's alternative designation as Eochaid, meaning horseman (Ó hÓgáin 1999, 60) and which according to Ó hÓgáin suggests links back to Bronze Age solar worship.

Strikingly similar is the combination of horses and intoxication in the Hindu inauguration ritual, 'asvamedha', meaning horse and mead, the Irish mythical landscape goddess of Tara, Meadhbh whose name means 'she who intoxicates', who raced against horses and who may be linked to Madhavi, a mythical Indian princess and consort of kings, and the Gaulish royal title Epomeduos, which again combines horse, sovereignity and an intoxicating substance, mead (Ó hÓgáin 1999: 133-134;

MacDonell 1968: 178). The sovereign goddesses Tailtiu and Eriu were both connected to lovers or husbands whose name or cognomen were connected with horses, such a Ro-ech, big horse, or Eochaid, the horseman (Hartmann 2001: 44), thus suggesting a link between sovereignty, horses and mating. This metaphor was still in use in the 12th century AD as evidenced in Giraldus Cambrensis' account of the kingship rite in Ulster in his Topographica Hibernica, which tells of the ritual union between a the King of Ulster and the 'banfheis rígi', the goddess of sovereignty, who is represented by a white mare. The white mare is sacrificed and the king eats and drinks from the meat and broth cooked from the sacrificed animal (Aldhouse-Green 2001a: 108). The link between white horses and royal status is also confirmed by the old Irish term for white horse 'gabor', which does not only denote the white colour but also the high, often royal status of white horses (Kelly 1997: 62).

Numerous tales in early Irish and Welsh vernacular texts feature supernatural white horses. The most striking example is perhaps the white horse of Rhiannon in the first branch of the Mabinogi. Rhiannon is a supernatural being, sometimes believed to be linked to the Gallo-Roman Epona, a goddess of fertility but also of death (Aldhouse-Green 2001a: 110; Wood 1997: 168-173) and whose name derives from the Celtic word 'Epos', meaning 'horse'. Epona was worshipped in Britain as well as France, Switzerland and Germany and was believed to have led human souls to the Otherworld, but she was perhaps also a goddess of sovereignity and a guardian of tribal boundaries (Green 1997a: 13-14).

The white horse in the first branch of the Mabinogi carries Rhiannon between this world and the Otherworld and is literally outside time. When the hero Pwll sees Rhiannon for the first time her horse moves slowly, but however hard he tries, he cannot reach it. The description of the colour of the horse, 'canwelw', meaning 'pale white', exemplifies according to Celtic linguist Sioned Davies its supernatural status (Davies 1997: 121-140).

Further examples of white horses crossing boundaries between this world and the Otherworld can be found in anthropological sources from Siberian shamanism, Greek myth and Germanic religion. Among the Altai a white horse was sacrificed to use its spirit for a journey to heaven (Eliade 1989: 191-192). Sometimes the burning of white horse hair or sitting on a white mare skin could help the shaman to cross the boundaries between the worlds (Eliade 1989: 469). Among the Buryat a shaman's drum, a tool which also assists in crossing boundaries to the supernatural, was often made out of the hide of a horse (Eliade 1989: 173). The idea of the horse being used as a means of transport to the Otherworld, or an altered state of consciousness is reminiscent of the myth of Bellerophon, who rides to the heavens on Pegasus, a winged white supernatural horse (Pindar Olympian Odes

---

[12] The link between white horses, sovereignty, fertility and death may just be one aspect of the wider metaphorical connections between sovereignity goddesses and death explored in detail by Máire Breathnach (1982).

13). Bellerophon is sometimes referred to as the son of or at least linked to Poseidon, a chthonic and water deity, and the mythical Pegasus is linked to both water deities and the heavens (Hesiod Theogonia 276; 285). According to Tacitus Germanic tribes kept white horses in sacred groves purely for the purposes of divination. It was believed that these horses knew the will of the gods (Tacitus Germania 10).

White horses also appear in Welsh, English and Irish folklore. There are a number of folktales of white water horses, such as the milk white horse which rises occasionally from the lake of Killarney to bring fertility to the land (Hartmann 1952: 64, 2001: 50), or the Ceffyll Y Dwr, a grey horse which dragged its rider for three days through water, brambles and briars (Brooks 1987: 93-94). Although this legend from Brecon in Wales does not specifically mention a crossing into the Otherworld, the horse is white, clearly a supernatural being and it transgresses boundaries which cannot be crossed without its help. Hartmann (2001: 56, 1952: 34) believes that these water horses which have their counterpart in Indian folklore are actually sun horses, conjuring the image of the sun sinking in the evening into water and building a cosmological unity of sun, water, truth and rebirth.

Other examples of white horses in Irish folklore link white horses to death.13 Hartmann (2001: 49ff, 1952: 90) gives examples of folk tales such as white water horses announcing imminent death, or customs which forbid the pulling of the funeral cart by a white horse or the riding of a white horse to a funeral. Hobby horse rites such as the rite of the White Horse in county Wicklow, where a hobby horse, made up of a white horse's head and a white cloth, was greeted with the exclamation 'White Horse' and had to jump over a fire (Hartmann 1952: 63, 2001: 50) and perhaps also the 'Obby Oss' in Padstow, where a large horse is taken through the town (Alexander 1982: 205) are according to Hartmann (2001: 50) reminiscent of the Indian and early Irish horse ritual mentioned above, although it is difficult to trace the actual meaning of such rites. One Welsh tradition still in existence is the so-called 'Mari Lwyd' or Grey Mare. A horse's skull draped in a white sheet is carried on Twelfth Night or Candlemas day from house to house accompanied by a group of men, one of whom operates the horse. They remain outside the thresholds and enter into a singing challenge with the people inside the houses. The ritual takes place at night and the darkness of night enhances the whiteness of the sheet and skull. The tradition also involves elements of feasting and drinking (Wood 1997: 164-167). Juliette Wood believes that the colour white does not automatically imply liminality. There are numerous supernatural horses in folklore and myth which have other colours which are often a counterpoint to the colouring of their owners or riders (Wood 1997: 176), but in the context of the Mari Lwyd the ghostly white colour must surely be a metaphor for liminal and interstitial time and activities, suggesting associations with boundaries to the Otherworld. This in turn would affirm the integrity and safety of the social group involved in the rite (Wood 1997:167, 175).

It is of course too simplistic to assume that there is a direct link between more recent folkloric rituals or ancient symbolism and rituals from other geographical areas and the British Iron Age without evidence of a continuation or connection (Wood 1997: 166). There are also numerous dissimilarities between the cited materials. Sometimes there is no mention of the horse being white, sometimes the connotations are merely with death or kingship or fertility in isolation. There may be further symbolic aspects in each of these rituals or tales, which escape us or have changed their meaning with time, and the White Horse of Uffington may have limited if any links to Irish sovereignty goddesses, the Welsh mythological figure of Rhiannon or the Indian Kingship rites.

It is not suggested that British Iron Age communities practiced the rituals cited above, but the ideology behind such practices and belief systems may have been similar and may have elicited similar responses. There are a number of common themes in these examples, which suggest such shared ideologies and which are echoed in the archaeology of the Uffington White Horse. The brightness of the white chalk set against the landscape may well hint at solar connections, a permanent white feature against a backdrop of seasonal and diurnal changes. The metaphors of white bone as a marker of both ancestral connotations and death and white milk or semen as life giving fluids, as well as the liminal position of the horse between burial places and the hill fort, which is clearly a place for the living, contribute to a cosmology which combines death, rebirth and fertility.

We have no written or archaeological evidence of any kingship rites having taken place in the vicinity of the Uffington White Horse. It is not clear from the iconography of the horse whether it was a mare or a stallion,[14] there is no evidence of any connotation with water, but the excavations in the vicinity have brought to light bones of horses and dogs which imply extraordinary practices, perhaps even sacrifice (Miles, Palmer *et al.* 2003: 191). It is evident from the lack of change in the outline of the horse, that the figure must have been periodically scoured. The excavations in the nearby hill fort suggest that it was not continually occupied, but intermittently and periodically used (Miles, Palmer

---

[13] The link between a white horse and death also appears in the bible: death, one of the four riders of the apocalypse rides on a pale horse (Revelations 6.8).

[14] Even the apparently gender specific iconography of horses on some Iron Age coins is ambiguous. Although there are clearly solar connotations (Green 1991: 156; 100, 1989: 146), the horses could either be male with triple phalluses or female with exaggerated triple teats.

et al. 2003: 124), perhaps coinciding with the ritual of scouring.

The archaeological evidence of perhaps votive deposition and breakage of pottery suggest a ritual consumption of food and drink (Miles, Palmer et al. 2003: 125) which again shows parallels with the Irish and Indian kingship rites. The Uffington White Horse was in the tribal area of the Atrebates (Cunliffe 1995: 58) and it is tempting to suggest that the horse was an integral part of the sacral kingship rites of the Atrebates, an ancestral horse set in a symbolic as well as actual landscape, rather than just a tribal marker as Cunliffe suggests.

In this context it is worth noting that the hill fort saw very little activity in the late Iron Age period, but was re-used again in the late Romano British period (Miles, Palmer *et al.* 2003: 124). At the same time the nearby landscape was re-used as a burial place. This suggests a return to traditional values. Perhaps in analogy with the interpretation of local British goddesses such as Rosmerta as permanent sovereignty goddesses united with less permanent Roman gods (Aldhouse-Green 2001a: 106), the renewed significance and ritual activity at White Horse hill could be interpreted as a return to the tradition of the sovereignty of the landscape, and as such an act of defiance against British rule.

The Yorkshire Chalk Figurines

Far removed from the monumental scale of the Uffington white horse are a number of small white chalk figurines found predominantly in East Yorkshire. They appear to be unique to Britain (Jope 2000: 261) and most of the fifty to sixty figurines, which range in height from 70mm to 170mm (Stead 1988: 13) were found during excavations at Bealands Nook, Rudston, Sherbourn, Harpham, Garton Slack, Wetwang Slack and Malton in East Yorkshire, the area occupied in the British Iron Age by the Parisii (Dent 1978: 50; Mortimer 1905: 198; Selkirk 1969: 170; Stead 1988: 12, 1971: 34). One similar figurine was found in Mill Hill, Deal in Kent (Parfitt and Green 1987) and one further figurine was found in Withernsea, East Yorkshire, which is about 40km to the south of Garton. However, the latter may have been deposited there with top soil or gravel, which came originally from Garton Slack (Stead 1988: 26).

The figurines are mostly wedge shaped, flat in profile with narrow shoulders and a wide base, although six appear to be slightly oval. Hands and arms are indicated by shallow carvings, but legs are absent. Only a few of the figures still have their head attached and numerous show surface scratches. Stead (1988: 13-19) identified several variants of type. More than half of the complete or nearly complete figures represent warriors, wearing a sword either suspended by a loop on the back or at the side (Figure 11c). Stead believes that the depiction of swords

was of greater importance than the limbs as some of the figurines have swords but lack arms. Most of the warrior type figurines, however, feature a belt (Figure 11d).

Five fairly well preserved figures are clearly not of the warrior type. They have barely any or no features carved into the body but one of them seems to wear a hooded cloak (Stead 1988: 19) (Figure 12a). It is beyond doubt, however, that none of the figures is overtly female. They are either male or sexless (Aldhouse-Green 2004a:, 106; Stead 1988: 25).

When the first figurines were discovered, dating appeared to be problematic. They were compared to the slightly larger, headless but much earlier chalk figure found in a Neolithic ditch at Maiden Castle (Stead 1971: 34; Wheeler 1943: 181), and the Grimes Graves Goddess (Longworth *et al.* 1991). The latter, if indeed genuine, is however not only much older, but also distinctly different. The figure represents a round, kneeling and smiling woman. Since then Dent attributed the figures found in Wetwang to the first century AD (Dent 1978: 50) due to the archaeological context of site, but Stead (1988: 23-24) argued plausibly for the middle Iron Age based inter alia on the central suspension loop of the back mounted scabbards depicted on the warrior type figurines. Similarly placed scabbards and swords have been discovered in nearby grave sites dating from the middle Iron Age (Stead 1988). The figures found in Romano British or later Iron Age contexts may therefore have been of already significant age, when they were deposited.

The function of these figures is uncertain and any interpretation can only be speculative. The same statement must apply to the interpretation and significance of their colour. However, exploring the whiteness of the chalk in the context of their biography, iconography, deposition and suggested function, a number of observations can be made which suggest colour perception on several levels and may lead to a better understanding of these little sculptures.

The figurines are not models, i.e. they are not reproductions of reality, but miniatures. Douglass Bailey summarized the cross-cultural key characteristics of miniatures as human creations which are reduced in size and abstract in detail, forcing the person viewing them to question the lacking detail. Miniatures are intimate, they make their viewers appear bigger and create a smaller, alternative world which can be accessed through handling the miniatures. They can offer comfort by minimizing and offering an explanation of the real world, yet at the same time they can unsettle the viewer by inviting thoughts about something larger. They are familiar yet at the same time strange (Bailey 2005: 29-42).

The brilliant white innate colour of the Yorkshire figurines is clearly their most striking feature. The whiteness of the material adds to the concept of abstraction and eeriness, but also vividly evokes the larger world of the surrounding environment. The chalk is a local material and had been quarried from the nearby landscape (Stead 1988: 24). The chalky landscape itself may have had ceremonial rather than agricultural usage (Fenton-Thomas 2003: 44), a landscape incorporating perhaps ancestral traditions (Fenton-Thomas 2003: 71), possibly by reference to the whiteness of bones (Aldhouse-Green 2004a: 107). Melanie Giles suggested that the figurines may have been used in story telling as representations of mythical ancestors (Giles 2007a: 247; Fenton-Thomas 2003: 71), although Stead (1988: 22-25) believes that the figures were intended to stand upright rather than be held. This could explain the dots on the underside of the base which may have helped in steadying them. Whilst the interpretation of the figurines as a story telling tool is incapable of verification, it is certainly the case that they had close connections to the locality. They do not appear to have been traded and occur only within a very limited geographical area. They have not been found in the context of graves and thus appear to have been used by and are meant for the living community (Dent 1978: 50; Stead 1971: 24). Unlike some goods found in Yorkshire Iron Age graves which appear to have had added importance due to their exotic provenance (Giles 2008: 73), the importance of the chalk figures seems to have lain in the very absence of any exotic or outside influence. They are closely bound to the locality. The only figurine outside the region of the Parisii which truly resembles the Yorkshire figures is the complete and genderless figure found in Deal, Kent which is also situated in a predominantly chalky landscape (Figure 12c). The association between a brilliant white chalky figure and the chalky landscape would therefore still make sense. The brightness and luminosity of the sculptures is inherent in their material and does not fade unless deliberately obscured, thereby conveying a sense of permanence.

The figurines are often perceived as crude (Stead 1971: 32), perhaps because of their simplicity and absence of any detailed decoration which features on so many Iron Age artefacts. It is of course possible that they may have been crafted by ordinary people without the necessary skill required for sophisticated chalk carving. I would argue, however, that the simplicity and minimalist aspect of these figures was deliberate and conveyed meaning. It is unlikely that they were painted. The surface does not show any traces of pigments and the figures do not feature any carved decoration other than certain criss cross patterns on belts, even though the material is soft and can easily be carved. The swirls, triskeles and patterns encountered so frequently on Iron Age bronze artefacts convey movement, agency and distraction for the beholder, sometimes playing deliberate mental games (Giles 2008: 60, 66) as will be discussed further in chapter 8. However, any such decoration, whether painted or carved, would have detracted from the brilliant whiteness of the chalk.

The figurines are standing still and the whiteness of their appearance appears to be an integral aspect of this serenity and stillness. The iconography of the figures seems to support this absence of any movement. It has been suggested by both Stead (1988: 13; 1971: 32) and Dent (1978: 50) that the warrior figures are the result of violent times, whether they represent warrior gods or are simply toys. It should be noted, however, that none of these figures is aggressive or inspires terror. The swords are firmly placed in their scabbards and none of the figures appear to draw their swords, thus contradicting an interpretation as a violent toy warrior. The majority of the figures featuring the sword worn on the back show a curious position of their arms; one arm is folded across the chest, the other arm is folded towards the back (Stead 1988: 3). Giles has interpreted this as a gesture of welcome and open-handedness, but at the same time a defensive stance. She sees the sword as a metaphorical backbone of the figure and perhaps the community (Giles 2008: 62). However, although some of the hands appear to touch the sword, it would be impossible to draw a sword from this position. Rather than posing a threat, some of the figures appear to create a protective circle around their body. The featured belts may have a similar function. One figure which raises one arm towards the shoulder as if to grasp the sword (Stead 1988: 19), still has its fingers on the front of its body rather than the hilt of the sword (Figure 12b).

The hooded appearance of the other type of figurine and the extremely minimalist Deal figurine, whose face is outlined as if hooded (Aldhouse-Green 2004a: 105-106), do not contradict this interpretation. Hoods can be metaphors for anonymity, concealment, disguise or shelter (Aldhouse-Green 2004a: 50), but they could also be a symbol for protection and safeguarding something within. Miranda Aldhouse-Green (2005: 67) suggests that the two types represent warriors and ritualists, but their lack of identity and identifying marks begs to ask the question whether they represent humans or perhaps rather spirits or ancestral deities. In summary, the figures seem to be protecting perhaps their very material and the brilliance contained within it, and thus the landscape they were a part of.

It is possible to argue a further layer of symbolic meaning inherent in the white colour of the chalk. Darvill (2002) argued convincingly for a continuity of symbolic meaning of white stones as a piece of the natural world becoming part of social constructions and thus deriving meaning and character. Although Darvill examined mainly quartz pebbles in the Neolithic, he convincingly argues for echoes of the same symbolism in later periods. It is interesting that the ritual of placing quartz pebbles in ditches or dark places has analogies in the deposition of the little chalk figures. Most of the figurines were found in ditches (Stead 1971: 34) or trenches filled with dark soil (Mortimer 1905: 198) and the 'Deal Man' was found in a pit (Parfitt and Green 1987). This juxtaposition of white material against dark places enhances the luminosity of the chalk and invokes metaphors of day and night, life and death and perhaps an aspect of numinosity of these objects. Stephen Keates argued in the context of the Italian copper age that brilliance and luminosity have associations with Otherworldly presence but perhaps also deified ancestors or spirits (Keates 2002). A similar interpretation of the chalk figures cannot be ruled out and two further contextual aspects of the figures support this suggestion:

The Garton Slack figures were found with a miniature chalk shield, again hinting at protection and the Malton figurine was found together with a miniature copper alloy shield in the vicinity of a spring. This would support an argument for the deliberate deposition of the figures perhaps as votive offerings rather than having been discarded with general debris. The association with water echoes the deliberate deposition of quartz pebbles in watery contexts in Iron Age Britain (Darvill 2002: 83) and perhaps also that of a little chalk head found in 1993 in the Thames near Battersea (Figure 12d). The head was carved from a small chalk nodule, but unlike the Yorkshire and Kent figurines, it is not part of a larger figure but complete in itself and shows an 'expression of brooding if not malevolent intensity' (Cotton 1996: 85). The Battersea head's deliberate deposition in a watery context would undoubtedly have enhanced its luminosity and suggests metaphors of boundaries and the spirit world (Darvill 2002: 83).

The second aspect is the apparent deliberate damage to the Yorkshire figurines. About two thirds of the Yorkshire figurines appear to have been decapitated. The high proportion of decapitated figurines suggests that this was not caused by accidental damage. In addition some of the figures seem to have been deliberately defaced by deep slashes and scratches (Aldhouse-Green 2004a: 107; Stead 1988). One figure in particular seems to be covered in cross hatching. Whilst cross hatching is sometimes perceived to create brilliance (Murphy 1992) as will be discussed in chapter 6, this figure does not show the precise and fine patterns of the fine criss-cross carvings which would produce such an effect. Rather, the figurine seems to have been a victim of prolonged and repetitive, but irregular slashing. The slashing has been compared to the deliberate rending of clothes or to ritual sacrifice (Aldhouse-Green 2004a: 107) and it may have had a similar effect to the ghost killings in nearby graves or perhaps even the ritual defleshing of a skull found at Folly Lane (Niblett 1999: 319-320). This violent act would have ultimately revealed the white cranium, perhaps perceived to be the seat of the mutilated body's ancestral power. The transgression against or defacement

of the bodies, or in this case the figurines, might have drawn attention to and perhaps reinforced underlying moral or social values (Giles 2000: 167). The slashing and breaking has a curious paradoxical effect. On the one hand the slashes would appear to break up and spoil the smooth texture of the figurines' surface, but depending on the light, they can actually appear whiter than the surface of the figures. Equally, decapitation would reveal chalk which might have been whiter than that of the figurine's surface, which may have become a little grubby through handling and exposure. Ian Stead drew comparisons to Middle and South American shamanic rites during which little figurines were smashed or decapitated to release the spirit inhabiting them (Stahl 1986; Stead 1988: 9-29).

It is tempting to accept such an interpretation from the perspective of colour. By deliberately scratching or smashing the figurines the aspect of smooth whiteness, brilliance and serenity is extinguished. Yet at the same time the deliberate violation of the sculptures may have provoked aggression and violence in the figurine's spirit or perhaps evoked and released the very essence of the chalky wolds and the ancestral powers linked to the landscape.

Conclusion

The Uffington white horse and the little Yorkshire figurines are very different examples of chalk relics from the British Iron Age.

Whilst the horse is monumental in size, extrovert, required repeated activity from perhaps an entire community to remain in existence and is still an integral part of the landscape, the figurines are miniatures, intimate, perhaps even private15, and appear to have had a finite lifespan prior to deposition. They are, however, both made out of the white chalk of their surrounding landscape. Loney and Hoaen (2005: 375) have argued that one of the defining aspects of British Iron Age society and social practice is the incorporation of past social memories through inclusion of earlier monumental architecture or other forms of material culture, even portable artefacts, which bind the community to older, perhaps no longer visible landscapes. Memories and relations with ancestors are played out in organization and dealing with such landscapes.

The interpretation of the white horse as a symbol of indigenous sovereignty is tempting, but at best speculative. However, there is no doubt that the Uffington White Horse is a place where periodic ritual activity involving large numbers of people took place and that these activities must have had social meaning to these people. This may have been purely a means of

---

[15] The figure from Deal, Kent, was found in a shaft with a niche cut into the chalk which may have been specifically intended for the figure (Parfitt and Green 1987).

communication to others or, as in the tradition of the 'Mari Lwyd', an expression and reaffirmation of the safety and integrity of the community through emphasis on liminality and boundaries.

The chalk figurines on the other hand evoke the landscape from which they were taken. They were carved in a deliberately minimalist style and placed against dark contexts to enhance the luminosity of the material, perhaps symbolizing protective ancestral deities. At some time during their 'life', possibly at a time of stress or violence, the figures may have been removed from their customary place, and their brilliance and whiteness were deliberately defaced and at the same time perhaps released in a ritual, following which the figurines or their fragments may have been deposited again in dark places. The white colour of both the horse and the Yorkshire figurines was clearly an important and integral element of and assisted in the conveyance of metaphorical meaning. However, these examples also demonstrate that a particular colour cannot be simply taken as a metaphor for a certain symbolic meaning, but that colour, material, landscape, time, weather and social relations are all interlinked revealing various and sophisticated levels of symbolism.

Chapter 6

Weaving with Light – Luminosity and Brilliance in the British Iron Age

The one remains, the many change and pass;
Heaven's light forever shines, earth's shadows fly;
Life, like a dome of many-coloured glass
Stains the white radiance of eternity
(Percy Bysshe Shelley, Adonais, I. ii)

Introduction

Research into colour in the British Iron Age would not be complete without an exploration of luminosity and brilliance. As already mentioned in chapter 1, brightness, shine and reflection of light may have had equal, or perhaps even greater, importance in prehistory than hue. Luminosity and brilliance are of course not just synonymous with gold or bright colours. The dazzling and reflective properties of highly polished materials, speckling, the shimmering rainbow effect on feathers or the sparkling of running water are only a few examples of luminosity in diverse materials. Certain surface treatments of metal can enhance the already shiny exterior of the material. As Goethe described in one of his experiments, if a highly polished surface of silver is slightly scratched and placed in the sun, in a certain angle the reflected light appears red and green. Goethe conceded however, that 'some form of light and dark must co-operate' with reflections (Goethe 1840: 157). In a society which depends very much on powers of observation for its survival, e.g. a society which is largely based on agriculture, changes in luminosity, even subtle ones, would not only have been recognized, but might also have been understood and interpreted as signifiers. On a very simple level changing light is an indicator of time, whether diurnal, nocturnal or seasonal.

Certain materials such as gold or quartz are inherently brilliant and this aspect may have played an important role in using such materials for certain artefacts. Gold, as has been discussed in chapter four, is resistant to tarnish and therefore eternally bright. Quartz can add aspects of brilliance to otherwise dull materials. For example, an Iron Age stone head found in a shrine in house VIII in Caerwent was carved out of sandstone containing a high quantity of quartz. The stone was found in a late Romano-British setting, but follows pre-Roman traditions (Boone 1976: 163; 171). In a dark room any source of light falling on the head would have been reflected by the quartz particles, thereby creating a speckled effect, enhancing the luminosity of the already light colour of the stone and emphasizing the contrast with the dark surroundings.

This chapter, however, is less concerned with inherently brilliant materials, but explores the various ways in which different materials and techniques were employed to create the effect of, or increase brilliance. It also considers whether the luminosity achieved by such methods may have had symbolic as well as merely aesthetic significance. Finally, I also want to consider if brilliance and the absence of brilliance had any meaning or might offer an explanation for the deposition of goods in watery and dry contexts. As a starting point, I have looked at references to brilliance and luminosity in classical sources and early Welsh and Irish myth which might provide a clue to its significance in Iron Age Britain.

Written Sources

Diodorus Siculus (Library of History 5.27-32) and Strabo (Geography 4.4,5) refer to the preference of the Gauls for striking garments with bright colours, striped or check patterns, dyed in various hues and embellished with embroidery. Both also mention a fondness for golden armlets, neck rings, rings, bracelets and even gold corselets worn by both men and women. Strabo tells us that dignitaries wore garments sprinkled in gold. Apart from this no comments are made by either of them as to whether there may have been political, value-related, functional, fashion related or symbolic reasons for this fondness of brilliance in garments and body ornaments (Sievers 1991: 438-439).

Diodorus Siculus and Strabo wrote of course about tribes in France. There is scarce literary evidence from classical writers as to whether this preference for shining clothes and jewellery was mirrored in Iron Age Britain, but in his Roman Histories (62.2) Dio Cassius describes Boudica, the Queen of the Iceni as wearing a gold torc and a brightly coloured coat which would suggest that gold adornments and bright garments were also valued in Iron Age Britain.

In classical myths as well as early Irish and Welsh vernacular narrative, brilliance and iridescence are often symbols of the sacred and divine. Gods, divine messengers, priests and apotheosized persons are frequently described as wearing golden garments, shoes and adornments, or are depicted as shining or surrounded by brilliant light. In Virgil's Aeneid (4.227-253), Mercury wears golden sandals. Chloreus, a former priest of the goddess Cybele, carries a golden bow and wears a red golden helmet, a saffron mantle and a tunic with golden thread (Virgil Aeneid 11.764-788). Venus is described as divinely shining (Virgil Aeneid 8.608-630) and her semi-divine son Aeneas stands before Dido in an aura of brilliant light (Virgil Aeneid 1.566-597). In Homer's Odyssey most gods or supernatural beings are referred to in terms of brilliance, such as the bright-eyed goddess Athena (Odyssey 3.330), golden Aphrodite (Odyssey 4. 13) or the golden sandal wearing Apollo (Odyssey 5.44). In the Mabinogi we encounter the queen of Arawn's supernatural court as dressed in shining gold brocade and eating from golden plates, the supernatural, perhaps even divine Rhiannon wears shining gold brocade and her son, Pryderi is initially called Gwri, meaning 'golden hair'. Lleu, another supernatural figure in the Mabinogi, has connotations with brilliance by virtue of his name which means literally 'bright' (Green 1992: 133).

In the Irish *'Tain Bo Cuailgne'*, the prophetess Fedelm wears a golden pin and a speckled cloak and is described as having the 'light of foresight' (Kinsella 1970: 60–61). Irish druids wore garments made of speckled or iridescent feathers. As already mentioned in chapter 5, in the Mabinogi Rhiannon's white horse is described in colour terms which emphasise the brightness of its coat. Even the bible mentions white speckled sheep as extraordinary. When Jacob places white rods made out of certain trees into the sheep's troughs at the time of their mating, the resulting sheep are striped, speckled or piebald (Genesis 30-31).

These examples are of course not conclusive evidence that Iron Age communities in Britain conferred a similar symbolic meaning to shining, iridescent or brilliant objects. However, these symbolic constructs are a common theme and, as will be seen later, operate cross culturally.

Shiny Surfaces

Wood is an excellent material for a discussion on luminosity of reflective surfaces. It is not inherently shiny, but requires some form of manipulation to make its surface glossy or smooth. This can be done by polishing, or, even simpler, carving. There is a paucity of wooden objects from the British Iron Age due to decomposition, but wetland archaeology has produced some exciting finds. The wooden figurines from Roos Carr are perhaps the most striking examples from the Iron Age (Figures 13a and 13b). The 35-40cm tall figures were found in 1836 six feet below the ground surface in a layer of blue clay (Coles 1990: 315-319, Bevan-Jones 2002: 155).

The figurines consist of five anthropomorphic figures, a boat with an animal head on which at least two of the figurines were fixed, and some shields. Originally eight figurines had been discovered but we have no knowledge of the whereabouts of the missing items and it is by no means certain if the surviving figurines all belonged together (Coles 1990: 315, Dr. Paula Gentil pers. comment). The figures have been radiocarbon dated with the Oxford Accelerator Mass Spectrometry System to a date between 606 BC and 509 BC. Originally the figures were thought to have been made out of pinewood, but further examination has revealed that they were carved out of yew (Coles 1990: 318-319). Quartz pebbles had been inserted as eyes in three of the figurines, one figure features one quartz and one limestone eye and the fifth figurine has just one limestone eye. All have asymmetrical faces, and are sexually ambiguous. The genital area is a broad orifice which could be a vulva or an opening into which a separately made penis may have been inserted. Some of the figures have quartz pebbles inserted into these genital holes.

Miranda Aldhouse-Green suggests that the sexual ambiguity and asymmetry could be interpreted as shamanic imagery and be linked to track ways which may have been perceived as trackways to the Otherworld (Aldhouse-Green 2005: 119-120). It is tempting to perceive symbolic connotations in the rich red colour of carved yew and the contrast with the blue clay in which the figures were found. Perhaps the ambiguity of the colour red as simultaneously symbolic of life and death corresponded to the ambiguous gender of these figures and the fact that they were made out of dead material but perhaps representing living beings. The colour of the wood may have enhanced the underlying symbolism of the wood species used, which itself may have suggested links to wood magic, boundaries, shamanism or gender, as Bryony Coles put forward (1998: 163–173) and as will be discussed further in chapter 8.

There are other wooden figurines, such as the Ballachulish woman (Figure 13c), dating from 728 BC to 524 BC and the Kingsteignton Idol (Figure 13d), dated from 462 BC to 352 BC, which were carved out of oak and alder respectively. These figures have however sufficient aspects in common with the Roos Carr figures, such as the sexual ambiguity, the deposition in watery contexts, and in case of the Ballachulish Woman a quartz pebble in the eye socket, the asymmetry of the face and the perhaps deliberate damage to the left side (Coles 1990: 319-326), to be grouped together with them. Whilst the colour of these figurines may well have had significance, the smooth finish of their carving is also of significance; perhaps they were even polished.[16] The carving of the Roos Carr figures had been carried out with a sharp tool

---

[16] The glistening surface of facets on yew can also be observed on the uprooted yew stump found in the Somerset Levels at Tinney's Ground in the vicinity of Bronze Age brushwood tracks (Orme 1982: 85-88).

applied to green wood (Coles 1990: 327) as shown by the clear facets. The wood had been worked on no later than a year or two after felling. All figures were carved out of single pieces of round wood with the pith running down the vertical axis from the centre of the head. The act of carving the figurines would not only have transformed a piece of rough wood into bodies and faces of the figures, but also created a smooth, shiny surface which in turn would have showed up the colour and grain of the wood, thereby revealing perhaps its very essence. The Roos Carr figures in particular show very small faceting, i.e. tool marks (Sands 1997: 11). They have been carefully crafted to leave the surface of the heads and limbs almost rounded and very smooth. The absence of individualistic features or carved decoration on the figurines allows an undisturbed reflection of light over virtually their entire bodies which depending on the light, creates a luminosity, which is further enhanced by the insertion of gleaming white quartz pebbles in the body cavities, representing eyes and perhaps semen.

The figures do not show much wear. It is probable that they were deposited soon after carving (Coles 1990: 332) and perhaps even made for the purpose of deposition. The process of making these wooden figurines, i.e. felling the tree, cutting it, carving and perhaps polishing it, involves several stages of transformation of the underlying material. This transformation does not only involve the death of a living tree with a rather rough surface, uneven to the touch, and a darkish red brown colour, but the human made creation of something different out of the 'corpse' of the tree. It may of course not have been necessary to fell a tree in order to carve the figurines. The figurines may have been carved from recycled wood or fallen branches. Nevertheless, the act would still have involved a degree of transformation.

Perhaps the act of carving the figurines out of trees, which themselves may have been sacred[17] and may have had fertility and longevity symbolism, would have been perceived as creating a second life of the tree, releasing the essence of the wood or tree and alluding to associations of death, rebirth and fertility (Aldhouse-Green 2004a: 96, 97). There would have been a clear link between the figurines and the trees from which they stem and thus the figurines would have represented a certain link to their past, but they nevertheless represent something new and human-made. Whether the figurines were meant to be deities or ancestral persons, the carving may have imbued them with some kind of energy. The ritual carving of wood and creation of energy is known from anthropological studies, such as Susanne Kuechler's account of the production of 'malangan' sculptures in Papua New Guinea. These wooden figurines, although carved as part of a funerary rite, do not simply represent

the dead person or even the ancestral dead but encompass a rich variety of symbolic associations ranging from fertility and rebirth to social structures, clan identity and landownership. The figures gain life through the act of carving, during which the life energy of the deceased is transferred to the sculpture. They are then symbolically killed by the public who throw money and shells at their base and finally they are left to rot (Kuechler 1992). In pre-Columbian Jamaica wooden idols, called 'Zemís' by the Taíno tribe, the indigenous people of Jamaica, were imbued with sacredness which stemmed from a combination of material, form, production process and use (Saunders and Gray 1996: 804). In Amerindian belief systems trees have a complex cosmological symbolism linked to myths of origin and access to the shamanic spirit world. The Brazilian Kuikuru believed that trees were once mythical people. The Taíno made wooden Zemís from trees believed to be occupied by the spirit of a dead chieftain. Trees were seen as anthropomorphic spirits and the act of carving only released what was already inherent (Saunders and Gray 1996, 808 - 809).

The rotting of wood as part of a ritual brings to mind Lucan's description of wooden images of deities rotted to white in a sacred shrine near Marseilles (De Bello Civilis 3.399-425), which is sometimes quoted in context with the wooden figurines found in Roos Carr. Miranda Aldhouse-Green likens the white colour of the rotten timber and the smell of decaying wood to the decomposition of human flesh and imagery of death (Aldhouse-Green 2004a: 89). The finite life span of wooden artefacts which decay or can be burnt (Aldhouse-Green 2004a: 24) would therefore suggest that they were not meant to represent eternal deities,[18] if deities at all, but that they represent some form of transformation, transformable beings or transformable aspects of deities.

Whilst this is a valid argument for wooden sculptures exposed to weathering, and there may indeed have been wooden figures exposed in sacred groves just as described by Lucan, the Roos Carr figurines and the Ballachulish Woman had a quite different fate. However, rather than being left exposed to decay like Lucan's idols, these figurines were deposited in a watery context, which would have had a different effect. The Ballachulish Woman had been weighted down with hurdles. It seems that she needed to be restrained or prevented from coming back to the surface, which would indicate that she may have been perceived to have beeen alive or at least a symbol of a living entity (Aldhouse-Green 2004a: 91). As will be discussed in further detail in chapter 8 the figures made of yew would have 'bled'

---

[17] Lucan describes the yew, alder and oak as sacred in his Pharsalia (3. 419; 440).

[18] It is not necessarily the case that deities have eternal life. Numerous gods in a variety of polytheistic religions are slain or are reconciled with the fact that their life span is finite, Odin, Kronos and Osiris being just some examples. Odin was sacrificed on a tree, Kronos was killed by his son Zeus and Osiris' human life as king ended by his murder at the hands of Seth before he was brought back to life by Isis.

into the water and the red colour of the figures would have been preserved. The immersion in water, especially during a time when the sun or moon would reflect on the surface of the water, would have enhanced the effect of brilliance and shine on both the wood and quartz and the shimmering effect would have been akin to movement. The significance of such depositions in watery contexts will be discussed below, but the combination of preserved colour and shine appears to have been important.

Twisting the Light – Metal Decoration

The transformation of materials to enhance their reflective qualities is of course not limited to wood carving. The simple act of polishing materials such as copper based and other metals, certain stones and minerals would have increased their luminosity. With the exception of inherently shiny material such as gold and quartz, the luminosity of brilliant objects is generally finite because of tarnishing, weathering or decomposition. However, repeated polishing or treatment with certain materials would have preserved their sheen. Some of the brooches found in graves in Arras in Yorkshire were decorated with chalk which appears to have been coated by a resinous material which would have preserved the soft chalk and would also have given it a shiny gloss (Stead 1965: 64; 65). Oiling or greasing might have renewed or prolonged the sparkle or gleam of certain surfaces such as wood or stone and such treatment may have had similar symbolic meaning as the initial creation of luminosity (Birkhan 1997: 803) although we have no archaeological evidence for such processes.

Polishing and treatment with resins are not the only methods to increase the brilliance of metal objects. The deliberate control of reflected light through technological manipulation is another example. Metalwork such as chasing or repoussé work on gold or bronze was used by smiths to create three-dimensionality and plasticity. Strands of gold or copper alloys of varying thickness were twisted and braided to create a highly decorative effect. The iconography created by such technology will be discussed in chapter 8, but the visual effect in terms of brilliance is evident in the following examples:

The crescentic bronze mount from Llyn Cerrig Bach (Figure 14a), the specific use of which is unclear but which may have been a chariot, wagon or shield decoration (Macdonald 2007: 122-12; Megaw and Megaw 1989: 2003) is a fine example of repoussé work. The metalworker would have modelled the bronze plaque to create the effect of three-dimensionality, which not only emphasizes the detail of the iconography[19] and its asymmetry, but it also alters the reflection of light. Depending on its position, different parts of the plaque are being brought to light or

cast into shade, drawing the eye to the illuminated and reflective parts. If the plaque was used as a decoration on a chariot, the movement of the chariot would have resulted in a the reflected light moving over the surface of the plaque, following the lines of the comma leafs and crescents in a dazzling display. The reflection of the rays of the sun or moon or the light of fire would have been controlled and harnessed, not only by the metalworker who carried out the repoussé work, but also by the person displaying the item on his or her chariot. The creation of a visual effect by the controlled use of the elements and the resulting effect on spectators would undoubtedly have inferred powerful status.

The ring terminals of the Snettisham gold and electrum torcs (Figure 14b) display fine chasing and repoussé work,20 but the main body of the torcs is made out of twisted, cabled or braided strands of gold (Brailsford and Stapley 1972). The braids and twists emphasise the roundness of the torc and, again, add a certain degree of movement and fluidity. In respect of reflected light, however, they achieve two things. Firstly, the terminals of the torc would have appeared to be brighter than the ring itself and the spectator's eyes would have been drawn to them. Secondly, the reflection of the light on the strands would have been broken up into tiny little facets, thereby creating the illusion of something shimmering. Anybody who would have worn such an adornment would have been bathed in reflected light, literally a kind of reflected glory. That the torcs were meant to be worn can be demonstrated by the way they can be twisted to be put round a neck and, as mentioned earlier, we know from the description of Boudica by Dio Cassius (Roman History 62.2) that she wore a golden neckring, which may have been a torc and which may have been passed down to her as an heirloom (Aldhouse-Green 2006: 34). Most of the Snettisham and Ipswich torcs are heavy. It is therefore likely that they would have been worn for ritual or ceremonial occasions only (Brailsford and Stapley 1972: 227, 228) and may have had meaning beyond that of mere decoration. However, some of the Snettisham Iron Age torcs are tubular (Jope 2000: 85). They are still dazzling, but cheaper to make, easier to wear and more likely to have been worn on a frequent basis.

Luminosity and Numinosity: the Symbolism of Brilliance

It is likely that luminosity and brilliance may have had symbolic as well as aesthetic and political value. In a primarily agricultural society there are immediately recognisable associations of sheen and brilliance with health and life. Healthy animals have shiny coats, healthy plants have shiny leaves, whereas illness, death and decay bring about dullness; eyes loose their sparkle, withering

---

[19] Whilst Megaw and Megaw (1989: 202) and Jope (2000: 271) belief the imagery to be based on birds heads, it is more likely to be a vegetal imagery as will be further explored in chapter 8.

[20] Unlike some of the Ipswich torcs, where the terminals were cast in cire perdue without further tooling, they appear unfinished (Brailsford and Stapley 1972: 221-222, 232).

plants become lacklustre. The Nilotic Dinka for example value sheen on cattle hides as indicator of health; they liken it to the morning dew glittering in the sunlight or the moon (Coote 1999: 253; 255). This imagery recalls further associations of brilliance and sparkling to the sun, moon, and stars and their reflection in water. The reflection of sun and moonlight on smooth surfaces creates agency, lightness and perhaps joy which, as Murphy has argued may be universally applicable (Murphy 1992: 202).

Murphy's study of the aesthetic values of the Yolngu of Northern Australia shows that material which provides a rich sheen, including fat and blood as well as inherently shiny objects such as cockatoo feathers or beeswax are possessed of spiritual or even ancestral power (Murphy 1992: 197-198). People who are fat and sleek, as well as objects made shiny by the application of blood or fat are thought to be endowed with spiritual power. In some North Eastern American tribes grease is a sacred material. It operates as a life giver and preserver of food (especially bone grease which can be gained from crushed bones) but it is also a symbol of immortality. It embodies the essence and the spirit of an animal. The bones of a bear for example are symbolic of its individual life, but its grease symbolizes its immortality. Shiny fat is used in rituals to contact the master spirit of an animal (Saint-Germain 2005: 111).

In pre-Columbian America the brilliance displayed by the sun, moon or rainbows had sacred meaning. Light was perceived to have supernatural qualities equating to spiritual life force, rivers and lakes were imbued with spirituality due to the reflective quality of water, clouds, mist and rain were perceived to have been glowing with spiritual essence. The Aztec rain god's paradise shimmered with reflected light from flowers and iridescent bird feathers. Shamanic visions and rituals were characterized by light and brilliance, thus displaying the essence rather than material surface of objects. For the Southern Chilean Mapuche light also had associations to time and the Kogi of Colombia regarded the dazzling snow peaks of the Andes as portals for the dead (Saunders 2002: 210-213).

The Bible (Leviticus 7.1-27) places a taboo on the consumption of animal fat which is reserved for ritual burning as a sacrifice to god, perhaps because of its shine. Indeed, luminosity appears frequently in the Bible in connection with the divine. When Moses descends from Mount Sinai his face is so luminous that he has to veil himself (Exodus 34.29-35). As has already been stated above sparkle and shine in Greek and Roman myth as well as early medieval Welsh and Irish vernacular literature can have numinous qualities or signify the presence of a supernatural being.

Brilliance and luminosity can symbolize ancestral spirits, life force or the supernatural, but as a whole such associations represent something intangible, metaphysical and elusive, yet appreciable and powerful. Stephen Keates has suggested that in analogy with anthropological studies in both Australia (Murphy 1992) and South America (Saunders 1999), luminosity in the context of European prehistory may have had connotations with an Otherworldly presence (Keates 2002). Especially in the context of burials he proposes a link between luminosity and transformation of the dead to ancestral status. Whilst this explanation might make sense in the context of burial and will be explored further in chapter 9, it is not necessary helpful in other contexts. Perhaps the association between brilliance and the ancestral dead is too simplistic. Saunders (2002: 209) believes that the sacred and spiritual dimensions of light and brilliance are universal. He suggests that in the context of prehistory brilliant objects may have been perceived as an earthbound material manifestation of sacred light and the spiritual qualities which such sacred light embodied (Saunders 2002: 214). Carl Jung considered light as an important part of the universal archetype of the spiritual father. According to his theories light as well as sun, rain and other iridescent phenomena formed part of a masculine symbolism as opposed to that of the earth mother, which is inherently dark (Jung 1992). In this context it is also worth noting Dobney and Ervynck's (2007) theory that fish was not consumed during the Iron Age in Britain because of the sanctity of shining surfaces. The scales of fish are highly reflective and iridescent.

The technological know-how involved in making objects brilliant may also have had ritual or magical significance. The manufacture, manipulation and the wearing of shining objects would have meant a continuing liaison between humans and the divine on the one hand, and metaphysical as well as political authority over spectators on the other (Saunders 2002: 216-217). In other words, brilliant objects equated to a manipulation of light and manipulation of others through light, an example of Alfred Gells notion of 'a technology of enchantment and an enchantment of technology' (Gell 1992). Such combination of religious and political power through technology can be illustrated by the example of the Cogi tribe from Columbia, who exposed their brilliant ornaments to the rays of the sun, thus gaining divine power which was then transmitted to the persons participating in rituals (Saunders 2002: 219). The wearing of shimmering golden necklets or torcs, such as the Snettisham or Ipswich torcs, may not only have been a display of wealth, but may have placed the wearer outside ordinary humanity and perhaps given him or her semi-divine status or divine power, akin to the coronation of Christian kings and Queens whose power was said to have been god given. Such apotheosis would in turn create political power over others.

If shine imbued material objects with numinosity or perhaps displayed their inner essence, then the very act of carving, polishing, chasing, hammering or any other technique that was used to create shimmering surfaces, may therefore have constituted a magical and powerful human interaction with the sphere of the supernatural, evoking, creating or releasing spiritual forces or even creating life. The German term '*Dingbeseelung*', i.e. giving soul to an object, might be an appropriate term, especially in the context of the wooden figurines from Roos Carr, where the addition of eyes and perhaps semen, would appear to have increased the potency of such activity. The manipulation may on the other hand have released or revealed something that was already inherent, hidden or imprisoned in the manipulated material, but it is in any event the human intervention which brings out such qualities.

Cross Hatching: Interfering with the Divine

One metalworking technique which is specific to the late La Tène period in the British Isles is the effect of cross hatching on bronze and gold artefacts. Even though cross hatching affects the brilliance and luminosity of the object, it must be treated separately from the techniques discussed above, as its effect is quite different.

Crosshatching and basket weave patterns in conjunction with compass designs were widely used in England and Wales in the first century BC and the first century AD even though compass design had by that time been largely abandoned in continental Europe. It is a distinctive feature of the patterned backed bronze mirrors dating from the late second century BC to the mid first century AD, coinciding with the resurgence of gold in Britain and the use of gold coins (Creighton 2000: 48-49; Joy 2008: 78 Megaw and Megaw 1989: 210-215).

The decorated bronze mirrors are specific to the southern areas of Britain, mainly in the regions occupied by the Catuvellauni or the Trinovantes, where the mirrors are generally kidney shaped (Jope 2000: 138, 146), but also in more western regions such as Gloucester, Dorset or Cornwall (Joy 2008: 94-95). Only one mirror of a similar type was found outside of Britain, in Nijmegen in the Netherlands, but it is possible that this mirror had been imported from Britain (Jope 2000: 137, 292).

The mirrors are large and heavy; the Birdlip mirror weighs one kilogram and measures about 30 cm in diameter. They were mostly found in the context of graves (Jope 2000: 146), but repair work carried out on some of the mirrors, such as the Dorton mirror (Farley 1983: 282) would indicate that they were not made specifically for burials, but had been used prior to their deposition in graves. Their very weight, however, makes it unlikely that there were used for everyday personal grooming.

The association between mirrors and magic or the spirit world is a cross cultural phenomenon, and some aspects of this symbolism may be a universally applicable construct. Mirrors invite the beholder to present himself or herself, in a very deliberate manner, but the reflected image is two dimensional, back to front, intangible and perhaps even distorted. Depending on the colour and material of the mirror the colour of the reflection may vary. The image appears therefore like a different reality, perhaps another world. In Lewis Carroll's 'Alice through the Looking Glass' the heroine climbs through a mirror into a world which appears initially just like the one she left behind, albeit transversed, but then becomes more and more surreal. Mirrors inspire curiosity as to the reality of this hidden world behind it, but perhaps also fear of the unknown and fear of being trapped in the mirror world. The reflected image may have been perceived as a reflection of the soul, but a distinctive and individual soul, the very personality of the beholder, perhaps the abstraction of the person's life. It is interesting to note that there is a close etymological connection between the words for mirror and life in the old Egyptian and Hittite languages (Vacano 1960: 8-9).

The fear of mirrors and reflections, as well as the belief that souls can be trapped in mirrors is a common theme amongst many culture groups. In rural Ireland even now mirrors are covered or screened as part of the funerary rite (Ó hÓgáin 1999: 32). In a society where metal or glass was relatively rare, the only other means of observing one's reflection would have been in water, which in the British Iron Age had its own symbolic associations with liminal boundaries and probably sacred meaning (Green 1986: 166). Perhaps mirrors with their sparkling and reflective surfaces were perceived to be similar to or a substitute for water, especially in the context of burial, which will be further explored in chapter 9.

The use of mirrors as a scrying tool is also known from various sources.

Pausanias (Description of Greece 7.21, 12) describes the rites at the temple of Artemis at Patrae. A mirror was suspended on a thread and dipped into a fountain. Once it resurfaced, the person wishing to consult the future would look at his or her image and find out their fate, depending on whether the reflection was healthy or ill looking. In Thessaly, witches saw oracles written in human blood reflected on moonlit mirrors, if St. Augustin (De Civitate Dei 7.35) is to be believed. The Elizabethan alchemist John Dee used a mirror of black obsidian to scry and try to converse with angels. It might have been similar to the obsidian mirror, which had been used by Native North Americans for magical purposes, and which was one of the exhibits in the 2007 'New World Exhibition' in the British Museum. The German Romantic Poets like E.T.A. Hoffmann made extensive use of mirror magic in their poetic take on fairy tales, 'Kunstmaerchen', no doubt based on the magic mirror in the folk tale of Snow White. Even now the internet gives abundant information for 'would be magicians' on how to use mirrors, crystals or other reflective surfaces for enoptromancy. Returning to the associations between brilliance and the essence of material discussed above, perhaps the image reflected in a highly polished bronze mirror would have been perceived to be an image of the soul or the essence of the person rather than its physical image. For the purposes of this chapter, it is however not so much the reflective quality of the front plates, but the shimmering effect of the decoration on the mirror backs, which is of interest.

There are no decorated mirrors known from the Northern parts of Britain. Mirrors found in Arras, Wetwang and Garton Slack in Yorkshire had iron plates and do not show any patterns. Although the Yorkshire mirrors were also found in grave contexts and may have had a shared symbolic function, they date from an earlier period. A mirror found in Llechwedd-Du Bach in Merioneth in Wales, even though dated to the later first century AD, has a plain bronze plate and back (Fox 1925: 255, 1958: 101; Jope 2000: 292). Two iron mirrors found in Ireland have bronze handles, but again differ stylistically from the Southern British mirrors in as much as their backs are not patterned and they feature animals on their handles. None of the southern decorated mirrors features zoomorphic handles (Jope 2000: 146, map: 7). The British decorated bronze mirrors differ from Roman mirrors of the same period not only because of their distinctively patterned backs, but also in their metallurgic composition. Whereas Roman mirrors average 63% to 72% copper, 21% to 26% tin and 6% to 14% lead, the British mirrors, as will be further demonstrated in chapter 9, contain virtually no lead at all, a smaller percentage of tin (8% to 13%) and a very high percentage of copper, 84% to 90% (Farley: 1983, 288). The Latchmere Green mirror plate for example is composed of 88.5% copper and 11.5% tin, its handle 87% copper and 12.4% tin (Fulford and Creighton 1998: 331). This composition of this alloy would result in a redder colour than that of the Roman mirrors.

What makes the mirrors so distinctive however, are their engraved decorations. The bronze front plates would have been highly polished, but the backs of the mirrors featured an abstract and intriguing maze of cross hatched areas. Whilst the pattern on mirrors such as the Mount Batten mirror from Stamford Hill in Devon (Cunliffe 1988: 87-88) show a relatively crude execution of the cross hatching and the Latchmere Green Mirror features irregular oblong blocks (Fulford and Creighton 1998: 331), the intricate detail on mirrors such as the Colchester mirror (Fox 1958: 87) the Desborough Mirror (Smith 1907-1909), the Holcombe mirror (Fox and Pollard 1973: 21-27) or the Old Warden I mirror (Spratling 1970) had been executed in a very precise manner with fine and even strokes creating a regular geometrical basket weave pattern within the curvilinear flowing pattern of the decorated design (Figure 14c).

John Creighton suggested that the basket weave patterns shown on some of the mirrors can be likened to the chevrons and curvilinear patterns produced during early stages of a trance, which may have been induced by the use of narcotics such as henbane or mandrake (Creighton 2000: 49-52). However, the drug induced geometric patterns described by Dronfield (1995) in the context of megalithic rock art, which Creighton uses as basis for his argument, are more simplistic patterns of the kind which Lewis-Williams described as dots, grids, zigzags, nested curves and meandering lines (Lewis-Williams 1997: 325). The patterns on the mirrors, certainly the later ones, have been carried out with the help of a compass and fine nosed gravers, a very precise and detailed action which seems at odds with the influence of drugs (Farley 1983: 284).

There is also a curious contradiction between the asymmetrical curvilinear and flowing outline of the crosshatched fields and the very precise and more or less geometrical basket weave patterns forming this field. The precise nature of this form of decoration becomes apparent when contrasted with the cross hatching displayed at the repoussé bronze disc of Monasterevin from County Kildare in Ireland which is now in the British Museum in London (Armstrong 1923) (Figure 14d).

The surface of the disc with the exception of the protruding scrolls and the scoop in the centre of the plate had been covered with very finely engraved neat strokes. These strokes, which give the surface a slightly matt effect and different texture and thus emphasize the shine of the scoop and scrolls, do not form any kind of pattern or basket weave, but they resemble fine hair or fur. However, the lower third of the plate is covered with much cruder cross hatching which resembles much more that found on the Yorkshire figurines discussed in chapter 5, than the finely detailed engravings of the British bronze backed mirrors. It is unlikely that this crude pattern was meant as a decoration of an otherwise skillfully and precisely crafted piece or that this was an attempt at emulating the basket weave pattern of the British mirrors. In my view this was the result of a deliberate act, perhaps even a ritual act, of spoiling or desecrating the surface, perhaps a ritual killing prior to deposition or an act of aggression which may have released energy. The intricacy of the basket weave patterns on the British bronze backed mirrors, however, does not allow an interpretation of a ritual desecration. None of the precise basket weave decoration on the British bronze backed mirrors could have been the result of an aggressive action.

Even so, Creighton's argument is not entirely negated. As he rightly points out, the British Iron Age features numerous examples of ritualistic behaviour and the engraving of mirrors may well have had such significance. It is conceivable that there was a temporal gap between a drug induced trance of the ritualist and the act of engraving, and that the more complicated basket weave patterns are merely a developed stage of the zig zags seen during a trance. The person experiencing the trance and the engraver may not even have been the same person. In my view, however, the meaning of the pattern may be more complicated than a reproduction of a trance induced vision and the visual effect of the cross hatching may shed some further light on this.

As Jody Joy pointed out in his recent work on British decorated mirrors, the decoration may not have representational meaning, but rather evoke the reflective properties of the object, its 'mirrorness' (Joy 2008: 94). In some societies cross hatching has the effect of creating brilliance. As Murphy showed in his study of paintings of the Yolngu in Australia (Murphy 1992), cross hatching on otherwise dull backgrounds (in his particular study yellow and black crosshatching against a red background) clearly defines separate sections of the paintings, the result of which is a shimmering brightness which the Yolngu associated with ancestral power and beauty.

However, in the context of the British mirrors, the effect is quite different. The surface of the mirror plate was already highly reflective, probably polished to a glossy shine. Even though the cross hatching clearly defines boundaries, it does not create an image of overall brightness, but a dichromatic effect which makes the hatched area appear darker, and emphasizes the brightness of the smooth part of the mirror back, bringing to mind yin and yang symbolism and creating the illusion of depth. The dark area would, however, not have been dull, but depending on the angle the mirror was held, might have created a shimmering reflection, which in turn would have given added energy and movement to engraved pattern. Jope describes this effect as a pleasing change of light and dark shapes with void and positive complex shapes and perhaps a half hidden plan (Jope 2000: 147; 193). I would argue that the effect goes beyond this interpretation and that the engravings were a powerful tool to harness and control supernatural forces.

The decoration was achieved by engraving even and short lines into the metal. This repetitive, perhaps even ritual action defaced the smooth unblemished surface of the mirror. Perhaps the cutting action released some of the inner magic or energy of the mirror, but also created a new pattern and controlled the areas which, depending on how the mirror was held, were perceived as brilliant or dull, thereby deliberately changing and controlling the reflected light itself.

The dichromatic effect achieved by cross hatching is mirrored in the difference in texture between the smooth surface of the undecorated part and the surface of the engraved parts. The overall effect is one of polarity between dark and light, smooth and rough, still and moving. The earlier Yorkshire mirrors were made out of blackish iron, yet the front plate would have been sufficiently polished to have reflective qualities and a similarly dichromatic visual effect of black and blazing white would have been achieved by the contrast between the dull black of iron and the shiny reflected light of the polished front. The decorated bronze mirrors may have been a development of the same theme, but perhaps with added meaning. The polarity between brilliant and dull, dark and light and stillness and movement might have alluded to death and life, which is conceivable for artefacts mainly found in the context of graves, but depending on the way the mirror would have been held against the light, the reflective areas would have shifted and changed, dull becoming bright and vice versa. This would have had an effect akin to movement, a fluidity which was perhaps enhanced by the redness of the bronze with its added blood symbolism and its associated ambiguity, which will be discussed further in chapters 7 and 8.

In addition, the often intricate decoration resembles weaving patterns and may have its own particular symbolic meaning which in turn may have enhanced the symbolic polarity of light and dark. Weaving in prehistory was generally done by women for the simple reason that unlike hunting, smithing or warfare it could be done in conjunction with childcare. Whilst both sexes might have been perfectly capable to do the other's work, women, especially nursing women, could not be relied on to hunt or go to war, whilst nursing children (Barber 1995: 25-30). Weaving only became an occupation for men in periods of increased specialization and commercialism such as the Late Bronze Age and Iron Age in Greece and Egypt (Barber 1995: 284) but there is no evidence of similar organized and commercialized manufacture from the British Iron Age and in any event, the mythological associations between weaving and spinning and the female sex remain even though the commercial reality may have shifted.

Weaving and spinning is an act of creation and transformation, yet at the same time a symbol of continuity and connectedness. Both in Greek and Norse mythology these activities are metaphors of fertility, life spans and fate. In the Odyssey Penelope weaves a shroud by day and then unravels her weaving by night (Homer Odyssey 2.100-110). Apart from the symbolism suggested by day and night, this passage also seems to suggest that Penelope's life remains in a stasis which is controlled by her actions. Weaving can also have magical qualities. In the Iliad Andromache weaves protective roses (Barber 1995: 155), which allude to apotropaic symbolism because of their thorns and blood red colour, into a garment for her husband Hector, although sadly too late to protect him. Ethnographic evidence shows that the analogy between weaving, spinning, life and creation is not isolated to Europe. The Batak in Sumatra also regard weaving as a metaphor for fertility and life giving. The making of cloth symbolizes life giving, the creation of something which has not existed previously (Barber 1995: 160). The cloth is also a metaphor for time as it shows the metric time invested in making it. Amongst the Batak women are given a 'soul cloth' during their first pregnancy, covered with designs which foretell their future and guard their and the children's wellbeing (Barber 1995: 161). The common theme in all these different culture groups appears to be that the thread stands for life span, but the weave is a metaphor of what one does with it (Barber 1995: 242, 243). This symbolic concept is a strong indication of a belief system where humans perceive themselves as not solely dependant on fate or divine powers, but as capable of actually influencing it and interfering with it. Perhaps mirrors had a similar symbolic concept. The affinities between weaving, mirrors, magic and the Otherworld are beautifully brought to mind in Alfred Lord Tennyson's fairy Lady of Shalott, who

> 'weaves by night and day
> a magic web with colours gay (…)
> moving thro' a mirror clear,
> that hangs before her all the year,
> shadows of the world appear(…)
> but in her web she still delights
> to weave the mirror's magic sights'
> (Lord Alfred Tennyson, The Lady of Shalott).

The similarities between weaving and engraving basket weave patterns are intriguing. Weaving is a repetitive act which, as evidenced by classical Greek writers and archaeological evidence from a piece of preserved Bronze Age cloth found in a bog in Denmark, was often carried out by more than one woman (Barber 1995: 30; 86). Engraving basket weave patterns is a similarly repetitive activity and might also have been used as a metaphor for time. Both may have been perceived as ritual and trance inducing activities. Both create a woven pattern and it is tempting to consider that the act of engraving had perhaps also been carried out by one or even several women. Unlike the initial smelting and casting of the mirrors, which was in all likelihood carried out by men, engraving was not as physically demanding, but may also have been compatible with child rearing as it was less dangerous.

The act of engraving and the resulting decoration of agency giving, fluctuating, dichromatic shapes which consist of differently textured voids and geometrically patterned parts may therefore have combined a complex symbolic polarity, ranging from life and death, movement and stillness to male and female. The symbolism is not reduced to these contrasting ideas but goes beyond it. The creation of the pattern was perhaps itself a ritual imbued with metaphors of human creation and fertility,

of human life and human interference with and even control over potent forces such as light, a negotiation between this world and the Otherworld. The handling of the mirrors may have had similar symbolic power. By holding the mirror up towards light and moving it, the reflective areas would have appeared to be changing and moving, dazzling and perhaps enchanting the spectator. Perhaps making, as well as handling the mirrors were acts of intervention with fate and supernatural powers. The ambiguity of the mirrors' symbolism may have been enhanced by flowing designs made out of basket weave, the shimmering effect of the engraved parts and the reddish colour of the mirrors.21

If we assume such symbolic meaning of the basket weave pattern on British mirrors, we have to ask the question whether this can be substantiated by other artefacts featuring such decoration. The bronze shield mounts found as part of the Tal-y-Llyn hoard show regular hatching although perhaps not as fine a workmanship as the mirrors. The main difference however, is that the triskele design on the mount is devoid of decoration and the hatching forms simply the background. Similarly, the cross hatching on the iron spear with highly polished bronze decoration found in the river Thames (Figure 15a) forms the background rather than the design. The cross hatching on sword scabbards, such as the Bugthorpe sword (Figure 15b), the chape frames of the Meare Sword or the Cambridge sword is in each case an intrinsic part of the overall design, which combines both the hatched and the void areas and bears a more pronounced resemblance to the mirrors. Finally, the cross hatching on the terminals of the gold torcs found as part of the Snettisham hoards or the tankard handles found in Seven Sisters, Neath, appears to be part of an elaborate design which again incorporates both void and decorated areas but also utilizes the three dimensionality of the work. It is interesting to note that the design on some of the mirrors such as the Dorton mirror and the Great Chesterford mirror is constructed by the cross hatched areas whereas the void areas form the background. Perhaps as the mirror plates show everything reversed the engravers wanted to show this reversal in the design.22

---

21 If we look at the figurative decoration on Etruscan bronze mirror backs, there may even have been a similarity in meaning, even though expressed in a totally abstract manner. The Etruscan so-called Athrpa mirror shows the nail of fate being driven into a wall by Athrpa, the goddess of fate, but there are also images of the mythical pairs Atalante and Meleager, and Aphrodite and Adonis, which have elements of gender bending, life, death, fertility, rebirth (Vacano 1960: 11-13) and even human interference with divine powers.It is possible that the belief systems associated with mirrors had their influence from Mediterranean culture groups and although the symbolism is similar, it was expressed in Britian in a non-figurative abstract manner.

22 These mirrors were found in burial contexts and the ritual of reversal of roles to prevent the deceased to come back in burial rites is amply documented (Morris 1987: 29-31; Parker Pearson 1999: 25). Perhaps the Mirror decoration had a similar apotropaic function and this may have been the reason why some of the mirrors were found upside down (Farley 1983: 281).

Apart from the triskele on the Tal-y-Llyn Shield mount, the patterns on all of these items seem to have a floral design, which in the case of the swords and scabbards seems at first glance to be at odds with the underlying function of the artefact but could again be a deliberate juxtaposition of opposites. All of the artefacts were found either in rivers, wet depositions, hoards or graves and may have therefore had a ritual rather than or as well as utilitarian function. It could be argued that the shimmering effect of cross hatching may have imitated the shimmering of water which was perceived to be a liminal area, thus perhaps ideally suited to a context which implies the transgression of boundaries from this world and the Otherworld. The cross hatching on the torcs may have imbued the wearer with the kind of shimmering effect usually associated with deities or supernatural beings. All of the designs which involve cross hatching, including the triskele design on the Tal-y-Llyn shield mounts are flowing and imply some sort of movement, action or agency and are therefore comparable to the mirror designs. It is not inconceivable that these artefacts had symbolic meaning similar to that of the mirrors and whilst they do not have the same reflective qualities as mirrors themselves, they were deposited in wet and therefore reflective sites.

Going Out in a Blaze: Dry Hoards and Deposition in Water

The examination of brilliance would not be complete without also exploring the deliberate concealment of luminous objects. Archaeological evidence for the deliberate wrapping of bodies and grave furniture in burial contexts is known from continental and British Iron Age sites such as Hochdorf in Germany or Baldock in Hertfordshire (Banck-Burgess 1999: 21-22; Stead and Rigby 1986: 53). As will be discussed in chapter 9 the act of wrapping may well have had symbolic function during funerary rites. For the purposes of this chapter, however, I want to examine the deliberate concealment of material objects outside burial contexts in the form of wet and dry deposition. There is ample archaeological evidence of the depositions of material objects in both watery and dry contexts in the British Iron Age and at first glance it would appear that both forms of deposition had the same effect in terms of brilliance and luminosity. Ultimately the objects are hidden from sight and their luminosity is thus extinguished.

During the La Tène period there does not seem to be a distinct separation of disposed objects in terms of material or use as to dry and wet deposition; bronze shields, swords and scabbards like those discussed above, as well as everyday objects such as tools, firedogs or currency bars were found in watery contexts such as the River Thames or the lake at Llyn Cerrig Bach (Bradley 1990: 165, 172). At the same time dry depositions reveal highly decorated gold and bronze artefacts, e.g. the

Snettisham and Ipswich hoards (Figures 14b and 15c), as well as work tools, currency bars and firedogs such as those found inter alia at the hillforts of Bulberry Dorset or Madmarston, Oxon (Manning 1972: 230).

If we look at the colour implications of the deposits, there does not appear to be a preference for certain colours or materials either. Iron in the form of tools or bars or even weapons is found both in watery and dry contexts, gold in the form of coins was deposited into the river Thames alongside other metalwork (Bradley 1990: 173) but gold coins were also found alongside weapons and torcs as part of the Essendon dry hoard. The Battersea shield (Figure 16a) and the bronze torcs which form part of the Snettisham hoard demonstrate that bronze was deposited in both wet and dry contexts.

However the development of hoards from the Bronze Age and throughout the Iron Age reveals certain differences. According to Bradley (1990: 136) during the Bronze Age depositions in wet contexts were the successors of grave goods and may even have had associations with male gender, whereas dry deposits may have had perhaps female connotations. Iron Age communities continued to deposit bronze artefacts in rivers, mainly swords. It is possible that there was still a connection with male gender and even burial contexts as the nearly three hundred prehistoric skulls which were found alongside weaponry in the river Thames, suggest. The skulls were placed into the river in de-fleshed condition and belonged mainly to young males between the ages of 25 and 35. Whilst there is no proof that their deposition was connected to that of the weapons, radio carbon dating shows that at least some of these skulls date to the early Iron Age (Bradley 1990: 107-109). The late Iron Age and Roman weaponry depositions and de-fleshed skulls of young males dating from the first century AD found in the river Walbrook, a former tributary river to the Thames, would suggest a continuation of a link between weapons, skulls and rivers throughout the Iron Age (Bradley 1990: 180-181).

Bradley (1990: 133; 251) suggests that wet deposits are most obvious in areas which lack raw material resources of their own. He argues that the metal artefacts found in wells and rivers are geographically far removed from copper and tin ores and there is therefore an element of exotic value attached to them. However, whilst his argument may be true for areas rich in finds such as the river Thames, the Tal-y-Llyn hoard was found close to an area rich in ores. Indeed, as the metal analysis of some of the copper alloys showed, the high zinc content of 19% found in one of the shield bosses is very similar to the high zinc content in copper ores found in nearby Aberystwyth (Savory 1964: 475, 1964a: 30). It is therefore likely that the copper alloy artefacts from the Tal-y-Llyn hoard were manufactured locally and are not an exotic product. Secondly, Bradley's theory also assumes that copper extraction and smelting was done at the same place, which is not necessarily the case as discussed in chapter 4.

It is perhaps more relevant to explore the distinction between the deposition of bronze swords in watery context and iron swords as grave goods which permeates the early Iron Age (Bradley 1990: 153, 257). Bronze and iron seem to have different ritual connotations and meanings. The gleaming, shiny and more durable bronze (perhaps linked to the gleaming white skulls) may have been perceived to have an affinity with the reflective and preserving qualities of water whereas the less luminous but easily rusted iron had closer associations with dry land and decomposing matter.

Metal depositions and in particular deposition of weaponry in rivers and bogs became much scarcer in Britain and Northern Europe during the middle of the first millennium BC which Bradley (1988: 258) attributes to a crisis in supply of metal, and thus supply to the votive sphere, but in Scandinavia there is evidence of deposition of food and agricultural equipment. In the later part of the Iron Age metal artefact deposition in rivers as well as burials with grave goods is again on the increase. This, as Bradley (1990: 170) suggests, coincides with the increased supply of metal in the economy. However, it appears that at this time, i.e. around 300 BC, the deposition of metal may have acquired symbolic association with food production, although in Britain a connection with burials remains (Bradley 1990: 171). During the middle Iron Age inhumation burials appear and the deposition of animals in dry contexts, either as complete skeletons, without any signs of butchering, or skulls, or articulated limbs, is often associated with corn storage pits and therefore symbolically linked to fertility or regeneration (Bradley 1990: 161).23

Iron hoards and deposits are a relatively late development. There were some isolated pieces of iron in the Llyn Fawr hoard such as a wrought iron socketed sickle, the design of which incidentally appears to be an attempt at imitating the bronze sickle designs in iron, but the main part of this early Iron Age hoard consists of bronze artefacts such as cauldrons (Howell 2006: 21; Manning 1972: 239). However, from the first century BC throughout the period of Roman occupation iron mainly in the form of currency bars was deposited throughout Britain, although concentrated in the South West during the Pre-Roman period (Manning 1972: 224-226). At the same time iron fire dogs appear as grave goods in the Welwyn burials (Manning 1972: 239, 240).

Manning (1972: 237; 238) remarked that the iron currency bars were usually shallowly buried, often in or near hill forts, but none were found in deep pits or wells, which would suggest that they were meant to be re-used rather than permanently buried. He believes that votive deposition of iron was relatively rare in the early Iron Age because iron was too valuable and only small quantities would have been deposited (Manning 1972: 240-241). However, iron corrodes much more easily than bronze and this still does not explain why the deposition of iron concentrated in hill forts or dry sites, and was relatively scarce in the context of lakes.

A visual distinction between wet and dry deposits becomes apparent if we examine the actual act of depositing objects. Deposition in a dry context would have eliminated brilliance. In dry hoards or any deposition in the ground any brilliant objects would become concealed and invisible. In time, most items would become either dull or even disintegrate. Metal items such as iron would rust, bronze would tarnish; wood and other organic matter would rot and decay. Iron Age people would surely have been aware of such transformation in the ground. There may even have been the accompanying smell of rotting wood or organic matter. The last memory of the object would be one of integration with the earth.

However, the deposition in a watery context is very different. Not only is the material object immersed into a substance which is already reflective and shimmering, but the contact with water will give most materials a shiny and reflective quality and enhance the brilliance of those objects which are already luminous. If luminous objects are deposited in water on a brilliantly sunny day or a moonlit night, they could with careful orchestration of the deposition literally disappear in a blaze of light. The immersion in water therefore does not obviate the luminosity, but enhances it. Even though the luminous object disappeared from sight, the last and memorable vision of it would have been a dazzling display of brilliant light. And as the preserving qualities of water would have been known, the object, even though no longer visible, would have been remembered as luminous and preserved.

In order to explore the symbolic meaning of this difference, the act of deposition requires further analysis. The reasons which Manning (1972: 238) proposed for the deposition of iron hoards are in my mind valid for deposition of all materials. The first one, rubbish disposal or disposal of something that is not wanted is an unlikely explanation for a society which probably had no concept of rubbish as such (Hill 1995) and even if we take into account that certain items were no longer wanted, these items or their deposition may still have had symbolic value and may have had to be treated in a certain manner.

The second reason, the preservation of objects during personal or general danger with the intention of

---

23 Peter Reynolds (1974: 130) demonstrated that underground pits were useful for seed grain storage whereas consumption grain would have had to be stored above ground. Any artefacts found in underground pits may therefore have had associations of fertility or regeneration rather than consumption as will be explored in further detail in chapter 9.

recovering them later may explain hoarding to a certain extent, but it does not explain the burial of objects which appear to have no value[24] or have been broken, nor does it explain deposition in storage pits, shrines or in rivers or deep lakes. The suggestion that bronze hoards were deliberately deposited to take surplus bronze metalwork out of circulation to create an artificial scarcity and therefore increase its exchange value in relation to new material, is, as Bradley argues (1990: 40; 41) also unlikely as it assumes not only a sufficiently sophisticated market co-ordination but also an understanding of the fairly recent concept of market economy, neither of which are likely to have existed in Iron Age Britain.

The third explanation is that of a votive deposit or religious offering. Hedaeger (1992) suggested that the difference between dry depositions and wet depositions in the context of the North European Iron Age is simply that the former are secular depositions whilst the latter are religious. Bradley (1990: 10-11) agrees that distinctions should be made between dry and wet hoards. He concedes that wet depositions may have ritual relevance and that locations such as bogs, springs, wells, but also those locations where material is buried at a great depth, e.g. burial mounds, have religious meaning, especially where the deposited objects are ornamented with cosmological references or musical instruments, like in Bronze Age Denmark. In contrast, the scrap metal and freshly made yet broken objects marked with marker stones in Danish Bronze Age dry hoards appear to have had utilitarian rather than religious value.

However, this argument implies a simplification which may not be entirely applicable. It presupposes a distinction between secular and ritual or utilitarian and religious which is a modern Western concept and cannot be assumed for the British Iron Age. Anthropological studies show that in many societies there is no distinction between the secular and the ritual. It is often not even the end result or the object, but the act of making or unmaking something, which could be ritual, although the result may be purely utilitarian (Brueck 1990: 320; Graves- Brown 1995:, 96; Sinclair 1995: 60).

I would agree with Bradley's argument (Bradley 1990: 39-40) that depositions in watery context and perhaps also shrines and burials had a different purpose to that of dry hoards. Bradley believes that those items deposited in the former context were meant to be taken out of circulation without expectation of a counter gift, perhaps with a lavish display, although I would not necessarily concur that this should only apply to special purpose artefacts, in order to make them economically dormant once they have served their special purpose. Bradley (1990: 40) cites marriage payments as one such special purpose, but marriage payments are usually intended to be used for further prosperity and not to be taken out of the market.

To my mind there may not have been a differentiation between votive and sacrifice offering as Bradley had suggested (Bradley 1990: 37), but the differentiation should be between the deposition of goods or living beings which are meant to be taken out of circulation and the deposition of goods which were meant to be either retrieved or were meant to remain with the community.[25] Although both may ultimately benefit the community rather than an individual, be it in the form of votive gifts to a deity or a sacrifice or merely as hidden goods (Bradley 1990: 40) they serve separate purposes.

Depositions in a dry shallow context such as in storage pits or dry hoards would have remained part of the community and the communal landscape. The deposits may have decomposed or weathered or disintegrated but this may have been perceived as a transformation to something which may still benefit and belong to the community. Artefacts may have played a role as propitiary deposits (Davis 2002: 23), an exchange mechanism invoking notions of regeneration and fertility but still very much in this world. Even the artefacts which were buried for the purpose of hiding and later re-usal would fall into this category. Their place is still with the community and after a time they would be returned into circulation, thus remaining beneficial to the community.

The deposition in wet contexts, however, has very different aspects. Firstly, wet places are geographically outside or at the boundary of the communal landscape. They are often geographical as well as political boundaries, but also liminal places and boundaries to the Otherworld (Brueck 1995: 260).

Secondly, immersion in water changes both inert objects and living beings. Water restores energies, it preserves, it is a live giving fluid, necessary for survival, but it also purifies and cleanses both literally and in many religions also symbolically. Christian baptism or ritual bathing in the Hindu religion, Judaism or in Ancient Egyptian religious practices are but a few examples. The act transforms and imbues with numinosity or divine spirit.

But the surface of water is also a reflective mirror, having perhaps the same magical qualities as discussed above in the context of mirrors. Its surface shows perhaps an entrance into a different sphere where the intangible soul of the person looking at his or her reflection could be trapped. The deposition into water is clearly an act which does not involve any expectation of retrieval. It is a deliberate permanent deposition of artefacts or beings with the intention of preserving them in this liminal zone. The essence as well as the material bodies are taken out of

---

[24] although the concept of value may have been quite different and not readily apparent to us.

[25] The deposition of grave goods is a separate issue as they are linked to an individual and will be discussed separately in chapter 9.

circulation and the community, and enter the Otherworld, perhaps in order to obtain divine intervention, perhaps as a gift to the gods, protection of the boundaries or as an act of preserving the very idea and the spiritual essence of the artefact. Thus they may have ensured the continuation of the material aspects of such artefacts in this world. In other words, the wooden figures from Roos Carr may have represented real people, perhaps an entire community; bronze artefacts may have stood for bronze working or even the usual contents of cauldrons, i.e. food or drink, the swords for military prowess and the skulls perhaps for victory in battle.

The connection between shiny metal objects the reflective and luminescent context of water in the Bronze and Iron Ages (Keates 2002: 122) enhances the symbolism of interaction with the supernatural. The entry into the Otherworld is literally highlighted by the sparkle of both the surface of water and the shimmering of the brilliant object. Whilst during the later Iron Age an increasing number of less sparkling artefacts such as workman's tools were ritually deposited in watery contexts such as Fiskerton (Field and Parker Pearson 2003), the fact remains that the immersion in water would still have imbued them with a certain luminosity, but it is also possible that the inherent brilliance of the artefact which is to be deposited was no longer perceived as important as it was during the Bronze Age and the early Iron Age.

Conclusion

As Melanie Giles (2008) pointed out, decorated Iron Age martial objects dazzle us with their moving and highly reflective designs. But it is not only decorated metal which provides us with such effects. Materials such as wood or stone can have equally brilliant effects through manipulation and the biographies of objects may reveal further rituals which enhance, prolong or create brilliance, shimmering or dazzling spectacles. The brilliance of such objects however should not be treated merely as a symbol of beauty, power or wealth (Saunders 1999: 253). Their biography shows that the creation of luminosity by a variety of means, the handling and usage of such objects and finally the deposition of objects in contexts where brilliance was an important factor, may well have had or added symbolic meaning, perhaps creating or revealing inherent numinosity or negotiation with natural forces or the supernatural. What is important to note, is the relevance of active rather than passive human contribution. There is always a human action, an act of intervention whether in the manipulation, the handling or the deposition of objects which creates or enhances such brilliance. This aspect of human interference suggests a strong belief in human power to interfere with and perhaps even control the natural and also supernatural world.

Chapter 7

The Power of Blood – Decorated Metal Ware

'Then Cronos' son brought them confusing signs of trouble,
sending down from high in heaven a rain of blood
dripping from the sky,
for his intention was to hurl the heads
of many brave men down to Hades'

(Homer Iliad. 11.53-55)

Introduction

The decoration of metal objects with coral or vitreous substances appears to have been of great importance in the Iron Age in continental European countries such as France, Austria, Switzerland and Germany as well as in Britain (Megaw and Megaw 1989: 21). Such decoration appears on a variety of items ranging from horse harnesses to scabbards and brooches. On the continent the majority of artefacts dating from the Hallstatt period which are decorated with coral inlays are fibulae (Champion 1976: 33). During the early La Tène period metal ware decorated with coral inlays appears to have had different uses in Switzerland and France. According to Sara Champion (1976: 33) in Switzerland nearly 95% of finds with coral decoration consisted of fibulas, whereas in France the percentage was less than 43. There, a far higher percentage of coral decoration was found on chariots and other decorative metalwork. The percentage of Iron Age coral found in Britain is only a small fraction of the overall finds in Europe and Britain and due to the paucity of finds there does not seem to be a clear indication whether there was a preference for coral on fibulas or other metalwork.

One of the finest examples of coral decoration found on the British Isles is the Witham Shield. The bronze shield features a central domed umbo into which various inlays of a red coral were pinned onto the underlying metal. The central part of the boss consists of three almond shaped pieces of red coral held together by a metal ring pinned onto the umbo (Figure 15d). The pinning rather than embedding of coral may have been typical for East Britain (Jope 2000: 55). On either side of the centre there are two round pieces of red and well preserved coral, which according to Jope (2000: 56) may have been treated with a resinous substance. The shield is generally dated to the third century BC (Jope 2000: 61) but Vincent Megaw argued that the umbo was a later addition to the shield to make room for a handgrip at the rear (Megaw and Megaw 1989: 198).

Enamel and Hot Glass

During the first century AD decoration made out of enamel or red glass appears frequently on British Iron Age objects (Hughes 1972: 98). Enamel or hot glass is rarely found on classical Roman or Greek artefacts, but the application of such decoration in a variety of colours seems to have been widespread in Britain (Megaw and Megaw 1989: 21).

Prior to any discussion of the colour of enamel and glass a brief discourse on the terms is required. The relevant literature about decorated metal ware usually uses the term enamel for any inlays composed of a vitreous substance. Herbert Maryon (1971: 169) defined enamel as 'a vitreous substance fused onto a metallic background'. Bateson (1981: 6) defines enamel similarly as a 'vitreous substance applied to a metal base and fused to it by the application of heat'. Hughes (1972: 98-107) questioned the use of the term enamel. He argued that the red decoration generally referred to as enamel could not be true enamel in the sense of a layer of powdered glass heated and melted *in situ* onto a metal surface. He was of the opinion that it would not have been possible to use this technique for any opaque red decoration as the inlay would have oxidised to a green colour during the process. Hughes believed that the decoration of metal with opaque red colours was achieved by applying molten glass. However, since Hughes' analysis of red enamel Bateson questioned the validity of his argument. He thinks that Hughes underestimated the skills of British enamel workers and showed with the help of experimental archaeology that sufficiently reducing conditions could have been achieved to apply the enamel in form of a paste or powder and heat it without oxidation (Bateson 1981: 111; 134), even though he concedes that the red enamel inserted into objects in the form of studs was probably melted, shaped and then set in place with the help of an adhesive (Bateson 1981: 111). Mary Davis (Gwilt and Davis 2008: 155) makes a clear distinction between the two techniques: The more substantive red inlay generally referred to as red sealing wax enamel is made of a heat softened block of red glass and should be referred to as glass, whereas the smaller area of polychrome decoration found on metal ware is made of ground glass and therefore aptly referred to as enamel. For the purpose of this chapter I shall therefore continue to use the terms hot glass and enamel accordingly.

One of the very few classical accounts for the decoration of metal ware appears to describe the technique of enamelling rather than applying glass inlays. Philostratus the Elder wrote in his Imagines (Book 1.28):

'Ταυτα φασι τα χρωματα τουσ εν Οκεανω βαρβαρουσ εγχειν τω χαλκω διαπυρω τα δε συνιστασθαι και λιθουσθαι και σωζειν α εγραφη'.

The translation by A. Fairbanks (1931: 109) reads: 'these pigments it is said, the barbarians living by Oceanus compound of red-hot bronze, and they combine and grow hard, and preserve what is painted with them'. This would imply that the pigments were made out of bronze. However, in another translation also attributed to Fairbanks (Bateson 1981: 122) the meaning is somewhat different: 'They say that the Barbarians by Oceanus pour (these Pigments) onto red hot bronze and the colours join together and harden and preserve what has been painted'. [26] Bateson believes that Oceanus means the Atlantic and that the Barbarians are either Atlantic Gauls or Britons. In any event the technique is perceived to be a native craft rather than Roman and involves some form of painting, or more precisely the application of a liquid or a pigment in situ. It is of course debatable if this source is reliable for the British Iron Age. Firstly, Philostratus was born in AD 170 in Athens and was therefore geographically and temporally rather remote. Secondly, his implication that the process of enamelling or decoration with glass or enamel is an entirely local craft may not be correct. Based on chemical analysis Hughes believed that at least the brilliant red opaque glass was most likely to be imported from a few small production centres in the Mediterranean, Egypt or Syria and then exported into Britain and Northern Europe in the form of cakes. He argues that these cakes would have been broken down into smaller lumps by local glassworkers and heated until they were of sufficient viscosity to be pressed onto the underlying metal (Hughes 1972: 104-105). If Bateson is to be believed, such cakes could also have been ground down to form a paste or powder as basis for enamelling.

In his Natural History (36.65-66) Pliny gives an account of the three principal ingredients of glass, namely soda, silica and lime (Bateson 1981: 75; Tatton-Brown and Andrews 1991: 21). Silica was probably just sand, nitrum could have been used as a naturally occurring soda and lime was likely to have been prevalent in the sand. The addition of certain metals such as lead, copper and antimony would have produced coloured glass (Tait 1991: 8). According to Margaret Guido (1978: 7) glass in antiquity was made in thick earthenware crucibles which could be filled with up to 2000lb of mixed pulverised quartz or sand quartz mixed with some lime and soda, potash or nitrum to which then lead, iron, copper, manganese or cobalt was added. This mixture was then fired to a red hot viscous state from which some material was then drawn out to make beads or cakes of glass which could be traded. The whole process of bringing silica and alkali together without melting it and then adding further components has been likened to the process of cookery where the whole activity and human touch is sometimes more important than the actual ingredients (Biek and Bayley 1979: 1).

The addition of specific metallic oxides, and varying heat conditions in the furnaces resulted in different colours (Henderson 1985: 281). Added copper caused colours ranging from turquoise or pale blue to dark green, ruby red or opaque sealing wax red. Cobalt resulted in a deep blue colour whilst yellow, pale orange or opaque white glass could be achieved with the addition of manganese or antimony. Added iron turned the colour of glass into pale blue, bottle green, amber or a dark blackish colour (Grose 1997: 12-13; Tatton-Brown and Andrews 1991: 21). Yellow enamel seems to have been achieved by the addition of lead antimonite with approximately 20% lead oxide (Hughes 1987: 11).

Coloration of glass with the addition of copper has been known in the Middle East since the 15th century BC. To avoid oxidation the glass would have to have been produced under reducing conditions, e.g. with the help of a charcoal blanket and the temperature would have determined the intensity or hue of the colour (Henderson 1985: 281). Based on his analysis of 33 examples of opaque red glass from either the British Museum or Castle Museum, Colchester Hughes found that the substance was consistently averaging 7% copper oxide and 25% lead oxide and he concluded that the composition was therefore deliberate rather than accidental (Hughes 1972: 101). There seems to have been a fundamental change of the composition of red glass in the European Iron Age in the second century BC. Higher traces of manganese oxide are found in artefacts from this period onwards and it is assumed that manganese oxide instead of antimony was used as a decolorizer, a trend which according to Henderson may be linked to the expanding Roman Empire (Henderson 1985: 284-285; Jope 2000: 351). Chemical analysis of the red hot glass in the swastika settings of the Battersea shield(Stead 1985: 50) shows no manganese oxide, thus suggesting a date not later than the second century BC. On the general assumption that red glass production in Britain and its use in military equipment appears mainly in the first centuries BC and AD the Battersea shield seems to be a unique piece. A

[26] Both translations are problematic. The work can also mean copper ore and χαλκον means untouched by fire. Perhaps the paragraph refers therefore to unworked copper-ore.

further change in composition of red vitreous decoration occurred during the Roman occupation. The duller red tesserae typical of Roman Britain, which Hughes also analysed, contained less cuprous oxide (Hughes 1972: 104-105).

In the British Iron Age, sealing wax red is the colour most commonly found on decorated metal ware. A survey of the 25 best known decorated terrets (Figure 1) shows that 14 of the objects are decorated with red glass only, eight have red and blue decoration, two display red and yellow, and only the Saham Toney terrets were decorated with all three colours.

Red appears most frequently on its own on curvilinear crescentic terrets such as the terret from Westhall in Suffolk or the terret from Whitton, Vale of Glamorgan (Figure 16c). Similar decoration can also be found on other decorative metal ware such as the eared mounts forming part of the Santon hoard, dating to the middle of the first century AD (Smith 1909: 146-63), the beautifully crafted enamelled harness fitting of the Polden Hills hoard (Brailsford 1975a: 227-230) (Figure 16d) both dated to the middle of the first century AD or the feline head of the tube handled bronze patera found in Snowdon in Wales (Jope 2000: 311-312) (Figure 17a). Red is also found in combination with blue or yellow as seen on the crescentic terrets from Bapchild, Lakenheath or Richborough (Henry 1933) or the strap junctions from the Seven Sisters hoard (Davies and Spratling 1976; Davis and Gwilt 2008: 179).

Yellow and blue are hardly ever found on their own and when encountered in combination with red, they are usually only in the form of small spots on objects with curvilinear red designs on crescentic terrets or relatively small angular cells in geometric designs on platform terrets (Bateson 1981: 67). The combination of red and blue, a fine example of which is the strap fitting from Westhall in Suffolk (Henry 1933) (Figure 16b) showing a number of blue spots and red panels and a blue central spot surrounded by a three pointed star, is found more frequently than red and yellow, but a combination of all three colours, usually in geometrical

Terret	Type of terret	Decoration	colour
Auchendolly, Kirkcudbright	crescentic	curvilinear	red with yellow spots
Balmuildy, Lanarkshire	platform terret	geometric square and oval cells	red and blue
Bapchild, Kent	crescentic	curvilinear	red with blue spots
Birrens, Dumfriesshire	platform	geometrical triangles and squares	red and blue
Bolton, Lancashire	crescentic	curvilinear scrolls	red fields, blue spots
Colchester, Essex	crescentic	plain diamonds patters set off against glass background	red
Ditchley,Oxfordshire	Lipped	Curvilinear and spots	red
Fremington Hagg I, North Yorkshire	platform	Round spots	red
Fremington Hagg, II, North Yorkshire	platform	four geometrical square cells	red and blue
Great Chesters, Northumberland	platform	swastika style cells	red
High Rochester, Northumberland	platform	geometrical triangular cells	red
Lakenheath, Suffolk	crescentic	curvilinear design and spots	red with blue spots
Middlebie, Dumfiresshire	platform	round annulus with inner spot	red with blue spot
Owmby, Lincolnshire	crescentic	curvilinear	red
Polden Hill, Somerset	lipped	glass spot	red
Richborough, Kent	crescentic	curvilinear	red with blue spots
Runnymede, Berkshire	crescentic	curvilinear, waves against glass background	red
Saham Toney, Norfolk	platform	petal like cells	red, yellow and blue
Snettisham, Norfolk	lipped	spots	red
Staines, Middlesex	crescentic	curvilinear	red
Traprain Law, East Lothian	platform terret,	geometric square cells	red and yellow
Westhall, Suffolk	crescentic,	curvilinear	red
Weybread, Suffolk	crescentic	curvilinear design over glass field, zigzag bordering	red
Whaplode, Lincolnshire	crescentic	curvilinear and spots	red
Whitton, Vale of Glamorgan	crescentic	curvilinear and spots	red

FIGURE 1: DECORATED TERRETS

or angular designs or in the form of petals, where red is no longer the predominant colour, can be seen on artefacts such as the terrets of the Saham Toney hoard (McGregor 1976: 26) (Figure 17b) or the Seven Sisters hoard (Davies and Spratling 1976; Davis and Gwilt 2008: 179). Whilst McGregor (1976: 26) argues for a date of AD 40/60 preceding the Icenian revolt for these designs, which appears to co-incide with the generally accepted date for the Polden Hill artefacts, Jope (2000: 155) believes that the use of multicoloured decoration is a new development starting in the mid first century BC. Davis and Gwilt (2008: 160) however, have argued that the objects decorated in geometric style from the Severn Sisters hoard date to the first century AD but were contemporaneous to the curvilinear red glass decorated items deposited in the same hoard. They suggest that Roman influences are clearly present in the new technologies used for decoration. This argument is further strengthened by the fact that objects with geometric designs in the Seven Sisters hoard are made out of enamelled brass whereas the artefacts decorated with red glass were made out of bronze. However, both sets of items were clearly native, made by indigenous craftsmen using very pure materials, and can thus be distinguished from the Roman items also deposited as part of the hoard. The reason for this overlap of styles could be a change in production, new consumers and a new elite competing with the more traditional technologies and leaders (Davis and Gwilt 2008: 160) but, as will be discussed below, the geometric decoration might suggest a different underlying cosmology.

Bateson is convinced that the three colours red, blue and yellow are the only colours used in the Pre-Roman Iron age. Any greens or whites found on artefacts of that period should be regarded as decayed colours (Bateson 1981: 67), but although red coral often fades to white (Megaw and Megaw 1989: 79), the use of white coral should not be ruled out. Bateson made the valid point that it is also not always possible to describe enamel or coloured glass with an exact colour term. Yellow orange and red merge into each other, greens and blues merge and light colours fade to white whilst dark blue colours merge with black. The colours cited in publications often differ from those evident in examination, possibly due to fading (Bateson 198: 68).

During the Romano British period a far greater variety of colour occurs, ranging from green and orange to black and white, and blue becomes the most common colour, whereas the use of red diminishes. This seems to coincide with a change in composition of the enamel (Bateson 1981: 67-69; Palk 1991: 306-307). As stated above, the copper content in red vitreous decoration diminishes, resulting in a much duller colour. In the post Roman Period the colour range drops back to just three, with red being the preferred colour, followed by yellow and rarely blue (Bateson 1981: 69). It is possible that the reversion

to such pre-Roman colours and colour combinations is an example of retro-ideology. Interestingly the use of red enamel on horse harnesses in Ireland seems not to have flourished until the fourth or fifth century AD (Palk 1991: 306).

Decoration with coral or vitreous substances is usually found on bronze artefacts or brass artefacts. Bateson (1981: 78) cites only one example of enamelled gold from a Romano British context, a gold bracelet from Rhayader, but none from Iron Age Britain. The only potential example of enamelled silver from Iron Age Britain is a brooch which was found with the Birdlip mirror , even though it is not certain that it had indeed contained red enamel (Bateson 1981: 78).

The combination of iron and enamel is frequently found on the continent, but relatively rare in Britain. Bateson cites the Trevone brooch, the Eastburn brooch, the iron frames from the Bugthorpe discs and a bronze coated terret from Aldborough (Bateson 1981: 79). Natalie Anne Palk believes that in the rare cases where iron, bronze and enamel or hot glass were used together for harnesses and horse trappings, iron was used because of its tensile strength, but for the purposes of decoration bronze, often inlaid with coloured enamel or hot glass was the preferred material. Iron fittings, such as terret rings and bridle bits would usually have been invisible to the observer. Where they might have been visible they would have been covered or plated in bronze. She makes the point that the covering of bridle bits with bronze may have been carried out for reasons of easier mouthing as horses seem to prefer the slightly garlicky taste of bronze to that of iron (Palk 1991: 311-312), but this does not explain the covering of terrets and other visible harness fittings. Even the Kirkburn sword and scabbard (Figure 17c) which is probably the most striking example of a combination of different metals decorated with red hot glass, arguably conceals the parts made out of iron. The hilt and pommel are made of horn covered with iron sheets, the back of the scabbard consist of iron and the front part of the scabbard and the chape are made of bronze. All of these parts are decorated with red glass (Gosden and Hill 2008: 10-11; Stead 2006: 116; 184). The back of the scabbard would have been mostly hidden from view and the hilt of the sword would have been covered when handled. The whiteness of the horn, the black iron and the red glass in the hilt and pommel would have formed a triad of colours which might have had symbolic meaning connected to life and death and which will be discussed further in chapter 9. The most visible part, however, would have been the front part of the scabbard which is made out of bronze.

It can therefore be concluded that the combination of bronze and red is the most frequently found combination in the British Iron Age and seems to have had more appeal than any other colour grouping. In order to explore if this combination had any specific symbolic significance we need to look first at the relationship between coral and vitreous decoration and also consider if there were mere technical reasons for the use of red in preference to any other colour.

Coral and Enamel

At first glance the argument that red hot glass simply replaced coral as a means of decoration appears attractive. However, as Sara Champion pointed out, there are fibulas of the Muensingen Type where both coral and enamel (rather than red glass) were used (Champion 1976: 34-35; Hodson 1995: 65). It is of course possible that due to a shortage of coral only some small pieces were used, and glass or enamel were employed as substitutes. We know from Pliny that during his life time coral was so rare that it was hardly ever seen in its country of origin, mainly because it was imported to India (Pliny Natural History 32.11). According to Sara Champion there is no evidence of the use of coral north of the Alps later than La Tène II (Champion 1976: 36).

Apart from the brilliant red colour, there are a number of similarities between coral and red glass. Both materials were imported and therefore exotic, which may have given them special value. Pliny (Natural History 32.21) mentioned that coral was found in the Red Sea and the Persian Gulf, the Gallic Gulf around the Stoechades Islands and the Sicilian Gulf around the Aeolian Islands. As stated above, red glass, according to Hughes, was also likely to have been imported from the Mediterranean (Hughes 1972: 104-105), but even if it had been produced in Britain, it still included non-local materials (Henderson 1991: 107). Like coral, it had a restricted functional use, but a small amount of material could be used for a large number of artefacts (Henderson 1991: 107). Both materials undergo a process of hardening and both materials retain their brilliant colour for a significant length of time.

There are, however, a few striking differences. Firstly, coral is a naturally occurring material. Pliny believed it to be organic. He tells us that the coral's shape resembles a shrub and that its 'berries' are white and soft under water, but they harden and turn red when taken out of the water, resembling a cultivated cornel cherry (Natural History 32.21). In a different part of the Natural History (37.164) he states that 'Gorgoneia' or gorgon's stone is the same material as coral and alludes again to the transformation of soft material into something which is as hard as a stone. The name Gorgon's stone is of course a reference to the petrifying stare of the Gorgon Medusa in Greek myth. This quality appears to have had significant symbolic value to the classical world and the East, if Pliny is to be believed. He tells us that coral was used to ward off thunderstorms and whirlwinds, and that branches of coral were worn by babies as protective

amulets. He further cites numerous healing remedies made out of coral. He mentions that red coral has the highest value and that Indian soothsayers regarded it as a powerful religious and apotropaic amulet. Interestingly, he also tells us that the Gauls 'used to ornament their swords shields and helmets with red coral' (Pliny Natural History 37.164; 32.21-24). The name 'Gorgoneia' and the association of the name with petrifaction suggest that certain belief systems may have been imported together with the actual material, perhaps even into Iron Age France and Britain, and the insertion of coral into shields such as the Witham shield might have been perceived as having the same effect as that of the Gorgoneion on the Aegis, Athena's shield, i.e. the petrification of one's enemies (Ovid Metamorphoses. 4.800-803).

Red glass is neither an organic nor a naturally occurring material; instead it is a human made material manufactured from a number of components. It was probably at least initially imported in the form of red glass cakes, although there is some evidence of glass making in Britain as early as the second century BC. Henderson concluded on the basis of semi formed glass beads and glass moulds that there was a workshop specialising in vitreous materials in Meare in Somerset. Evidence for another glass workshop, albeit dating to the first to second centuries AD, was found at Culbin Sands in Scotland (Henderson 1991: 124).

Even if the base material had been imported in the form of glass cakes, the decoration of the metal base still involved processing and melting the glass cakes. There is evidence that this may have been carried out by the metalworker who cast the bronze alloy. Natalie Ann Palk (1991: 310) mentions that some items of the Stanwich hoard were miscast and therefore unusable, but they still show red glass inlays. She argues convincingly that the decoration may have been done at the final stage of bronze production just before cooling of the bronze objects.

In contrast to coral which hardens naturally without human manipulation, it is the metalworker or glass worker, perhaps one and the same person, who has power to make glass soft with the help of fire and then harden it again. The apotropaic qualities of red glass may have been perceived to be the same as those linked to coral, but here the smith/craftsman is in control, thus perhaps being seen as interacting with and possibly controlling the supernatural, which would have made him undoubtedly a powerful person. The red colour of the decoration also echoes the colour of fire, which the craftsman would have used in the process and perhaps the ambiguous qualities of fire as a destructive as well as transformative and positive force might have been transferred to the decoration. If this were the case the preference of red enamel and glass over coral by the specialists who carried out the decoration becomes entirely rational.

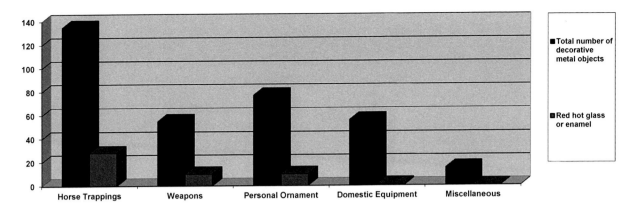

FIGURE 2: DECORATED METALWARE FROM NORTH BRITAIN AS LISTED BY MACGREGOR (1976)

Red Hot Glass – Symbolic or Technical Reasons?

We have to pose the question if the preferred use of red vitreous decoration over other colours was driven purely by technical reasons. Both glass and enamel are after all vitreous substances and opaque yellow glass was regularly used in Iron Age Europe from the eighth century BC onwards. Cobalt blue glass is the most common glass colour in Iron Age Europe and both yellow and blue glass were widely used in the European Iron Age for bracelets and beads during the third and second century BC (Henderson 1987: 183-185; Venclova 1991: 445). There does not seem to be any reason why differently coloured glass could not have been used, and indeed, in the first century AD there is an increasing number of metal artefacts decorated with more than one colour, both glass and enamel. It is therefore safe to say that technical reasons can be ruled out and the reasons for the use of red glass must lie elsewhere.

Effect of Red Glass

On a mere visual examination of decorated artefacts there are immediately recognisable effects. The deliberate addition of brilliant red to bronze makes the underlying metal appear more dazzling, but also warmer. The addition of blue or yellow, especially on brass, would have had the opposite effect. By way of illustration, Figures 17d and 18a show what the eared mount from the Santon Hoard would have looked like, had it been made out of yellow coloured brass decorated with blue instead of red on bronze.

This juxtaposition of colours and the resulting effect may well have been a deliberate choice. Pliny (Natural History 37.126) describes the effect of a certain yellow gem called Chrysolithus on gold. According to him the best specimens are those which make gold assume a white silvery appearance when placed next to them. In view of the Romans' preference for silvery and colder colours (Pliny Natural History 33.58) this not only makes sense, but begs to ask the question if the deliberate use of red on bronze would have appealed more to people

living in a colder climate and may have coincided with the increasing use of using copper in gold (see chapters 4 and 8).

Another clue for the preferred use of red on bronze may be found in the type of decorated object. The main group of objects with this kind of decoration dating from the British Iron Age forms part of military or equestrian equipment, such as horse harnesses, chariot parts, scabbards or shields. Although red glass is also found on mirrors, fibulaes and other miscellaneous objects, decorated horse harnesses and objects such as terrets are far more numerous than any other type of artefact (Bateson 1981: 7; 1987: 3). Of the 343 decorative metal objects from Northern Britain listed by Morna MacGregor 49 are decorated with hot glass or enamel. Of these 38 are horse trappings or weapons, 10 are personal ornaments and only one, a tankard handle from Catterick, North Riding of Yorkshire, belongs to the group termed domestic equipment (MacGregor 1976) (Figure 2). Of the 38 horse trappings and weapons 11 are decorated with red only, one fragmented mount, possibly cruciform, is decorated with angular cells of blue and yellow [27] and the others feature combinations or red and yellow, red and blue or all three colours.

Natalie Anne Palk commented that there are no known horse harness parts decorated with stone or other organic matter; decoration is restricted to coral, albeit rarely, and hot glass (Palk 1991: 303) which would suggest a very specific meaning for red hot glass. Palk thought that the rise of decorated bronze in the late Pre-Roman Iron Age may have been a deliberate attempt to undermine the prestige of bronze on its own (Palk 1991: 330). This is of course plausible, especially if we assume that the ability to decorate bronze with hot glass may have given added power to the craftsman or metalworker, as stated above. However, this argument in isolation does not justify the obvious preference for red enamel.

---

[27] It cannot be ruled out that the missing parts of the mount included red decoration.

In the context of decorated military and equine equipment such as the finds from the Santon or Polden Hills hoards, we encounter a combination of gleaming reddish golden metal decorated with often asymmetrical swirling patterns of brilliant red which convey a sense of flowing movement and do not allow the eye of the beholder to rest even when they are not in motion. If one imagines such pieces on a chariot or horse at full speed, especially if sunlight reflects on the metal pieces, such dazzling spectacle would have been very impressive and awe inspiring to spectators or enemies.

Red and Blood

The connection between the use of red inlays (or at least the early red coral and glass studs) on horse gear and weaponry such as shields and swords and other items of military display leads to one further thought. Red glass may have had important ritual or symbolic functions (Henderson 1982: 20). There is a distinct resemblance between the round coral or enamel inlays and spots or drops of blood (Giles 2008: 73). If red coral or enamel on decorated metal ware were indeed symbolic of blood, this symbolism could have a variety of further associations which can perhaps be best explained by recourse to classical writers and early Irish and Welsh myth.

Pliny mentions a certain Zachalias of Babylon who claims that to be smeared with an ointment containing haematite or blood stone, so named after its colour, is beneficial in battle. There seems to be a connection between blood, red colour and protection. (Pliny Natural History 37.169). Whilst this custom comes from a geographically remote culture, a similar belief system connected to red enamel might have been transferred from one culture group to another, perhaps together with the technical skills of metal decoration with coral and enamelling which ultimately came from the Middle East and Mediterranean culture groups.

The classics scholar Tamara Neal has recently explored the symbolic meaning of blood in the Iliad (Neal 2006: 17). In book 11: 53-55 of the Iliad Zeus sends blood dew as a portent of many deaths to occur. The presence of spots of blood on armour even in the form of imitated blood spots such as the early round coral inlays on the Witham shield may therefore have been perceived as a warning to the enemy of their imminent death. This symbolism is echoed in early Irish mythology where the colour red is often used as a signifier of impending death. The 'redmouthed' and bleeding Badbh, the warrior aspect of the Irish mother goddess, who appears as the scarecrow of battle and who may have been identical to the Gaulish Cathubodua combines the colours red and black as symbols of war and death (Green 1992: 38; Green 1995: 43; Ó hÓgáin 1999: 67). In the 'Taín Bo Cuailgne' the seeress Fedelm uses the words crimson and red in her prophesy of forthcoming battles (Giles

2008: 73; Kinsella 1970: 61). However, as Neal suggests, there are further blood associations in the Iliad. If blood is connected with a non fatal injury it gives the warrior value. The spilling of one's own blood and bleeding wounds symbolise survival and blood is thus seen as a badge of honour, endurance and bravery (Neal 2006: 18-19). It is conceivable that bright red decorations on weaponry and horse gear may have been rooted in such a belief and replaced actual blood as a symbol of such honour, bravery and endurance and ultimately survival.

Following this trail of thought, the link between red decoration and blood can be taken a step further. Blood is an ambiguous bodily fluid. It can symbolise death, but can also stand for life and life force. The colours associated with blood mirror this ambiguity. Blood in the context of death literally leaves the body, dries up and ultimately turns black, whereas blood symbolising life is liquid and bright red. Similarly hot glass retains its brightness and is a material which could at will be made liquid again with the help of heat. It becomes a preserved liquid. The viscosity of heated red glass could even be perceived as reminiscent of slightly coagulating but still 'life' blood. The sense of this preserved liquidity in hot glass is followed through in the iconographic development of red enamel decoration from the early studs which symbolise perhaps drops of blood, to the swirling patterns of pieces such as the harness mounts from the Santon or Polden Hill hoards, which convey a sense of flowing movement, and, as will be seen in chapter 8, perhaps suggesting associations with liminality.

One further link between red glass and blood symbolism may have been the use of copper as colorant in the production of red enamel. As outlined in chapter 4 there may have been symbolic affinities between copper and blood. The process of applying red hot glass, as discussed earlier, may have taken place simultaneously with the smelting of copper and copper based alloys such as bronze. Copper ore and lead would have been used for the production of both bronze and sealing wax red glass (Biek and Bayley 1979:12) and there may have been symbolic synergies resulting from the correlation between material and production which may be a further explanatory factor for the predominance of red glass on bronze rather than any other metal.

One of the earliest pieces of vitreous decoration in the British Isles, the Battersea shield, suggests a connection between red glass and solar symbolism. The bronze swastikas surrounded by red glass (Stead 1985: 16) are surely solar symbols, but perhaps the bronze colour refers to the setting sun rather than the bright golden colour of the noon sun. As already mentioned in chapter 4 Hesiod used bronze as a metaphor for the threshold to the Underworkd (Hesiod Theogonia 807; Ó hÓgáin 1999: 55). The reddish colour of bronze could be indeed be likened to the colour of the setting sun, but perhaps the ambiguous quality of bronze, i.e. that its colour is not consistent and can become duller and dark if left unpolished or untreated, may have added to this symbolism. This ambiguity may well be the reason for the threshold symbolism of bronze, not only in the sense of a threshold between life and death but also between this world and the supernatural, which can be found both in classical and early Celtic myth.

In addition to the metaphorical value of bronze and copper in the Odyssee and in relation to the Irish mythical hero Conchobar already discussed in chapter 4. We encounter in the Aeneid a description of the 'twin gates of war' being locked with a 'hundred bolts of bronze' (VII: 588ff) and the godless spirit of discord having his hands tied behind him with a 'hundred knots of bronze' (I: 293-294). The temple dedicated to Juno in Carthage had a threshold, door and door posts of bronze (Aeneid I: 428-454); Aeneas, the son of a mortal father and the goddess Venus and thus semi-divine, nails a shield of bronze to his door when he settles on the shores of Actium (Aeneid 3.267-293). The combination of red glass and bronze might therefore have alluded to a rich and varied symbolic language, evoking at the same time associations of blood, protection, honour, survival, warning, battle frenzy, liminality and impending death.

If the link between red sealing wax glass, blood and related associations with liminality were correct, how then can we explain the use of different colour enamel which occurs increasingly in the first century AD and the use of multi-coloured geometric decoration? The idea of preserving liquidity can of course be transferred to other liquids. Blue glass or enamel, especially translucent blue glass may have stood for water. Yellow glass, as will be further discussed in chapter 9 may have had similar associations as and perhaps even replaced amber, perhaps functioning as a representation of the reflection of sun on water. The symbolic references are all to liquids, or in the case of amber, to a petrified liquid. Certainly the slightly earlier multicoloured pieces such as the Richborough concentric terret show blue and yellow mainly as spots, often translucent. All of the above mentioned liquids have protective or live giving qualities and may have had apotrapaic powers similar to those of red glass. The addition of a second or third colour to metal ware required obviously enhanced technical skills and the earlier pieces would indicate that the experimentation with other colours did not negate but may have even enhanced the underlying belief systems.

If we were to assume the validity of the argument that curvilinear vitreous decoration represented blood and possibly other fluids, the symmetrical, geometrical and angular patterns such as petals, lozenges, triangles and squares found on horse harness equipment such as the terrets from Saham Toney (Figure 17b) or the Seven Sisters hoard may indicate remoteness from such underlying

symbolism. Macgregor (1976: 23-30) dates horse harnesses of this type of small cell angular multicoloured decoration firmly to the time of the Roman conquest. As has been stated above, certainly in respect of the Seven Sisters hoard, the curvilinear and geometric parts were both created by native craftsmen, and used concurrently. The impression of flowing and dazzling movement of the predominantly red curvilinear decoration is replaced by rigidity and orderliness combined with equal amounts of red, blue and yellow on brass, a much colder metallic colour, on the geometrically decorated objects. The latter seem to be either devoid of any symbolic language of fluids, and perhaps reject it on purpose. Even though the pieces are not Roman but indigenous, stylistic influences from the Roman world cannot be ignored. The aesthetics of the colour combination is much closer to that preferred by the Romans if Pliny can be believed (Natural History 33.58), but it may also indicate an acceptance of a world where everything is straight and where order and hierarchy are firmly in place, as opposed to a cosmology where order, power and life itself is in a state of fluidity and negotiation.

The shift to geometric patterns could therefore have been the result of a change of production techniques hand in hand with growing urbanisation, the exchange of technology with and exposure to the cosmologies of the Roman world. Whether or not such influences were voluntarily absorbed or imposed, they may have resulted in abandonment of certain belief systems in favour of new belief systems or simply in favour of new technology without any underlying symbolism. The whole new range of colours of enamel appearing throughout the Romano British period is perhaps a further indication of technology and innovation taking precedence over symbolic meaning of colours. Colour, it appears, becomes a mere decoration. On the other hand, the return to the initial triad of colours red, yellow and blue with emphasis on the colour red during the post Roman Period in Britain might be an indication of a return to old symbolic values.

Conclusion

In conclusion, the role of colour in decorated metal ware may have changed during the British Iron Age. Initially the innate colour of material may have contributed to the inherent symbolism of the material itself, but the colour is perhaps incidental or secondary to the material. Then human made decoration in the form of hot glass introduces the notion of representation of other materials by reference to colour, thus separating colour from material whilst still alluding to the represented material's symbolic values. Finally, the appearance of a different combination of colours, shapes and underlying metal suggests outside aesthetic influences and perhaps the abandonment or rejection of traditional symbolic values.

Chapter 8

Yellow Stars and Red Journeys – Colour, Iconography and Cosmologies

'For a very long time after that they were travelling over the waves, until they came upon an island with trees in it like the willow or hazel. There were marvellous fruits on them with great berries. Then they stripped a small one of the fruit trees and cast lots next to see who should tase the fruit of the tree. The lot fell to Mael Dúin. He squeezed part of them into a vessel and drank, and it sent him to sleep from that time until the same time the next day; and it was not known whether he was alive or dead, with the red foam round his lips until he woke up the next day.

(Unkown; The voyage of Mael Dúin, Irish eighth or ninth century AD)

Introduction

Iron Age archaeology does not appear to provide a straightforward and easily recognisable link between certain colours or coloured materials and iconography. For example, astral symbols like crescent moons or solar symbols are found on both gold and bronze coins, vegetal style decoration appears on scabbards and swords made from bronze or iron; triskeles, birds' heads, dragon pairs and trumpet scrolls, to name but a few typical Iron Age motives, feature on a variety of materials. However, this does not mean that there are no correlations. The following chapter will explore certain patterns and more subtle correlations between Iron Age depictions and colours, and possible reasons behind such correlations. In this context I will also deal with shamanism which may well have been an important part of the British Iron Age belief systems (Aldhouse-Green 2005: 111-142), and the possible implications of shamanic rituals on colour and iconography.

Patterns of Art and Patterns of Colour

There are two developments in the British Iron Age concerning coloured material and art which may be correlated. Firstly, gold, which was a very important material in the early and middle Bronze Age, especially in religious and funerary contexts (Eluere 1995: 30), virtually disappears between the end of the eighth century BC and the third century BC (Northover 1994: 21). When gold re-appears in the archaeological record from the second century BC onwards, it is mainly found in hoards such as the Snettisham or Ipswich hoards which are made up of torcs and coins (Jope 2000: 80; Northover 1995: 529). The absence of gold in the late Bronze Age and early Iron Age has been explained by some as a result of climate change (Hawkes and Clarke 1963: 227-229; 240), others as a result of depletion of native raw gold resources (Raftery 1994: 161), but as yet there does not appear to be a conclusive explanation.

One possible reason might have been a shift in belief systems. As already stated, during the Bronze Age gold was used in religious and funerary contexts. In many cultures gold was reserved for the gods and seen as their property (Betz 1995: 21). The glistening quality of gold, its durability and purity and its colour connects it nearly universally to the sun (Betz 1995: 25; 27) or, as already discussed in chapter 4, to Otherworldly realms. The tendency towards bronze as primary material might be an indication that metalworkers were less concerned with a material which belonged perhaps to a divine Otherworld, but in any event represented something pure, untarnished and enduring, something that was to a certain extent beyond their control. Instead they may have been more interested in a material with qualities and colours which lend themselves to experimentation, variation and ultimately a degree of human control. Such human interference with and control over a material substance would undoubtedly have been perceived as powerful and perhaps magical. It might also explain the increasing tendency of alloying gold with copper which started during the late Bronze Age (Hawkes and Clarke 1963: 208) and which, as will be discussed later, played an important role in the production of gold coinage in the later Iron Age.

The second development is the emergence of new styles of decoration in the Iron Age. Enormous efforts have been made in the past to classify the various styles of decoration stylistically and chronologically by adopting a Classical methodology (Jacobsthal 1944: Jope 2000; Megaw and Megaw 1986; 1989), but more recent studies of Iron Age art have justifiably taken a much wider approach in considering also visual and sensory impact, agency and social effects of decorated artefacts (Gosden and Hill 2008: 12).

One of the striking characteristics of much of the British Iron age art is the ambiguity of its imagery. Mansel Spratling (2008: 194-195) provides a good example by discussing the various interpretation of the repoussé bronze plaque from Llyn Cerrig Bach (Figure 14a) which has been in turn perceived as an asymmetric triskele with comma shaped finials, heads of birds, puffins and by Spratling himself as a quadruped animal, possible a horse. It could however, also be interpreted as a circle showing a sequence of berries with unfurling leaves in various stages of development together with solar and lunar elements which may hint at seasonal cycles or time.

Whatever the imagery meant to represent, it emphasises some of the typical features of British Iron age decorative art. Firstly the meaning of the imagery is not readily apparent to us. It is perhaps codified or deliberately hidden. As stated by Fitzpatrick (2007: 345) the colours, textures and fantastic animals in British Iron Age may have been part of a visual language, which was only spoken and read at certain times. Perhaps it was also meant to be read by certain people only, but whoever the onlookers were, they would certainly have been drawn in by the imagery and invited to think about it. This is supported by the second feature of Iron Age art. The images are rarely static. They seem to move and shift, swirl, turn or grow or alternatively represent something that is growing, living or moving, such as plants or shape shifting animals and humans.

As already discussed in chapter 4 the colour of bronze is not static; it can change depending on its composition from golden to reddish, it can be polished to a high shine but it will also tarnish and in time oxidize and turn bluish green. The makers of Iron Age decorated objects may have been deliberately drawn to use bronze as a preferred material as it is as ambiguous, changing and changeable as the images they created. There are, however, further and perhaps more complex links between certain imagery and colours which can best be demonstrated by a number of examples:

Astral signs, Dragon Pairs, Birds, Triskeles: Polarity and Negotiation

Even though there are no exclusive direct links between colour and coloured material, and iconography, John Creighton (2000: 38-40) noticed certain connections between gold coins and imagery in the later Iron Age. The gold of the earlier coin series known as imagery A - J was a strong yellow rather than white or red gold. The same yellow colour is also prevalent in the gold and electrum torcs found in the Snettisham and Ipswich hoards.[28] The fact that the colour rather than the composition of the material was important is demonstrated by the

fact that the alloying percentages had changed in the Durotrigan series, even though the yellow colour had been maintained. Many of the coins show solar or lunar symbols such as crescent moons, circles, stars, horses or boars with erect dorsal fins, and perhaps the connection between the yellow golden sun and moon would explain the preference of the colour yellow over a more reddish or whiteish golden colour. However, the later Iron Age coins, namely British Q and L series, not only show a revised imagery, but are also made out of new alloying compositions which resulted in either red gold or silvery white colours. Interestingly, only the red gold coins are inscribed with the names of rulers (Creighton 2000: 38; 40; 55) (Figure 8.1).

So why was yellow gold so much more important than white or red gold during the earlier series and why did this change in the later Iron Age? Creighton (2000: 42-43) draws from ethnological examples from the Andes, and sees the making of coins and their imagery as an attempt to recreate a trance world of otherwordly shimmering and shiny objects relating to astral symbolism like the sun and moon.

The argument for a link between yellow golden colour and astral symbolism is strengthened by the yellow or silvery colour of the astral symbols on the stamped anthropomorphic swords examined by Fitzpatrick, although in this particular instance in stark contrast to the colour of the underlying material. Anthropomorphic short swords were not a common weapon and were probably used for specialised purposes. About 15% of these weapons found in Europe and Britain and dated to Mid La Tène show engraved or chased decorations which are inlaid with other metal, usually gold but sometimes silver or even brass (Rieckhoff 2002: 155). The two brightly golden coloured stamps, depicting an animal, perhaps a horse or a dragon on the iron blade of the Isleworth sword are made of brass foil. As already mentioned in chapter 4, it is suggested that this is the earliest example of the use of brass foil in Britain (Craddock et al. 2004; Stead 2006: 123; 168).

The stamps on these swords usually depict a circle to the left and a right facing crescent to the right of a vertical line, perhaps depicting the full and new moons (Fitzpatrick 1996: 373; 378; 381-382; Rieckhoff 2002: 155). The small handles of the swords suggest a symbolic rather than functional purpose and Fitzpatrick suggested that the line between the circle and crescent could be the distinction between waxing and waning moons or lucky and unlucky days. Perhaps they even referred to the passage of time. The swords may have been used by druids for practices associated with time keeping or predicting propitious days (Fitzpatrick 1996: 375; 388; Stead 2006: 49). Allusions to night and measuring of time can be found in relation to the Gauls in Caesar's De Bello Gallico (4.18). He tells us that the Gauls see

---

[28] Gold Torcs found in hoards from the later Iberian Iron Age are of impure gold alloyed with silver, copper and other impurities, but they have a good 'golden' colour. They were made in a region which had substantial natural gold sources which were heavily exploited at that time (Pingel 1995: 393). Other gold objects found in the same hoards have much finer gold. It is therefore probable that the torcs were deliberately alloyed resulting in much lower caratage in order to obtain the correct colour (Pingel 1995: 394).

themselves as descendants of Dis Pater, the god of the Underworld and that they therefore measure their time in nights rather than days.[29] Although Caesar does not refer to colours as such, his narrative still evokes the black Underworld and the night sky with moon and stars.

The knowledge of time keeping and the determination of propitious days or nights is not only a powerful knowledge (Fitzpatrick 1996: 389; Green 1998) but is also a human control over natural forces. The colour correlations between astral imagery and golden colour against the dark background of the iron blade handle stands in contrast to the bronze of the anthropomorphic handles. Fitzpatrick thinks that the symbolism of these swords suggested male, possibly divine figures (Fitzpatrick 1996: 374). I would, however, dispute that the anthropomorphic figures with their handlebar moustaches represent divine beings. These male representations are the essence of the sword handle, the part of the sword which is actually held by humans, and they are placed along the vertical line between the two opposing astral signs. I suggest that they are more likely to be representative of the people who handled the swords. It is even possible, that such swords were personalised and had their own innate power, their own 'life' (Bradley 2002: 53 - 55; Fowler 2004: 6; 59-60; Wells 2007: 474).

Fitzpatrick draws parallels between the astral stamps on the British swords and the gold inlaid dragon pairs found on the continent, e.g. on the scabbard of the anthropomorphic short sword from Baron sur Odon or the short sword from grave 15 in Radosevice (Fitzpatrick 2007: 350). He believes that dragon pairs and perhaps also bird pairs are an expression of heavenly symbolism and symbolise perhaps the polarity between good and evil, courage and fear, light and dark. They may also hint at shape changing. He suggested that placing a hand on a shield or sword between such opposing animals might have transferred power to a mortal man (Fitzpatrick 2007: 352). If this argument is taken a little further, one could suggest that there is a tension between opposing astral or divine forces which are represented by gold or golden coloured brass stamps on dark iron and human powers which are represented by the handle. The person handling such swords would be interfering with and perhaps derive some supernatural power through the interaction with the supernatural. Perhaps he or she would even be believed to be in control of such tension by the act of handling the sword. This element of human control might have been symbolised by the anthropomorphic handle, and the metaphor of human agency might have been re-enforced by the ambiguous colour of the bronze. Unlike pure gold or silver bronze is a human made alloy and the ambiguity of its reddish

colour may have represented forces which, although interacting with divine forces, originated in this world rather than the Otherworld or Underworld. This notion of reddish colours belonging in the sphere of the living or at least crossing the boundaries to and from this world and other realms is echoed in early Welsh and Irish myth. The supernatural hunting dogs of Pwyll, lord of Dyfed in the *Mabinogi*, are described as dazzling white with shining red ears. Similarly there are descriptions of supernatural white cattle with red ears in Irish myth (Ó'hÓgáin 1999: 93).[30] Whilst these animals are not from this world, they are transgressing liminal zones and perhaps their red ears are indicators that they are controlled by humans from this world.

Could such symbolism be the reason for the change in colour of Iron Age gold coinage? Creighton argued that the change was linked to political change in South East Britain as a result of which earlier British gold coins were withdrawn, Roman gold was probably used for the minting of new coins and further alloying agents were added (Creighton 2000: 68-70). Another argument is that the increase in copper not only changes the colour, but it also lowers the melting point of the metal and makes is harder. The hardness of the metal may well have played a role, but neither of these arguments explain the development of two distinctive colours in gold coinage. Reverting to the iconography of the coins the importance of the astral and solar imagery on gold coins cannot be negated. Perhaps the round shape of the coins themselves only added to such symbolism. It could of course be argued that British Iron Age bronze and silver coins also show astral symbols, but this does not necessarily invalidate the connections between golden colour and astral symbolism. Bronze and silver may have been used to express certain aspects of solar or lunar imagery such as sunset, sunrise or a silver moon.

The argument that the coins are merely an introduction from the Hellenic worlds, and any symbolic iconography would have been imported, is too simplistic. There must have been some aesthetic and symbolic principles which caught the imagination of the British Iron Age communities, for whom gold may have been a material reserved for certain objects only. Therefore, if we accept that the astral iconography as well as the gold colour of the gold coins had symbolic significance for Iron Age Britons, then the development towards gold coins of two distinctive colours may have been the visible expression of the emergence of two different attitudes towards such symbolism. On the one hand, the white gold may have been the recognition of ancient symbolic values; white gold standing for pure, celestial and perhaps even ancestral forces. The red gold, on the other hand, may have acknowledged the importance of human power.

---

[29] The Gaulish calendar of Coligny refers to light and dark phases of the moon, representing favourable and unfavourable times in each month (Zimmer 1997: 1050).

---

[30] Although Ó hÓgáin suggests that the description may refer to an actual breed of cattle which can still be found in Britain.

The red coinage frequently shows inscriptions of the names of human leaders. Perhaps this was meant to exult such leaders to the spheres of the astral world akin to the apotheosis of Roman emperors, whilst still recognising their human origin. Or it recognises such leaders' ability to cross boundaries to the Otherworld and interact with the divine. The fact that alloying gold with copper makes the material stronger and harder might just have added to the power of such symbolism.

Shamanism and Colour

The transgression of boundaries between the natural world and the metaphysical world and the importance of human magic as opposed to divine magic is a frequent feature in Iron Age British art. The ram headed snakes and zoomorphic beings, triple horned bulls and triskeles all hint at transformation, shape shifting and powerful magical dimensions, which suggest shamanic connotations (Aldhouse-Green 2001: 222; Clottes and Lewis Williams 1998; Green 1989: 179; 204, 1995: 476; Megaw and Megaw 1995: 370). The tension created by such imagery may not only be a metaphor for the tension between the natural world and the spirit world, but perhaps also a symbolization of the risks associated with crossing the boundary to such worlds during shamanic trances (Aldhouse-Green 2001: 218; Green 1995: 488, 1998a: 898-911). It is, however, not just symbolic imagery which is important in shamanic rituals. Sound, smell and colour are all parts of rituals (Watson 2001: 178-179) and the following part of this chapter will explore if the use of colours supports the suggestion of shamanism in the Iron Age.

Definition of Shamanism

The terms shamanism and shaman are widely used in archaeology and anthropology, but they are not used consistently. In order to avoid confusion I want to commence with a definition of the term 'shaman' used in the context of this research. It is not applied in the strict sense of the central Asian Tungus shaman, but rather as a classifier of certain people with special powers who have access to alternative realities, who use their powers to interact with spirits and supernatural entities, control the lives and movements of animals and people and are often also healers (Lewis Williams 1997: 323-324). The shaman, medicine man, witch or whatever name such people are known by, is a mediator between the natural and supernatural world in belief systems where all difficulties can only be relieved with the help of journeys to the Otherworld (Parkinson 2002: 21; Price 2001a: 6; Siikala 1987: 319; Straus 2004: 74). One other factor which seems to permeate such shamanic belief systems throughout the world is that the cosmos appears to consist of three levels. The upper level is a place where ancestral beings or gods reside, the lower level is the world of the dead, and the middle level is the

natural world. Shamans can travel to both the lower and the upper level. The latter journey, sometimes referred to as shamanic ascent, appears to be a journey to an unchanging and eternal reality (Aldhouse-Green 2005: 10-14; Harvey 2006: 140).

Shamanic Dress

Shamans' attires can be important, both as a marker of the shaman's status in the outside world, but also as an integral part of his or her magical persona. Colours can play a significant part in such attire. By way of example Siikala (1987: 116-117) described the dress and trinkets of a typical Siberian Yukagir shaman. Attached to his apron would be a variety of metal pendants. The uppermost would be in the form of a copper man which represented the soul of a dead ancestral shaman. The next pendant would be an iron heart symbolizing the shaman's courage, followed by three bird amulets, symbolizing his spirit helpers and, hanging from the bottom of the apron two metal discs engraved with human faces to protect against diseases of the stomach. Often the shaman would also wear an amulet in the image of a swan round his throat in order to protect him from sore throats and chills. Metal badges called the shaman's sun, moon and star would be attached to his coat and these were meant to light his way to the Underworld. Apart from the copper man and the iron heart Siikala's account unfortunately does not specify which metal such pendants were made of. Attached to the arms of the shaman's cloak were fringes called wing feathers, with the help of which the shaman would be able to fly like a bird.

The symbolic images on this dress not only evoke imagery in Iron Age art such as birds, faces and astral symbolism, but suggest that the material and perhaps the colour of the metal pendants must have had their own significance. The description brings to mind Irish druids and seers in early Irish myth. In the 'Tain Bo Cuailgne', the prophetess Fedelm is described as holding a golden weaving rod (perhaps a divination rod), her tunic is held together by a golden pin, and she is wearing a speckled cloak. Her eyes are described as having triple irises which not only draws attention to them and alludes to triplism and its connotations with other dimensions, but it also suggests unfocused eyes in a trance like state (Kinsella 1970: 60). The speckled appearance of the cloak is echoed in the description of a druid poet in an eightht century AD account whose robe had 'colouring of bright bird feathers in the middle, a showery speckling of bronze on the lower outside and a golden colour on the upper part' and another account which describes a druid's toga as skins of white and multicoloured birds from the girdle downwards, and of the neck of mallards and of their crests from the girdle upwards to the neck (Ó hÓgáin 1999: 125). The iridescence and the rainbow colours, especially in association with a trancelike state alluded to in the image of Fedelm suggest perhaps spiritual journeys to the Otherworld over a rainbow bridge, a symbolism still encountered in Siberian shamanic tradition (Eliade 1989: 135; Ó hÓgáin 1999: 69). The fact that Fedelm had learned the 'imbas forasnai', literally translated as the light of foresight, would not only support her status as a powerful and magical persona and possible shaman, but also enhances the metaphysical aspect of brilliance and light in her appearance.

We have no archaeological evidence of shamanic dresses of the British Iron Ages, although it might be possible that the Llyn Cerrig Bach bronze disc with its ambiguous imagery might have been worn as part of a ritual dress and perhaps by a shaman. There are however some accounts by Pliny and Tacitus which give us some idea about the dress codes of Iron Age people who were concerned with the supernatural. Tacitus describes the 'wild haired' women, possibly priestesses, of the sacred island of Mona as wearing black robes (Annales 14.28). Pliny tells us that druids wore white at least for certain rituals, such as the gathering of mistletoe or selago (Pliny Natural History 16.249-251; 24.103). Such descriptions differ significantly from the iridescent cloaks of the Irish druids or the fringed cloak and decorated apron of the Siberian shaman. However, they suggest that colour, and as will be discussed later, certain metals played an important role in certain magical rituals.

Shamanic Trances and Rituals

As stated above, John Creighton (2003: 42-43) argued that certain imagery on Iron Age coinage and the shimmering qualities of its metal echoed the experiences of a class of people who are familiar with trances. Imagery like zigzags, dots, meandering lines and curves which flicker, scintillate, expand and contract are encountered in states of altered consciousness independent of cultural background (Lewis Williams 1997: 325, 2001; Dronfield 1995a). Such altered states of consciousness and resulting alternative reality are often associated with shamanic journeys (Lewis Williams 1997: 323-324).

Shamanic trances, whether they are drug induced or a result of certain other techniques, do not only include certain recurring imagery, but colours also play an important and perhaps symbolical role. Sereptie Djarvoskin (2003), a shaman from the Siberian Nganasan tribe tells of his journey to the Otherworld, where he encounters tents covered with white frost, copper and iron smoke holes and 'red stuff', all tied with black rope. He learns that each of these components heals certain diseases. He then comes across a weak fire, which to him makes reference to the ritual of purification of newborns by fumigating them; he sees a man forging iron, which symbolizes the origin of the shaman, and then he notices red plants which turn out to be red stones. He takes one of them and the colour red indicates to him that he can return to the living. In his view, if a man dies, his

face turns blue and changes; a shaman cannot do any more. Redness therefore symbolizes life in the natural world. However, red can also mean illness and danger. When curing illness, the shaman perceives the man who recovers as having breath like a white thread and the man who dies with breath like a black thread (Djarvoskin 2003: 38). This account of a shamanic trance appears to have numerous symbolic colour references. They include black and white dualism, the importance of certain metals, but above all the colour red features as an ambiguous colour representing at the same time danger, illness but also life (Siikala 1987: 175-185).

Michael Harner, an anthropologist who was initiated in the ways of South American shamanism by the Jívaro of the Ecuadorian Andes, describes one of his shamanic trances after drinking Guayusa tea, a hallucinogenic substance. He saw images in brilliant reddish hues; curvilinear designs intertwining, separating and turning in 'a most enjoyable fashion', small grinning demonic faces appearing, swirling and disappearing amongst the changing patterns. He felt that he was seeing the spiritual inhabitants of the place he was staying in. On the following day he was shown prehistoric pot sherds from the local area which showed painted red designs identical to those he had seen the previous night (Harner 2003: 48). Harner's account of red moving and swirling curvilinear designs, faces appearing and dis-appearing is reminiscent of Iron Age imagery on bronze artefacts. Perhaps the imagery as well as the warm reddish gold colour of bronze played the same role as the red designs on the Ecuadorian pot sherds; an evocation of a colourful experience from a trance captured in metalwork.

Whilst there are no accounts of shamanic trances relating to the British Iron Age in classical sources, there are a number of colour references in the context of Gaulish rituals which may support the suggestion of shamanism and shamanic colour symbolism in Gaul. If the classical writers are to be believed there are religious similarities between Gaul and Iron Age Britain, and therefore the rituals might have been similar. In De Bello Civilis (3.399-425) Lucan describes a grove – 'untouched by men's hands from ancient times (…) a space of darkness and cold shade' where water fell from 'dark springs', and 'images of gods, grim and rude were uncouth blocks formed of felled tree trunks. Their mere antiquity and the ghastly hue of their rotten timber struck terror. (…) When the sun is in mid heaven or dark night fills the sky, the priest himself dreads the gods and fears to surprise the lord of the grove'. Lucan's imagery of rotten timber against a dark background brings to mind the polarity of black and white and with it perhaps associations of decay, decomposition, bodily fluids (Aldhouse-Green 2004a: 89-90) and ultimately white bone, life and death. There are also hints at a third colour. He writes of gods which 'were worshipped with savage rights, altars heaped with hideous offerings, every tree sprinkled with human gore'. Not only does this intensify associations with the symbolism of bodily fluids and synergies between wood and flesh (Aldhouse-Green 2004a: 90), it also recalls the image of sprinkled blood and blood sacrifices which Lucan refers to elsewhere (De Bello Civilis 1.444) in connection with the god Teutates, and therefore allusions to the colour red which acts as a perhaps magical intermediary between black and white or this world and the Otherworld.

In his Natural History (16.249-251) Pliny mentions the Gaulish ritual of gathering mistletoe grown on oak trees. It could only be cut on the sixth day following the new moon by a druid in white clothing using a golden sickle. The mistletoe is then caught in a white cloth and two white bulls are sacrificed. Pliny tells us further that the Gauls believe the drink made out of mistletoe berries to be a panacea. The imagery presented by Pliny gives us a number of colour associations. The golden sickle may represent the waxing moon both in terms of shape and colour and furthermore resembles the golden leaves of the mistletoe, whereas the white cloth mirrors the colour of the berries (Figure 18b) and the colour of the bulls (Perrin 2002: 16). The account also presents us with a perceived hierarchy of colour. The mistletoe is not allowed to fall on the ground, thus inferring a higher level made up of gold and white, hinting at ancestrality and astral connotations, an intermediate level of red, represented by the sacrificial blood of the white bulls, and a lower level of black, represented by the black earth into which the sacrificial blood soaks. The symbolism of bodily fluids and their associated life, death and fertility symbolism may not only be represented by blood, but also by the white juice of the mistle berries resembles semen or milk. This hierarchy of colours is played out in front of an oak tree, which itself is highly symbolic and could be likened to the tree of life within shamanic traditions (Eliade1989: 117). The druid's actions against the backdrop of the three tiered cosmology represented by this imagery and its associated colours may even have been tantamount to a shamanic ascent.

In another account Pliny tells us of the Gaulish ritual of harvesting a plant called selago, which was used as a charm against evil. The plant had to be gathered by a harvester dressed in white. The harvester had to fast prior to the ritual and pick the plant with the right hand but through the left sleeve of his garment. Furthermore he was not allowed to use iron implements (Pliny Natural History 24.103). A number of symbolic associations spring to mind. Firstly, the harvester is dressed in white and the dress had perhaps similar symbolic qualities as referred to above in relation to the gathering of mistletoe. Secondly, the plant was not allowed to get in contact with iron in order to retain its magical qualities. In comparison with the rite of gathering mistletoe, it is likely that it is the black colour of iron, resembling the black colour of the earth or the red colour of rust,

resembling blood, which may be the crucial element. Thirdly, the polarity between black and white is alluded to again, perhaps representing the upper and lower tiers in a three tiered cosmology. Interestingly, Pliny does not tell us what implement should be used to cut the plant but it is conceivable that it was bronze. Even though his narrative is set in a different cultural background Virgil provides us with an interesting analogy. In his Aeneid (4.504-527) Queen Dido cuts magic poisonous herbs with a bronze knife, perhaps indicating that bronze rather than iron was to be used for magic rites as the boundaries to the Otherworld are crossed.

The plant mentioned by Pliny has interesting colour connotations. Selago or 'lycopodium clavatum'[31] is a moss-like green creeping plant without flowers, but bifurcated stems bearing needles. These stems contain powdery yellow spurs which are highly flammable and explode when ignited and are still used today as flash powder. Selago is also a narcotic poison and is known to staunch blood flow (Willfort, 1959: 62). This usage not only suggests the throwing of sparks in rituals, but it brings to mind also the red colour of fire, and its transformative and ambiguous qualities. The act of slipping the right hand through the left sleeve hints at masking and concealment, but also sinistrality. In many cultures magic made with the left hand is used to propagate death or neutralising bad fortune. The left hand is concerned with "sinister' powers, the occult and illegitimacy. It often inspires terror and revulsion (Hertz 1960: 104-105).

Sinistrality, narcotics, a journey and the colour red all feature in the wooden Roos Carr figurines already referred to in chapter 6 (Figures 13a and 13b). The figurine's faces are asymmetrical, and the left side of one figure had been badly damaged. Bryony Coles believes that this may have been deliberately inflicted before deposition of the figurine in order to destroy or negate whatever the left hand side may have symbolized (Coles 1990: 315-319; 332). Their sexual ambiguity, the bulging quartz eyes which suggest a drug induced trance, the snake boat found with them and the deposition on a trackway all give further credence to the suggestion of a shamanic journey (Aldhouse-Green 2005: 119-122; 128). But equally important is the material of the figures. They are carved from the wood of a yew tree, an evergreen tree with red berries, numerous symbolic connotations and unusual qualities (Figure 18a). Unlike most other trees, the yew has separate male and female trees; all parts of it apart from its ripe berries are highly toxic and cause nausea, dizziness, disorientation, increased heart beat and ultimately often death, yet at the same time it has been widely used for healing purposes[32] (Bevan Jones 2002:

---

[31] Selago is known in German as Hexenkraut or Drudenfuss; both terms refer to its use in magic and witchcraft.
[32] One of the chemicals identified in yew, taxol, is used in chemotherapy. Hageneder (2007: 112-113) included in his book the account of a

1, 9; Hageneder 2007: 48, 110-114). There are some reports of hallucinogenic effects experienced by people who were merely sitting or working underneath yew trees, even though the psychoactive effects of yew are as yet unconfirmed by pharmacology. The visions included vampires and diabolic scenes which were replaced by visions of paradise, heavenly music and euphoria (Hageneder 2007: 49), all of which are reminiscent of shamanic journeys. The various names for the yew tree in Indo-Gemanic languages refer invariably to either life-force or eternity (Hageneder 2007: 139). The colour of the yew berry is a vibrant red, and the colour red is also echoed in its bark and the seemingly animated grain of its wood (Figure 18c). It is also known to 'bleed', i.e. ooze a bloodlike thick liquid from openings in its bark (Hageneder 2007: 146). If a piece of yew is inserted into clear water the water will turn blood red within a short space of time. In a simple experiment I inserted a piece of yew wood into clear water. After five days the colour of the water turned to a bright red (Figure 18d).

The other wooden figurines from the British Iron Age, i.e. the Ballachulish woman and the Kingsteignton Idol (Figures 13c and 13d) were carved out of alder and oak respectively, as already stated in chapter 6. Although Bryony Coles suggests a gender difference corresponding to the tree species, i.e. yew for sexually ambiguous and thus perhaps shamanic figurines, and oak for ancestral male figurines (Coles 1998: 170), in my view both the Ballachulish Woman - who would incidentally not even fit into either category of wood species - and the Kingsteingnton Idol are also sexually ambiguous. Whilst the underlying material of these figurines may well have had significance, it may be a more complicated and even localized symbolism rather than a mere gender difference. Oak and alder may have different symbolic values to those of yew, but it is worth noting that alder, when inserted into water turns from a pale beige colour to a reddish colour. Even oak turns a reddish colour after insertion into water, but less so.

In a further experiment I exposed pieces of alder, oak and yew for two years to the elements, and immersed an identical set of pieces of wood for two years into water. Whilst the pieces of wood exposed to the elements had turned a silvery pale colour, those inserted in water had a dark reddish colour (Figures 19a, b and c).

Coles and Orme (1985: 12) stated that yew was very rarely found in the Somerset Levels, and if so, as an artefact rather than part of a construction. The Somerset

Levels do not appear to be isolated in this respect. Yew is not often encountered in British prehistoric archaeology, even though it survives well in peat and wetland contexts. The rare finds suggest that it was predominantly used for boats, weapons such as bows, or figurines (Cole, Heal and Orme 1978). It is possible that this is due to the fact that yew is a very hard wood and does not have the material qualities required for constructions such as trackways. On the other hand, it may be significant that most yew artefacts seem to be associated with movement, whether as a tool, a boat, or a living being, as suggested by the figurines; perhaps the red colour and fluidity of the grain had some significance which made yew an obvious choice of wood for such artefacts. Whilst it cannot be ruled out that the figures had been painted before deposition, there is no evidence for such treatment and in my view it is highly unlikely. There is no reason to assume that organic material such as wood would have been as richly decorated as Iron Age metal or pottery (Evans 1989: 185) 33 and the innate colour and grain of yew are striking without added decoration. I would suggest that the redness of the yew added to and enhanced the already present shamanic symbolism of the figurines.

Whether red is a universally applicable colour associated with shamanic trances is not certain. The perception of the world as a shimmering place is an entoptic phenomenon experienced during one of the phases of a trance (Lewis-Williams et al. 1988: 203), but unlike the visions of zig zags, meanders, swirls and other geometrical patterns which are universally experienced in trances (Dronfield 1995a; 1996)[34], there does not seem to be an equivalent consistency relating to the experience of various colours[35]. The hallucinogenic stages of trances seem to be in any event subjective and variable experiences (Lewis-Williams et al. 1988: 203). However, there are some further observations which can be made in respect of colour: Firstly, during a trance colours appear to be vibrant and saturated (Lewis-Williams et al. 1988: 203), and red is the most vibrant and vivid colour imaginable. If certain Iron Age art or objects such as the wooden

cancer sufferer who underwent such treatment and painted the inner images she experienced during this time. These images are mainly geometrical, round, perhaps even solar, patterns and the dominant colours are yellow and blue, which, as will be discussed in chapters 9 and 10, may have had connotations to healing in the Iron Age. Interestingly, the treatment of cancer with yew appears to have been mentioned in ancient Sanskrit texts dating to the first half of the sixth century AD.

[33] Evan's distinction between decorated metal and pottery which had been transformed by fire and undecorated organic material such as wood is interesting, but not necessarily conclusive. Stone is a non organic material which was not transformed by fire and could be decorated such as the, admittedly Irish, decorated monoliths from Truroe or Castelstrange (Jope 2000: 103-105) or of minimalistic and nearly abstract design, void of decoration such as the Yorkshire chalk figures (see chapter 5). His reasoning that there are more decorated artefacts in the Iron Age due to a higher stability in domestic production and less of a ritual aspect (Evans 1989: 196) is also flawed as it presupposes a clear distinction between ritual and utilitarian which, as discussed elsewhere, is unlikely.
[34] Although the influence of hallucinogenics and the applicability of the three stage model initially suggested by Lewis-Williams et al. (1988) is still under debate (Helvenston and Bahn 2003).
[35] Certain drugs such as foxglove can lead to acyanoblepsia, a form of colour blindness where blue tones are filtered out (Bernd Hertling pers. comment) and a number of hallucinogenic drugs may lead to visions of bright white light coupled with feeling of calm and euphoria, but this is not consistent (Ben Fergus-Grey pers. comment).

figurines are the result of a recollected trance, then red would be an obvious choice of colour. Secondly, during a different stage of a trance the shaman will try to make sense of the entoptic patterns he sees and his 'vision' is linked to and constrained by personal experience, his state of mind and what he desires to see (Lewis-Williams *et al.* 1988: 203; 210). If the person undergoing the trance had seen something red immediately prior to the trance, for example sacrificial blood, then it is conceivable that this colour might have an impact on his or her experience. Lastly, red blood can be an important element in trances. For examples, ritual bloodletting can induce a trance (Boyd and Dering 1996: 256), or, as in the case of the San of Southern Africa, some shamans experience nasal bleeding during a drug induced trance (Lewis-Williams *et al.* 1988: 210).

The associations of the colour red or bronze with altered stages of consciousness or liminality feature frequently in early Irish myth and Roman literature. In the Taín, Cú Chulainn is overcome by such rage, that he literally becomes a red bowl with red mists hanging over him (Kinsella 1970: 150-151). In book VII: 20ff of the Aeneid, Aeneas' mind is described as in feverish conflict and likened to the reflection of the sun or moon in quivering water in a bronze basin. This imagery is even more fascinating as it combines astral symbolism and shimmering water with the liminality of reddish bronze and mirror imagery, all of which suggest an altered perception of reality.

None of these accounts mention the use of hallucinogenic drugs but we can assume that selago, yew and henbane[36] may have been used as mind altering drugs. Traces of ergot, a highly hallucinogenic fungus which infects cereal grains, was found in the gut of Lindow man II (Figure 20d), an Iron Age bog body discovered in 1984 in Lindow Moss in Cheshire. Traces of cannabis and Artemisia, another psychotropic substance were found in Romano-British sites (Aldhouse-Green 2005: 112-113, 123; Green 1997: 108-109). At first, there does not seem to be any connection between the use of these plants and the colour red. Cannabis does not usually have strong hallucinogenic effects. Artemisia has healing properties as described by Pliny (Natural History 27.45), but it is also the main ingredient in absinthe which is said to have hallucinogenic effects. The colour usually associated with it is green, rather than red[37]. However, ergot infested grains have a distinctive dark purple colour (Aldhouse-Green 2005: 112) which

stands in stark contrast to the light colour of the grains. Also, when ingested, ergot can cause a burning sensation which coupled with synaesthesia, which it can also cause, suggests links to fire and perhaps the colour red. The associations between selago, fire and the colour red, and the numerous connotations between yew and the colour red have already been discussed above. I would therefore suggest that the ingestion of certain drugs does not necessarily result in the experience of the colour red. Yet there are certain, albeit more subtle connections through synaesthesia, personal experience and subjective perceptions which might lead to the experience of redness. However, the symbolic value of red as a link between the polar opposites black and white and its connotations with blood is perhaps a more potent reason to use the colour as a representation of the middle tier in the shamanic world order or a representation of the transgression of boundaries in shamanic objects or art.

Conclusion

In summary the tendency towards more fluid and ambiguous iconography, features such as asymmetry and triskeles with their allusions to three-dimensionality, or the depiction of strange animals which hint at shape shifting, coupled with the increasing importance of the colour red, suggests a cosmology which still recognises divine forces such as those symbolised by the sun and the moon. But the simple polarity between day and night, life and death or good and evil, has been replaced by a cosmology where boundaries are fluid, where everything is in motion, where the tension between such opposites is acknowledged and where the harnessing of, or influence over divine powers through human agency comes to the foreground. There may have been an elite, perhaps metal workers, religious leaders or druids, who had the ability and power to transgress boundaries to other worlds. They may have experienced shamanic trances which were then documented in art or objects. Whilst drug induced shamanic trances and shamanic art did not start in the Iron Age, the emphasis on the colour red and reddish metal as opposed to gold, coupled with the imagery of shape shifting suggest that subjective and personal human experience, as opposed to the vision of the divine, increased in importance.

---

[36] According to Schrijver (1999: 17-46) the hallucinogenic herb henbane may have been connected to the Gaulish sun god Belenus. Its German name, 'Bilsenkraut', still retains the Celtic root B(h)el which is generally associated with white and shimmering. Henbane may have been used in shamanic rituals as it leads to the impression of flying, perhaps towards the sun or astral zones.
[37] Absinthe used to be called '*la fée verte*' in France and during the height of its popularity the hour between 5 and 6 pm was referred to as '*l'heure verte*'.

Chapter 9

Black White and Red – Colours of Death

'She opened her Torc on him
And opened her fen
Those dark juices working
Him to a saint's kept body'

(Seamus Heaney, The Tollund Man)

Introduction

Death and funerary rites are linked to certain colours in most culture groups. The deceased and the mourners may wear specifically coloured clothing or shrouds, the grave goods or grave furniture may be fashioned in prescribed colours. The Remembrance Day ceremonies in modern day London provide a useful example for the importance of colours involved in a ritual honouring of the dead. The black clothes and the vibrant red poppies worn by the participants stand in stark contrast to the whiteness of the cenotaph. The underlying symbolism of the colours, i.e. the red poppies representing the flowers of the first world war battlefields in Flanders as well as the blood shed by soldiers killed in action and black symbolizing death, may not be immediately recognizable by everyone, but the colours are nevertheless evocative and give the ceremony both structure and formality.

In this chapter I want to explore the colour implications in the context of death and burial in the British Iron Age. The colour transitions undergone by the body in primary funerary rites, such as excarnation, cremation and inhumation will be looked at, followed by a detailed exploration of specific inhumation and secondary burials, including mirror burials, bog bodies and pit burials with references to specific sites. The colours of grave goods and their potential meaning including possible gender related symbolism will be examined and contextual landscape colours of burials will also be taken into account. In order to set a framework against which the archaeological evidence can be read, the initial part of the chapter will contain a general discussion of funerary rites, the phenomenon of death, and aspects of personhood.

Funerary Rites

Funerary Colours

Colours used in funerary contexts are not universal, although the colours red, white and black seem to be predominant and, as suggested in this chapter may also

have had symbolic importance in the British Iron Age. Mourners in most modern Western societies wear black, whereas the colour of mourning in Japan and China is white (Watson 1988: 109-134). Shrouds in modern Western societies are white and linked in our imagination to the appearance of ghostly apparitions. The Tandroy in Madagaskar drape a red funerary cloth which is referred to literally as a 'red shawl' over the open coffin in the grave, before both coffin and grave are closed (Parker Pearson 1999b: 12).

In ancient Greece shrouds appear to have been red (Banck-Burgess 1999: 85-86), although Homer mentions in his description of Patroklos' funeral in the Iliad, that the hero's body was wrapped first in a red shroud and then in a pale cloth (Banck-Burgess 1999: 85-86; Barber 1991: 377; Homer Iliad 18.350-360). The body of a high status person found in the Hallstatt wagon grave at Eberdingen-Hochdorf in Southern Germany was wrapped in a blue and red chequered fabric and then covered by a red shroud (Banck-Burgess 1999: 107-109).

The use of red ochre in funerary rites appears to be a cross-cultural and enduring phenomenon. There is evidence of its use in Paleolithic burials such as the so-called Red Lady of Paviland which was actually the remains of a young man (Aldhouse-Green 2000a; Turner 1967: 86); during the Bronze Age the faces of the dead were occasionally masked with red ochre (Harding 2000: 120), and there is evidence of the use of red ochre in funerary rites of the Plains Indians, who associated the application of red ochre with the separation of body and spirit. In their belief system the body returned to the earth, but the spirit was believed to have been reborn or travelled to the Otherworld (Bancroft-Hunt 1981: 16).

Funerary Symbolism

As will be discussed later in this chapter, in the British Iron Age the majority of the dead were in all likelihood exposed to excarnation. Even though there is an increase in inhumation and cremation burials in the later Iron Age, there is not only a lack of archaeological data but also a great deal of regional diversity. Due to this lack of material as well as lack of written evidence we have limited knowledge of funerary rites in the British Iron Age and no record at all as to the secondary participants of funerals, i.e. the mourners. Therefore any conclusions in respect of colours employed in the context of funerals and burials cannot present a comprehensive picture. However, the exploration of funerary rituals and especially the treatment of corpses are important tools to understand the constitution of personhood within a particular culture group (Jones 2002: 162). Burial rites are intrinsically linked to symbolic contexts which can operate at various levels, and as such the colours employed during such rites may also have multi-level symbolic importance. Funerals give meaning to both the deceased and his or her relationship with the mourners, in a political, economical and religious sense (Parker Pearson 1993: 203; 1999a: 83). They are associated simultaneously with remembrance and forgetting, express belief systems, may represent social and political structures and may operate as protection against dangers associated with the liminal status of the deceased. There are, however a number of issues related to this multi-level symbolism which should be taken into account.

Whilst it is undoubtedly the case that funerals are a manifestation of cultural identity (Woodward 1997: 9-10) and as such they must follow certain traditions in order to be understood by the participants, funerals are also an ideal platform to gradually introduce deviations from such rituals, perhaps in order to sustain the very importance of the ritual or as a demonstration of political power shifts (Parkin 1992: 16-18). We also have to bear in mind that the society reflected in a burial may differ from the actual society of the living community at that time. Funerals can create an idealised social structure in which social identities are given symbolic recognition. Hodder, for example, argued that modern Church of England burials present an ideal of equality, humility and non-materialism which is in stark contrast to the way modern society actually operates (Hodder 1982: 200), perhaps as a symbolic inversion with which to mark the special nature of the day and to differentiate it from ordinary life (Chapman 1995: 7-28). I would also agree with Hodder (1982: 197) that the complexity of artefacts associated with funerary rites does not necessarily reflect the complexity of social structures and roles within society and vice versa. In our own very complex society funerals and burials are often very simple affairs. Ashes of cremated bodies may be scattered without any permanent marker and inhumations in cardboard coffins are becoming increasingly fashionable.

The deceased may be also be given an identity as part of the burial which is different from his or her identity when still alive (Hodder 1982: 201; Morris 1987: 43). Clothes and burial furniture or grave goods project and represent values or identity decided upon by the

mourners (Parker Pearson 1999a: 9). Grave goods can be either possessions of the deceased or gifts from the mourners, sometimes even specifically made for the burial (Parker Pearson 1999a: 7). These artefacts may express the identity of the deceased, but perhaps also the relationship between the deceased and the mourners (Jones 2002: 170). In this context colours can be employed to symbolize differences and transformations, perhaps by the perceived disassembly and transformation of the coloured objects themselves over a period of time. Colours used in funerary rites may also have mnemonic values, perhaps evoking memories of the relationship of the deceased within society (Jones 2002: 171) and the colour changes of the body itself over time may also be recognized.

Funerary Rites as Rites of Passage

Whilst social relationships undoubtedly play an important role in funerary rites, the religious aspects and belief into afterlife are equally important. Aspects of east-west positioning or gender-bending are important patterns in many cultures in funerary rites and often symbolize beliefs in the afterlife, cosmologies and fertility association beyond the mere biological birth and death of a person (Hodder 1982: 172; Parker Pearson 1999a: 10; 26-27). Colours may well be employed to strengthen such symbolism. It is therefore important to read the material evidence and the colours employed in the context of burials as a whole and not in isolation of each other.

Van Gennep's theory of burials as a rite of passage with a tripartite structure is generally accepted (Van Gennep 1969: 209; Parker Pearson 1999: 22; Turner 1967: 95). The first stage is the stage of separation, beginning with the time of death, where all participants leave behind their normal social roles and enter an altered stage. The deceased becomes a decomposing corpse, the survivors become mourners. The second or liminal stage is in many cultures connected with fear for the dead body's soul and dread of the deceased coming back to haunt, but also of actual and symbolic pollution (Parker Pearson 1999a: 24). This pollution or fear is often dealt with by special rituals such as reversal of roles and cross dressing of the mourners, turning clothes inside out (still followed by modern day gypsies) and simultaneously cutting the pockets of their clothers, or disorientating the coffin to prevent the dead from coming back (Endicott 1970: 25-26; Goody 1962: 71; Morris 1987: 29-31; Parker Pearson 1999a: 25). The deceased reaches the third stage, also referred to as rite of aggregation, when the remains resume a stable form, i.e. all that is left are bones or cremated ashes. The soul becomes then associated with the Other-world or joins the ancestors depending on afterlife believes. The survivors, who until then stayed in a transitional stage of mourning, resume their roles within society (Morris 1987: 32). Each one of these stages of transitions has numerous colour implications and these colours are often echoed in the burial rituals themselves.

Death

The colour implications in the various forms of burial in the Iron Age may be linked to the concept of death itself. Whilst in the modern Western world death is generally perceived to be the time when a person stops breathing, this is by no means a simple and universally applicable concept. Even in our society, there are certain ambiguities and exceptions from this general perception. A missing person may be declared legally dead after a period of time, even though there is no proof that the person is indeed biologically dead. In medical terms the stoppage of the cardio pulmonary system generally defines the point of death, but there is doubt as to whether patients who continue to live only with the help of external life support apparatus are in fact still alive (Haley 1999: 1). Organ transplants and resuscitations of clinically dead patients only add to the debate.

In Japan brain death is recognised as the time of death from a medical point of view, but in a social context it is seen as a mere signal to warn the family of the impending death (Lock 2004). In the Hindu belief system death occurs when the 'vital breath', the essence which animates the body leaves the skull. The actual death therefore only occurs at the funeral when the chief mourner cracks open the deceased's skull (Haley 1999: 2). Amongst the Patanuma tribe on the borders between Guyana and Brazil in South America a person who is the victim of a *Kanaimà* attack (a highly complex and violent ritual killing leading to a very slow and painful death) is perceived to be dead as soon as the attack happens, although he or she is physically still alive and may remain so for days. For the Patanuma personhood and being alive is linked to the ability to speak and hold one's bowels (Whitehead 2001: 238-239; Butt Colson 2001: 224).

The idea of separation of body and spirit, or a pluralistic concept of the soul is prevalent in many culture groups. There can be several spiritual entities of which at least one may be transferred to another existence after physical death (Graeslund 1994: 17). For example the Tarahuamara tribe of Mexico believe that men have three souls, whereas women have four souls. In Chinese traditional beliefs each person has an animal or life soul called Po and a spiritual soul called Hun. The Po remains until a body is decomposed but the Hun lasts as long as the deceased is remembered (Haley 1999: 3).

For the Cheyenne in North America death involves various stages of transition. Death terminates the human physical life, but the individual spirit continues to exist in a different sphere and may return to the tribe through re-incarnation. Equally the tribal identity continues. Those who die a good death remain part of the community (Straus 2004: 74).

Personhood

The Cheyenne's tripartite division into ancestral human life, tribal life and individual physical life (Straus 2004: 71; 73) is alien to our modern understanding of personhood. Individuality is a modern concept which may not necessarily have been shared by prehistoric societies (Fowler 2004: 4). Fowler suggests that persons may be dividual and parts of the body may be permeable. A dividual person is a person who has parts owed to others, for example its community and is continually interpenetrated by flows of substance and vital essences. Even non-human inanimate objects like houses or pots, animals and even landscapes may be interpreted as persons produced through social activity (Fowler 2004: 8; 128). Bodily substances such as faeces, milk or blood may be seen as dividual and permeable, i.e. they are substance codes which express relationships between persons, or as dividual and partible, in other words objectified (Fowler 2004: 32-33). All these bodily substances are defined and recognized by their specific colours and the colours may well be used to symbolize or represent both the bodily substances and the part of the personhood or social relationship implied or expressed by such substances.

Literary Evidence on Death and Afterlife

We have no literary evidence of any belief in personhood, death or the afterlife in Iron Age Britain. There is some written evidence from classical writers, although from a later period, that the people who were referred to as Celts by the classical world, were in awe of their deceased. Nicander of Colophon, as quoted in the second century AD by Tertullian in his De Anima (57.10), claimed that the Celts spent the night near the tombs of their famous men because they received special oracles from the dead by staying there (Koch 1995: 9). Julius Caesar who was closer to the Gauls both temporally and geographically than Nicander, described in his de Bello Gallico the druidic belief system that the soul does not perish, but that is passes to another body after death. Caesar quite cynically and perhaps correctly thought that these teachings had the purpose to stop men from fearing death rather than being an expression of a belief in the afterlife (De Bello Gallico 6.14). Caesar also tells us that the druidic order originated in Britain (De Bello Gallico 6.13) and we can therefore assume that a belief in the survival of the soul, or parts of the soul would have existed in Britain, even though one must take into account that Caesar's knowledge may have been from incorrect or incomplete sources, that he may have been biased or even that he superimposed his own very rational mindset on druidic belief systems. Nevertheless, it is possible that death in the British Iron Age may have been seen as transition rather than a termination, perhaps even involving several stages, and that there may have been a dualism or even pluralism of aspects of physical and spiritual life and death, and a separation of personhood into various aspects.

Burials

Compared to the Bronze Age where there is ample material evidence for cremation burials, evidence of burials in the Iron Age is much scarcer. Even though an increasing number of burial sites especially dating from the later Iron Age are discovered, it is now commonly assumed that in the early and middle Iron Age in Britain the dead were rarely disposed of by inhumation burial or cremation, but that excarnation was the normative rite (Cunliffe 1995a: 72). However, cremation burials increase in the later Iron Age, inhumation burials seem to have become the norm in Dorset in the first century BC, cist burials are found in South West England and sword and cart burials in Eastern Yorkshire (Carr 2007: 444; Cunliffe 1995: 72; Dent 1983: 125). In addition to the regional differences and changes in burial practices within the same communities over time, the treatment of the dead is sometimes not even homogenous within the same communities and within the same temporal space. In sites such as Suddern Farm, Hampshire and Yarnton, Oxfordshire cremation and excarnation may have been practiced simultaneously (Cunliffe and Poole 2000; Haselgrove and Moore 2007: 9-10; Hey et al. 1999).

Excarnation

Excarnation as form of burial is difficult to prove because of the very absence of material evidence for such disposal. However, evidence of animal gnawing on bones, isolated fragmented, weathered or splintered bones, disarticulated or incomplete skeletons lacking limbs are all indicators for this particular burial rite and are frequently found in Iron Age Britain (Carr and Knuesel 1997: 170). There is also some archaeological evidence of four or five post structures, which may well have been excarnation platforms such as the five post structure just outside a ditch which enclosed a well furnished cremation burial in Clemency in Luxembourg (Carr 2007: 447-448). It has been suggested that only five percent or less of the Iron Age population of Britain is represented in burials. Some sites were occupied throughout the entire Iron Age period, yet their cemeteries have been attributed to only a part of this period (Carr 2007: 448-449). This would indicate that the remaining dead were excarnated.

In terms of colour, the absence of actual material evidence means that we have no knowledge about the colours employed in the excarnation ritual such as the colour of the fabrics in which the body may have been wrapped or the colour of the mourner's garments. Funerary

excarnation rituals can be very complex as demonstrated by a recent account of a so-called sky burial in Tibet, where excarnation is still being practised today. The deceased is tied to a pole on the top of a hill. Vultures pick on the flesh until only the skeleton is left. The remaining bones are mixed with flour, sugar and butter and are then also devoured by the vultures (Eldar 2005). It is not clear from the account what the underlying belief system of this ritual is but it is worth noting that no parts of the body are left behind, yet there is a clear separation of the body into flesh and soft tissues and white bones, which are mixed with equally white coloured food stuffs. We don't know if excarnation was similarly practised in the British Iron Age or if bodies were manually de-fleshed or simply left to rot on platforms until they all but disappeared. The importance of scavenger birds like crows in early Irish myth and evidence of bones of ravens, buzzards, starlings, crows, peregrine falcons and red kite found at some Iron Age settlements may hint at the role of scavenger birds in disposing the dead (Carr and Knuesel 1997: 170). There is some written evidence from geographically and temporally closer sources for excarnation by scavenger birds, even suggesting that this particular way of disposal of the dead may have meant an honorary death. Silius Italicus wrote 'The Celts, who have added to their name that of the Hiberi, came also. To these men death in battle is glorious; and they consider it a crime to burn the body of such a warrior for they believe that the soul goes up to the gods in heaven, if the body is devoured on the field by the hungry vulture.' (Punica 3.340-434). Archaeological evidence from tomb paintings and funerary urns from Celt-Iberia depicting human corpses and vultures support the suggestion of excarnation by scavenger birds in a Celt-Iberian context (Simon 2008: 61; Sopeña 2005: 380) (Figure 20a).

Whatever form excarnation in the Iron Age took, there are a few basic and generally applicable colour observations to be made. The transition of the body can be divided into various stages. The first stage begins with the physical death, i.e. ceasing of breath and heartbeat. The body of the deceased becomes immediately very pale as the blood pools, with red splotches in areas where the blood has sunk to. If the death is a violent death, a death caused by an injury or perhaps by childbirth, red blood would visibly and literally drain away from the body. This draining of blood or, to put it in simple terms, the red colour leaving the body, is associated with loss of heat and perhaps with the coppery smell of blood. This stage would be the first stage of Van Gennep's tripartite rite of passage, i.e. separation, and seems to be associated with the colour red or rather the colour red leaving the body.

During the following period the body would either have been defleshed by birds or other scavengers, which would then leave just the white skeleton, or the corpse may have been left to decay. This process can be separated into various stages. The Australian Museum has published on-line the results, including photographic evidence, of an experiment whereby a dead baby pig was exposed to excarnation by decay (Australian Museum 2003). Pig flesh and skin have similar qualities to human skin and flesh; human decay would therefore not differ much at all.

Initial Decay

During the first stage of decay, up to three days after death, bodily matter, faeces and urine will leave the body and the colour of skin turns slowly to a dull bluish green. Flies lay eggs in body cavities and the eggs begin to hatch inside the body shortly after.

Putrefaction

During this stage, between the fourth and tenth day after death body tissues are broken down, gases will leave the body and fluids are released into body cavities. This stage is accompanied by the sickly sweet smell of rotting.

Black Putrefaction

During the next stage, between ten and twenty days after death, the bloated body collapses, the digestion of the flesh by insects increases, the colour of the exposed surface turns black and a large volume of blackish fluids leave the body. The smell of decay becomes very strong. This smell is repulsive to modern Western society, but may not have been perceived as offensive or disagreeable to Iron Age communities. It may have been simply related to the notion of transition to an altered stage and, if this transition was seen as the deceased passing to the ancestors or the Otherworld, it may have had positive connotations (Carr and Knuesel 1997: 168). The Kanamawi in Panama for example call the smell of decay the honey of death and perceive it as food for their Jaguar god (Whitehead 2001: 239).

Butyric Fermentation

During the following step, twenty to fifty days after death, the remaining flesh is removed by insects and the body dries out. Beetles will then feed on the skin and ligaments and the body is covered with a whitish mould. The colour of the remains change from black to white and the accompanying smell is that of a cheesy fermentation.

Dry Decay

In the final period of decomposition, between fifty days and one year after death, the remaining skin and hair is removed by insects until only the white bones are left. The parts digested and recycled by insects would leave black traces on the ground or underneath the skeleton.

This period of transition from initial decay to the dry stage, which equates to Van Gennep's second stage of in the burial rite of passage and during which the corpse

loses all individual features, is often associated with pollution and danger (Parker Pearson 1999: 24). The dead may be a source of fear which could take the form of fear for the dead body's soul, or the survivors' fear of the dead. Among the Azande tribe in Sudan the death must be symbolically avenged during this period. It is a time when magic is made, oracles are consulted and taboos are imposed (Evans-Pritchard 2004: 121).

It is arguable the case that during the British Iron Age excarnation platforms were probably erected on the edge of the settlement itself or other liminal places. There is some, albeit scarce evidence of such structures from a number of sites. Martin Bell (2000: 72) argued that a late Bronze Age or early Iron Age structure of 12 wooden posts made of six or seven different species of wood from Goldcliff, Monmouthshire may have been used for the exposure of bodies. Two skulls found in the vicinity seem to support his argument. Goldcliff lies in the Severn Estuary in a wetland landscape likely to have been seen as a liminal area. Four-post-holes structures or two-post-hole structures situated on the edges of settlements in sites such as Rotherly, Wiltshire, Grimthorpe, Yorkshire or Little Woodbury, Wiltshire have also all been interpreted as possible excarnation platforms on the basis that the conventional interpretation of storage facilities did not necessarily make sense for these structures (Ellison and Drewett 1971). On the assumption that these interpretations were correct, then during the transitional stage the decaying body may have been confined to a special liminal place on the edge of the settlement but still within the tribal area. The body would have been elevated and thus would no longer belong to the earth but be placed in a liminal position between earth and sky, perhaps echoing the boundaries between life and death or the boundaries between this world and an ancestral Otherworld.

After the third and final stage of the rite of Van Gennep's rite of passage, i.e. the time when the corpse resumes a stable physical form, the skeleton, bones or ashes may be crushed or dispersed by animals or birds, but, as will be discussed later, they may have a role to play in a secondary burial.

During this process the corpse is no longer an entity but is divided into distinct separate parts, namely blood, flesh and bone. We do not know if these parts or their decay were associated with aspects of soul or individual personhood, but there are a number of observations we can make. The first part, blood, is associated with the first stage of Van Gennep's rite of passage, the threshold between life and death. It is a red liquid, perhaps still flowing or pooling. The second part, the flesh, is soft. During the transitional stage of decay it turns black and seemingly disintegrates into the earth. The third part of the deceased, the skeletal remains, is hard, white and seemingly permanent.

As already discussed in chapter 8 the polarity of black and white may have had cosmological symbolism. For example, the Nigerian Yoruba people associate the colour white with the spirits of their ancestral dead, whereas the colour black represents the world of the living (Keates 2002: 115). However, black and white may also have gender associations. Societies which practise burial by excarnation are often exogamous. The decaying black flesh might symbolize the transience of external relationships whereas the white dry bones can represent the permanency of a male royal line and also ancestral notions (Brueck 1995: 261). The Merina tribe in Madagascar perceive the decaying black flesh as female. It is given back to the earth near the village and has associations with fertility. The dried white bones are seen as male and are taken to ancestral tombs (Fowler 2004: 109). As already referred to in chapter 8 Tacitus described the priestesses of Mona as wearing black robes (Annales 14.28) and Pliny stated that the presumably male druids wore white garments during certain rituals, such as the gathering of mistletoe (Natural History 16.251) Perhaps the polarity of black and white played a role in the garments of priests and druids, indicating either gender or concern with the black Underworld and the white Otherworld or both.

Black and white dualism is frequently associated with death in both classical myths and early Celtic Vernacular. In Virgil's Aeneid, the hero Aeneas describes a dream in which the slain Hector appears blackened with dried blood and dirt (2.257-280), black blood tears flow out of a myrtle sapling as harbinger of the death of Polydorus, Priam's messenger who was killed in Thrace (3.24-51), and in Book 4 the Sybil and Aeneas sacrifice four black skinned bullocks to the Underworld Goddess Hekate and a black lamb to Night and her sister Earth. In the Odyssey Odysseus must travel to the entrance of the Underworld which is described as a dark place where 'dreadful night spreads her mantle' (Homer Odyssey 11.10-20). There he must sacrifice a black ewe to the dead seer Teireisias (10.520-530). After his return to Ithaka Odysseus encounters his dog after twenty years of absence and the 'black hand of Death' descends on the dog as soon as he sees his master (17.326). The opposite association of the colour white with Jupiter, a sky god is also documented in Virgil's Aeneid (9.617-640) when Ascanius promises Jupiter a sacrifice of a snow white bull with gilded horns.

Similar associations of dark with night, death and the Underworld and the opposite associations of white with daylight, this world, life and issues of fertility feature in early Celtic Myth such as the tales of the fights between Fionn and Donn, whose names mean literally white and black (Ó hÓgáin 1999: 126). Donn often appears in Irish tales as the lord of the dead, presiding over an offshore island (Ó hÓgáin 1999: 58). The Welsh equivalent can be found in the tales of the fights between Gwynn and Gwythyr and Arawn and Havgan. Gwythyr means victor, but Gwynn like Fionn means white. Gwynn is assisted by Annwfn who represents the dark Underworld and thus both colours are combined (Ó hÓgáin 1999: 126). Arawn who is clearly a supernatural figure and is possibly related to the Underworld, wears dark green and brown garments and is the enemy of Havgan, whose name means 'summer white'. The polarity of colours, which in the latter tale is not actually spelled out, but must clearly be intended by association, hints at a mythical perception of time, whether daily or seasonally (Gantz 1976: 15; Ó hÓgáin 1999: 127), which does not contradict but rather enhances the polarity of life and death. Night, autumn and winter are often associated with death, whereas daylight, spring and summer stand for life, fertility and rebirth.

If we were to assume that the belief systems in Iron Age Britain included such symbolism we can summarize the associations of the separate body parts as shown in Figure 3.

Cremation

Prima facie cremation appears to be a totally separate treatment of the body and it is therefore tempting to interpret it as the result of a separate belief system or a special rite linked perhaps only to particular individuals or special circumstances. There are, of course significant differences between excarnation and cremation. The natural process of decay is replaced by a controlled process which involves human intervention (Brueck 1995: 261, Pearce 1997: 175). However, there are still a lot of similarities in terms of colour. Firstly, the initial stage in Van Gennep's tripartite stage, i.e. the actual moment of death, evidenced by the flow or pooling of blood, is still the same. The second stage, the rotting of the flesh, is not necessarily replaced by cremation. The cremation may not have been carried out immediately after death. In modern day Bali cremation still takes place as a secondary burial rite. The bodies of the deceased are initially interred, then after a certain interval exhumed and burnt (Downes 1999). Gillian Carr (2007: 445-447) suggested that during the later Iron Age the dead may have lain in state in shafts or shrines, as is believed to

Blood	Liquid	Metallic smell	Perishable	Red	Not Gender Specific	Individual life force, magical mediary
Flesh	Soft	Fermenting smell	Permeable	Black	Female	Underworld, Fertility and regeneration
Bone	Hard	odourless	Permanent	White	Male	Otherworld, ancestral and kingship

FIGURE 3: BODY PART ASSOCIATIONS

have occurred e.g. at Folly Lane (Niblett 1999: 58-59), or as discussed above, exposed on platforms or de-fleshed prior to cremation. It is even possible that cremations took place only at specific times,38 which may explain the fact that cremation burials in the Iron Age generally do not contain whole bodies, but only token bones, the majority of the bones having already been dispersed (Carr 2007: 447).

Cremation is therefore perhaps not a replacement of excarnation but a variant of the already existing funerary rite with an additional step. Even though it has been argued that cremation was re-introduced into Britain from the continent towards the early first century BC as a new form of burial, Gillian Carr suggested that cremation was not so much a radical new rite, but the continuation of an existing tradition by the integration or reformulation of a new rite into existing systems. She bases her proposition on the fact excarnation and cremation burials are not mutually exclusive but overlap both geographically and temporally, that humans and animals were cremated and then deposited in a similar way, that only parts of the bodies were cremated rather than the whole body and that the rectangular shrines housing the deceased prior to cremation resembled excarnation platforms (Carr 2007). I would go even further and suggest that the colours found in the excarnation process are echoed in the cremation rite. The pyre would have had a moving and seemingly living red flame which, as alluded to elsewhere, may have been perceived as alive or even life-giving. White or black smoke, depending on the dryness of the remains and pyre, would rise into the air and the burning of the corpse or corpses would have been accompanied by a distinctive acrid smell. Once the fire had died down, the body or what was left of it would have been separated into black and white ashes and debris, most of which might have been discarded into the wind or used as fertilizer, and bones. Unlike the modern cremation process, where the ashes contain the fragments of bones which have been ground up by a special machine (Mays 1998: 11) the process of burning on pyres would not have de-fragmented the bones into ashes. They may have become brittle but the fragmented pieces would still be of a size that would allow them to be readily recognized as bones and quite distinctive from the ashes. In certain instances the bones or parts of the bones would also have been collected and may have played a role in a secondary burial, as will be discussed later.

The colours apparent throughout the process and the sequence of their appearance imitate the colours and

sequence already mentioned during the natural decaying process. However, during cremation the process is not only sped up, it is also interfered with and controlled by humans. The separation into red and ultimately black and white is no longer left to nature or even supernatural forces. Similar to the processes of metallurgy as outlined in chapter 4, during which humans 'create' material and were perhaps even perceived as creators of life, here humans are actively involved in the process of death. Cremation therefore artificially repeats and thus reinforces the natural process of death and decay.

There is however, one difference in colour terms which must not be overlooked. After excarnation the bones, which may ultimately be collected and deposited are always white. However, during cremation the colour of the bones may alter depending on the state of the corpse prior to cremation. If the body is still 'wet', i.e. if it still has remnants of flesh and fat, the bones will remain white. However, if the body has already been exposed to excarnation for a long period, then the bones would turn black during burning (Carr 2007: 447). In addition, the temperature of the pyre also has an impact on the colour of the bones. Experiments with goat bones showed that lower pyre temperatures would have resulted in reddish/brownish colours, followed by black and dark blue coloration and ultimately, at temperatures in excess of 645° C a white or pale yellow colour.

This poses a number of questions. If white bones were indeed seen as symbolizing ancestral and male connotations, as has been suggested above, would the deliberate burning of dry bones or burning at a lower temperature, i.e. turning them black or at least darker, have meant a change towards a different belief system, where the division into female soft flesh and ancestral male hard bones was no longer relevant or not desired? The female mirror burial from Chilham Castle, Kent (Parfitt 1998), for example, contains white bone fragments as well as blue-grey bone fragments. The question whether bones have indeed ancestral connotations has been subject to debate. Brueck (1995: 262) argued that bones found in ditches may have had fertility symbolism, although her argument relates to the Bronze Age period; Fitzpatrick and Parker Pearson suggested that the deposition of bones in ditches represented continuity and tradition, i.e. the bones had ancestral qualities (Fitzpatrick 1997a: 83; Parker Pearson 1996: 123). Carr (2007: 449) even argues for individuality of personhood rather than notions of ancestrality. In my view these arguments are not mutually exclusive, but the symbolic interpretation of the bones may have depended on their treatment and the context of primary or secondary disposal, as will be discussed later, but perhaps also on their colour.

Given the fact that the separation of the body into different parts is still a feature of cremation, it would be hard to argue that there was a total break with tradition

___
38 Hill argued similarly that depositions of body parts in ditches and pits were only made at ten year intervals (Hill 1995). Considering the argument that the construction of and possibly depositions at the Fiskerton causeway co-incided with the Saros cycle, a lunar eclipse which is repeated approximately every 18 years (Chamberlain 2003; Chamberlain and Parker Pearson 2003), the idea of long intervals between certain rituals may not have been unusual in the British Iron Age.

or that notions of dividuality of personhood would have been replaced with the idea of individuality. The persons who were responsible for the cremation ritual, perhaps priests or druids, had the power to deliberately make bone brittle and black, thereby changing that part of the body which in the natural decay process would have been white and enduring, perhaps imbued with notions of masculinity, kingship and ancestral symbolism, into brittle, perishable or permeable fragments of various colours, which could have been used in further rituals. Ash, for example, could have been smeared over mourners or used as fertilizer. Remnants of bones might have been used in the transformation of iron into steel as discussed in Chapter 4. Perhaps the symbolic connotations would have been changed to female gender, creation and fertility. If this control over symbolism were indeed the case, the persons performing the rite would have been very powerful indeed, harnessing and controlling physicality, politics, cosmology, and eschatology. The increase in cremation towards the latter part of the Iron Age and the argument that cremation was only performed at certain intervals would suggest that the power was perhaps initially only used at certain times and for specific purposes, but perhaps during the later Iron Age demonstration of power became more important due to the perceived threat of Rome.

Inhumation

The third type of primary disposal of the dead in the British Iron Age is inhumation burial. Inhumation burials are not confined to the late Iron Age, although like cremation, they appear more frequently during that period. There are numerous different inhumation practices ranging from pit burials in central Southern England, to square barrow burials in Yorkshire dating to the mid 5th to 1st centuries BC or inhumation burials in cists from South West England, which are dated to the 3rd and 1st centuries BC. Some burials are without grave goods, others have specific grave goods such as weapons, carts or mirrors (Bevan 1999b: 132-133; Creighton 2000: 48-49; Whimster 1981). Some burials appear isolated, others are grouped within cemeteries. Some are within settlement areas, others outside. All of these types of burial and their differences are discussed in their specific context below, but they all share certain properties. The treatment of the corpse is fundamentally different. Unlike cremation and excarnation where the second and third stages of Van Gennep's tripartite rite of passage are visibly recognisable and confined to certain periods or moments in time, the rite of inhumation takes place in the earth and there is no visible trace or acknowledgement of these stages. There is no topographical or temporal separation between the rites of liminality and aggregation by means of a secondary burial rite at a different location, the body does not become visibly divided into separate parts or separate colours. Instead it is treated in a holistic way. The visual

memory of the body, and perhaps with it all aspects of the deceased's personhood, is fixed at the moment of burial in the grave and there is no visible closure of the process of transition (Barrett 1988: 32). Whilst there may have been subsequent closure rituals, they have no impact on the remains themselves.

This could be interpreted as a radically different model with different underlying belief systems. However, inhumation burials appeared in Britain alongside excarnation and cremation throughout most of the Iron Age, even in the same geographical settings. Indeed, inhumation burials may have been more frequent than commonly suspected (Hey et al. 1999: 551), but the percentage of the dead disposed through inhumation, as mentioned above, is relatively small. Inhumation, like cremation may have been an additional or special rite rather than a replacement, where the known ritual and its associated symbolism may have been deliberately altered to express something different. If so, we have to ask the question whether this deliberate denial of separation of the body and closure had a negative or positive connotation.

Van Gennep (1969: 229) stated that persons, who do not have proper funerary rites, are the most lamentable, because they are not allowed to make the transition to the world of the dead. They stay in a permanent liminal period and are therefore at their most dangerous, like hostile strangers. Van Gennep likens their fate to children who have not been baptized or those without denomination in Christian terms and who are in accordance with some Roman Catholic doctrines forever confined to limbo. On the other hand, it is simply possible that different burial types were reserved for specific people depending on their standing within the community whilst alive and also the interest they have for the community after their death (Fowler 2004: 95-96). It is also possible that the denial of separation into divisible parts recognizes and retains the individuality or individual qualities of the deceased.

Gillian Carr argues that cremation or inhumation is not necessarily for special people, but that deposits in pits or cremations only took place once in a while (Carr 2007: 448-449). However, this does not explain the use of cemeteries used for more than one generation and we also have to take into account that a person, who may not have been special during his or her life, may achieve special status after death, whether the whole aspect of his or her personhood in the individual sense, or dividual aspects of that person. Depending on the circumstances these special burials and the colour aspects associated with them may all have different meanings and we therefore need to explore each type in the context of locality, grave goods, gender and circumstance of death.

Burials

Inhumation or deposition into the ground as part of a secondary funerary rite differs widely both geographically and temporally throughout the Iron Age period. Attempts have been made to group them into different categories and roughly they can be divided into the following groups:

- Square barrow burials and crouched inhumations, such as those found in Yorkshire (dating to the mid 5th to 1st centuries BC)
- Crouched inhumation burials, found mainly in Dorset, Scotland and Hertfordshire (dating to the later 1st century BC to the 2nd century AD)

- Crouched cist burials in the South West, (generally dating from the 3rd to the 1st century BC)

- Flat inhumation graves, found mainly in Dorset (dating to the 1st century BC)

- Cremation burials, such as the Aylesford Swarling or Welwyn rites in South East England (dating from the 1st century BC to the 1st century AD) (Bevan 1999b: 132-133; Creighton 2000: 48-49; Whimster 1981: 147-166; Whimster 197: 317-327).

Sometimes weapon burials are classified to as a separate category, but in my view burial with weapons permeate the categories already listed. Whimster (1977: 327) also includes pit and related burials into his categorization, but I suggest that pit burials are not mortuary rites in the same sense as the above mentioned practices and I will therefore deal with them separately in a later part of this chapter.

It goes beyond the scope of this book to analyse each and every Iron Age burial or even each category of burial found in Britain in terms of colour. Apart from the scale of such a project, the reliability of the statistics would be questionable due to the fact that we have still comparatively little archaeological evidence of burials. There are also further reasons which would make such an analysis a futile exercise:

The rough categories outlined above are vague. There are numerous inconsistencies within each rite and divergences within each geographical area. For example, in South East England there are four main types of cremation burial and mortuary structures, namely human remains accompanied by between one and five pots, human remains with some grave goods such as toiletries, vessels, wooden buckets, decorated mirrors and personal objects, cremations in large grave pits with a wide range of grave goods including at least one amphora, a quantity of pottery and imported glass or metal vessels – known as Welwyn cremations, and the deposition of cremated

remains in shafts or chambers with unusual objects, which are either deliberately broken or of which only a symbolic part had been deposited – known as the Folly Lane rite (Brookes 2004: 210-211; Niblett 1999: 394). The grave goods in the inhumation burials in Burton Fleming in Yorkshire are usually brooches, sometimes pots, bracelets, beads or rings, but the graves may also contain swords, carts or mirrors. Sometimes the bodies had been placed in wooden coffins without metal fittings, but generally the bodies were laid down directly onto the soil in a crouched or contracted position (Stead 1979: 14).

Some burials are part of large cemeteries such as Westhampnett which features over one hundred and sixty cremation burials (Brookes 2004: 30; Fitzpatrick 1997: 35), yet others are isolated or belong to a restricted number of burials even though they follow the same rite. For example, in North Shoebury only three cremation burials were found and excavated (Brookes 2004: 34). Some graves contain grave goods, but there are also numerous burial sites without any grave goods. Only half the inhumation burials in Burton Fleming in Yorkshire contained such objects (Stead 1979: 14).

Many burials with grave goods do not show significant or sufficient evidence of the use of colour to allow us to draw any conclusion as to the symbolic use of colour. Some graves contain no objects other than perhaps a part of a pig, or a bronze brooch which may have fastened a covering or a shroud. We have very little knowledge of organic material such as shrouds, wrappings, plants or flowers used in burials or the colour of such materials. There is evidence of straw or grass on fragments from burials in Westhampnett (Fitzpatrick 1997: 112), the archaeology of the La Tène III burial at Welwyn Garden City suggests that the deceased may have been wrapped in a bear skin prior to cremation,[39] part of the floor had been covered by a kind of mat made probably from oak bark and a fragment of animal skin, possibly belonging to a black stoat was found in a corner of the grave (Stead 1967: 34, 40, 42). In analogy with Roman sacrificial rites where animals sacrificed to sky gods where white, those sacrificed to chthonic gods or dead persons black and those offered to the fire god were red in colour (Wilkens 2004: 74), it is possible that the colour of animal skins or pelts had similar symbolic importance in British Iron Age burial rites.[40] On the other hand, the colour and pattern of hides and pelts may have symbolized social status or relationships. The Bodi of Southern Ethiopia for example associate the appearance of their cow hides with personal and group identity and attribute great

---

[39] Evidence of a body wrapped in bear skin prior to cremation is also known from Verulamium (Stead and Rigby 1986: 53).

[40] The association of colour black with chthonic cults and the dead is also an essential element of Greek ritual. Black Night is the mother of death, the world of Hades is black and he is honoured with nocturnal sacrifices, black sacrificial victims and worshippers wearing black clothes (Stratiki 2004: 108).

importance to them during rituals such as sacrifices or blood letting (Sharples 2008: 203). At present we do not have sufficient material evidence from Iron Age burials to draw any meaningful conclusions.

Grave Goods

Despite the variety of burial rites, grave goods can be categorized into five main categories:

- Vessels made out of pottery, silver, bronze or glass, objects concerned with grooming such as razors, shears, mirrors[41]
- Personal objects such as brooches or bracelets
- Furniture and fittings such as boxes, couches, hearth furniture, keys and lamps
- Objects of leisure and warfare such as gaming pieces, musical instruments, swords, spears, and shields

(Brookes 2004: 208-209).

However, some grave goods, such as brooches, may have had a mostly functional role, such as holding together garments or shrouds, and colour may have had no relevance. Other goods, such as toiletry articles may have had symbolic meaning as agents used in the process of transformation of the deceased's appearance (Hill 1997: 101), but their colour may have been irrelevant. Finally, just as there are different rites and symbolic values of grave or pyre goods, there are also different and complex responses to the dead, which may well have an impact on the symbolic interpretation of grave goods and their colours.

The process of mourning the dead can be regarded as a combination of loss, imagination and recovery (Steinhoff Smith 1989: 326-343) and this can be expressed by way of sorrow, grief and elements of nostalgia (Maschio 1994: 198). These responses can lead to a variety of actions which impact on the material aspects of the mortuary rite. The breaking of objects may be an expression of grief or sorrow and the placing of objects connected to the dead or the retaining of such objects are acts of remembrance and perhaps nostalgia.

A pure statistical database approach to colours in the context of burial would therefore not provide significant answers. Nevertheless, the importance of colour should not be overlooked but perhaps a different approach should be taken:

Firstly, an examination of the possible reasons for specific rites and the context of the wider geographical location may provide some evidence which a mere statistical analysis of colours of grave goods cannot

offer. Secondly, even though there is a disparity of burial rites, the use of certain grave goods and the tendency towards certain orientation pervades these rites and there are certain colours which re-occur and may have been part of a symbolism or belief system that transcended localized rituals. Thirdly, some burials provide such striking colours, that a more specific contextual analysis may contribute to a better understanding of their use.

Wider Context

The context of graves and depositions lends itself the various levels of symbolic analysis. According to Härke (1997a: 193) these levels can be summarized as

- Location and landscape context
- Grave form and monument
- Grave goods
- Decoration of artefacts in grave

I would suggest that there is a level even above Härke's summary, namely the effect of the particular rite on the body and funerary objects. As stated above the effects of inhumation and cremation on the body are rather different. In the inhumation rite the body of the deceased does not undergo a visible transformation; it remains intact, enclosed together with all the grave goods and furniture in a dark place. The mourners remember the deceased as a whole and most of the individual aspects of the person or at least those aspects which are important to the mourners and recognizable to them, are preserved in memory.

During cremation as primary rite the body and the pyre goods undergo a visible transformation not only in substance but also in colour, brought about by the red and white flames of the fire. Cremation includes an element of dispersion as not always all of the cremated bones are collected from the pyre sites (Brookes 2004: 113). The secondary rite, the burial of the cremated remains, however, equates again with darkness, containment and preservation, but only in respect of certain parts of the deceased, perhaps perceived as only certain aspects of his or her personhood. The differentiation between grave goods and pyre goods becomes obvious. Pyre goods are cremated and accompany the deceased, his spirit or whatever part of the dead person is passing on into the Otherworld (Huntington and Metcalf 1979: 15). There is evidence that during the later La Tène period weapons and jewellery, perhaps personal adornment, were cremated on pyres. It has been argued that the burning of metallic objects as part of cremation burials in the Bronze Age, evidenced by spot staining, may have been seen as a spiritualization of personal belongings. As the resulting copper alloy was not found it is possible that it may have been collected for re-use (Graeslund 1994: 21; McKinlay 1994: 133).

---

[41] Although mirrors may well have been used for activities such as communication with the Otherworld as suggested in chapter 6.

If the cremated pyre goods were intended for the afterlife of the deceased, the goods which were buried with the cremated remains therefore played a different role and had perhaps a more symbolic value. Graeslund suggested that shaving instruments in Scandinavian Bronze Age cremation rites were not cremated, either because they had a symbolic meaning as an agent of transformation or because they were polluted due to their usage in preparing the deceased for burial (Graeslund 1994: 20-21). In any event, it appears that such objects together with cremated remains also required containment and preservation.

Location and Monument

Looking then at the location and landscape of certain Iron Age burial grounds, some observations can be made. The importance of visible monuments in the landscape in the British Iron Age can be demonstrated by the reuse of earlier Bronze Age monuments in Iron Age settlements (Loney and Hoaen 2005: 374) and certainly some, though not all burials would have had visual impact.

Burials and cemeteries are often found near water, trackways or boundaries which would suggest an element of liminality both in terms of political and geographical boundaries, but also perhaps symbolic boundaries between this world and the Otherworld (Brueck 1995: 260). The seasonal appearance of water for example in the gypsy races in Yorkshire adds to this symbolic liminality (Bevan 1999c: 90). The square barrows set above some of the Yorkshire burials even suggest that the remains of the dead may have been taken out of the seasonal cycle, which may have been represented by the round dwellings for the living (Parker Pearson 1999: 51). But, more importantly in terms of colour, in Yorkshire the dead are buried in white chalklands (Dent 1984: 30) and burials in Kent, Cambridgeshire and Wessex are similarly located in white chalklands.

In direct contrast to excarnation where the dead are dispersed above ground without any lasting traces (if secondary burial of bones is disregarded) in the wolds and chalklands some of the dead are buried in a fairly high location in a landscape which is striking because of the brilliant whiteness of its underlying substance, and which may have been perceived as a landscape for the dead. If we follow the interpretation of the little chalk figurines from Yorkshire or the Uffington White Horse as having ancestral connotations, as discussed in chapter 5, the ancestral aspect of the dead in such locations may have been all important.

Any barrows or mounds erected on top of the graves as part of the burial site, might not have been allowed to be grassed over and the whiteness of the chalk mounds in the landscape would not only have been perceived as a highly visible mnemonic marker, but these features

themselves may have had ancestral connotations (Bevan 1999c: 79; Fenton Thomas 2003: 51-52; Tilley 1994: 157).

Not all inhumation burials occur in chalk lands and the landscape context of some inhumation burials differs greatly. For example, the cist burials predominately found in Cornwall are constructed out of local stone and the cists found on the isles of Scilly were made out of whiteish granite boulders (Ashbee 1954: 7-10). Again, it could be argued that the whiteness of these boulders had ancestral connotations. However, the Trevorne cist burial in Northern Cornwall is made of local dark blue slate (Dudley and Jope 1965: 18-19) and the argument is therefore not conclusive. In any event and disregarding the material of any cists or graves, most graves would have a different visual aspect even without any deliberate markers, as the soil disturbance created by the grave would resulted in a change of colour of any vegetation, which would have stood in contrast with the surrounding landscape.

Recurring Colours of Grave Goods

As already stated above, grave goods appear in a variety of materials and colours. In East Yorkshire for example, burials revealed objects made out of bronze and iron, blue and yellow glass beads, coral and red glass inlay, red pebbles, black jet, shale and chalk. At first glance there seems to be little consistency in colour terms and one could easily come to the conclusion that colour symbolism either played no role in burial rites or that the colours and grave goods were incidental or highly personal as adornments of the deceased. But despite such diversity in rites, colours and materials, there are a number of re-occurring features which appear to transcend localized rituals. Some of them have no or little impact on colour, such as the correlation between the direction in which bodies are laid out and the accompanying grave goods (Parker Pearson 1999: 53; Whimster 1981: 288) or gender differences such as the placing of pots at the feet of male corpses but in the area of the heads or hands of female corpses, suggesting perhaps a social relationship between genders of provider and server (Parker Pearson 1999: 53). Parker Pearson suggests that in analogy with the symbolic and geographical location of round houses, the orientation and lay out of graves may have demonstrated social difference or segregated groups (Parker Pearson 1999: 44-45).[42]

Weapons such as swords or shields are used as grave goods in a variety of burial rites and in numerous geographical locations, such as the crouched inhumation and barrow burials in East Yorkshire or Dorset or cist burials such as the burial found in Gelliniog Wen in Anglesey (Collis 1973; Whimster 1981: 2). Although

---

[42] Although the roundhouse orientation theory has come under some criticism (Pope 2007).

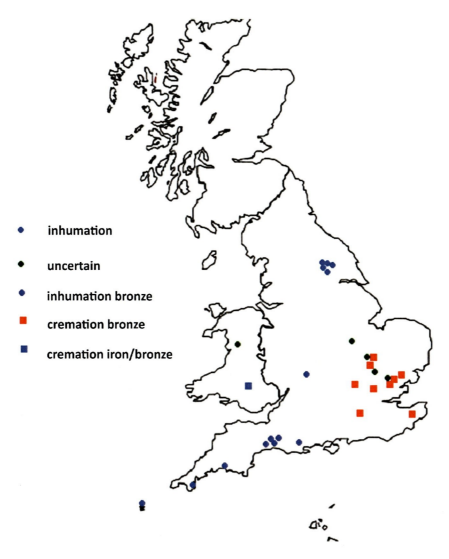

FIGURE 4: DISTRIBUTION OF MIRROR BURIALS IN ENGLAND AND WALES

weapons are not frequently found in cremation burials (Brookes 2004: 212), there are incidences of weapons used as grave goods such as those found in Snailwell, Cambridgeshire or Ham Hill in Somerset (Collis 1973; Letherbridge 1953). Not all swords, scabbards or shields are decorated and we do not know the colour of leather scabbards or shields, but the prominent colour in decorated weapons is red, in the form of either coral or red hot glass inlays. The most striking example is the Kirkburn iron sword and bronze scabbard already mentioned in chapter 7, which was found in a grave beneath the skeleton of a young man in his late twenties.[43] The blade, handle and bronze scabbard are decorated with intricate bar, roundel, crescent and tendril designs of red hot glass inlays and red glass studs (Giles 2008: 64; Stead 2006: 60, 184) giving the overall impression of a blood spattered weapon (Figure 17c).

Mirror Burials – case study

The prevalence of certain colours or colour inferences being spanning diverse burial rites and geographical locations can be demonstrated by a more detailed analysis of mirror burials. Mirror burials range from inhumation graves with Iron mirrors in Yorkshire to La Tène inhumation or cremation mirror burials found for example in Colchester, Birdlip and Billericay in Southern England, St Keverne in Cornwall and as far west as the Scilly Islands (Fox and Pollard 1973: 38-39, Johns 2002) (Figure 4).

I analysed 30 mirror burials in terms of the colour of the mirrors *per se*, the colour implications of the burial context, location of the mirror, gender connotations, burial rite and evidence of wrapping or containment (Figure 5). There are a number of observations which can be made.

Out of the 30 mirror burials examined, 24 mirrors are made out of bronze (Figure 6). As already outlined in

---

[43] The position of the sword is reminiscent of the swords suspended from loops and carried on the back as depicted by the chalk figurines discussed in chapter 5.

Mirror	Mirror material	decorated	decorated side up or down	Burial type	Male/female	Grave goods/colour	Wrapped
Arras, Yorkshire	iron with 2 bronze mounts on handle, bronze connects plate and handle	no	n/a	chariot burial, inhumation	female	two iron and bronze horse bits, one iron and bronze terret, bronze cap, perhaps end of a whip	?
Arras, Yorkshire	iron, now lost	no	n/a	barrow burial, inhumation	?	?	?
Aston, Hertfortshire	plate: copper 87.5, tin 11.6 handle: copper 85.5, tin 12.6	yes	mirror plane nearly vertical	cremation	suggested female, not conclusive	infill charred material, red burnt clay, one pot with grey core and brown surface, another pot heavily over-fired or re-burnt, grey core, grey brown surface, no finish survives	?
Billericay I, Essex	copper alloy, handle: 11.75 tin	yes	?	possibly cremation	?	no urn, possibly associated with pottery, both British and Roman	?
Billericay II, Essex	copper alloy, handle: only 8,75 tin	yes	?	possibly cremation	?	no urn, possibly associated with pottery, both British and Roman	?
Billericay III, Essex	bronze	?	?	?	?	?	?
Birdlip, Gloucester	copper alloy	eight pairs of red hot glass dots on plate	?	cist inhumation	suggested female	silver brooch with red enamel decoration , four bronze rings and bracelet, bronze knife, necklace of large ring beads of amber, jet and grey marble	possibly wrapped
Brecon Beacons, Powys	iron plate and Bronze handle	decorated handle	?	possibly cremation	?	Roman lamp, carinated bowl, bronze mini terrets, bronze Roman toiletry set	?
Bridport West Bay, Dorset	bronze mirror handle	no	?	inhumation of male and elderly female	probably female but uncertain	small beaded rim jar	?
Bryher, Isle of Scilly	bronze	yes	mirror angled, reflective side towards face of deceased, tin underneath, mirror possibly wrapped	cist burial	not certain, assumed male because of sword	iron sword with bronze scabbard, brooch, spiral ring, shattered unidentified tin object, sword belt ring, shield fittings. Three pieces of haematite with signs of wear, perhaps red pigment	mirror wrapped in cloth bag, possibly goat hair

Mirror	Mirror material	decorated	decorated side up or down	Burial type	Male/ female	Grave goods/ colour	Wrapped
Bulbury, Dorset	bronze	yes	?	inhumation burial?	?	uncertain context but said to include bronze ornament, two bronze cast figures with bulls heads and horns, two large bronze rings with small rings encircling thems, bronze horse gear, bronze tankard hangle, bronze bindings,, sword hilt, iron hammers and hatchets, an iron anchor, black pottery, eight glass beads of transparent amber coloured glass	?
Chilham Castle, Kent	bronze	yes	plain side upwards	cremation	female	two La Tène III copper alloy brooches, Belgic style grog tempered jar (brownish?)	position of brooches suggest possibly wrapping
Colchester, Essex	copper alloy, allegedly traces of gilding when found	yes	?	cremation burial, Aylesford Type	?	large pedestal urn, coral mounted bronze cup, bronze pin, pair of large jugs or flagons of red ware, mica coated, narrow mouthed cordoned vessel, cordoned bowl 'Belgic ware'	possibly?
Desborough, Northants	plate and handle copper alloy	yes	?	?	?	small bronze brooch – uncertain if connected with mirror	possibly
Dorton, Bucks	plate: copper 90%, tin 9% , handle: copper 85%. tin 8.6 %	yes	mirror with decorated side down in box, cremated bone beside	cremation burial	?	box made from hardwood, possibly oak, but not certain, iron band possibly part of bier, three red amphorae, two red double handed flagons, biconical cup with flat piece of board, several pieces of timber	boxed in
Garton Slack, Yorkshire	iron	no	?	inhumation burial	female	?	?
Great Chesterford, Essex	copper alloy	yes	?	burial context uncertain	?	?	?

Mirror	Mirror material	decorated	decorated side up or down	Burial type	Male/ female	Grave goods/ colour	Wrapped
Latchmere Green, Hampshire	plate: copper 88.5% tin 11.5% handle: copper 87.6% tin 12.4%	yes	mirror probably placed on top of urn	cremation burial	one adult and one child, uncertain sex,	cream coloured bone, grog tempered pedestal jar, initially burnished, but probably reburnt, blackened on one side, pale reddish brown colour, remains of iron fibulae	possibly wrapped?
Llechwedd-Du Bach , Merioneth	bronze	no	?	assumed burial context because of platter and good condition, no indication of human remains	?	bronze platter	n/a
Nijmegen, Holland	bronze	decorated with red enamel	?	?	?	vessel of blue green glass	?
Old Warden I, Bedfordshire	bronze	decoratedwith red Enamel	?	uncertain	?	Roman coins and amphorae	?
Old Warden II, Bedfordshire	bronze	no	?	possibly cremation	?	?	?
Pegsdon, Shillington Bedfordshire	copper alloy	yes	decorated side down on bottom of chalk pit, body on top	cremation burial, unsure if remains in pots	not certain, only one fragment of bone	La Tène III silver brooch, pedestal urn and flat-based jar, surface treatment no longer ascertainable	possibly
Portesham, Dorset	plate: copper 88.6% tin 11.2% handle: copper 86.4% tin 12.9%	yes	mirror placed decorated side upwards on woman's waist, brooch pinned through terminal loop of mirror	crouched inhumation	mature person, probably female	2 brooches, toiletry set, pan iron knife, pottery bowl, pig and sheep bone, brooch on mirror made of brass	possibly wrapped
Portland, Dorset	bronze	plain	?	cist inhumation	?	none	?
Stamford Hill, Plymouth, Devon	remains of three bronze mirrors, two handles, one plate	yes	decorated side up	crouched inhumation,	?	brooch found in the same grave, bracelets decorated with red glass	possibly
Trelan Bahow, St. Keverne, Cornwall	copper alloy	yes	?	inhumation	not certain, sexed female on basis of grave goods	vitreous beads one blue, the other striated black and grey, part of a brooch bronze or brass, described as gilded when found	possibly
Wetwang, Yorkshire	iron	none, but tassel of horse hair decorated with blue beads and coral	n/a placed across lower legs	chariot burial	female	chariot wheels removed, bronze horse strap unions, bits and terrets decorated with red coral studs, black birch bark adhesive, more coral than any other grave, pig bones	covered

Mirror	Mirror material	decorated	decorated side up or down	Burial type	Male/ female	Grave goods/ colour	Wrapped
Wetwang Slack Yorkshire	iron	no	?	chariot burial	female	rectangular box (probably vehicle) covered central area of grave, iron and gold pin decorated with coral, two horse bits and decorated bronze case with chain	covered
Verne Portland, Dorset	bronze handle	yes	?	probably cist inhumation	?	?	?

FIGURE 5: ANALYSIS OF COLOUR AND COLOUR CONNOTATIONS IN MIRROR BURIALS

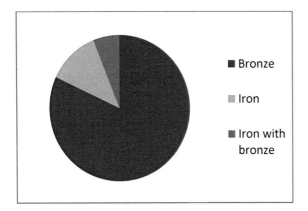

FIGURE 6: MATERIAL OF MIRRORS

chapter 6, where the material has been analyzed, the copper content of the mirrors and mirror handles is relatively high, resulting in a reddish colour. Only the five Yorkshire specimens and one unpublished mirror found in the Brecon Beacons in Wales are made out of iron, but one of the Arras mirrors from Yorkshire has bronze fittings which connect the handle to the plate, and the Brecon Beacons mirror has a decorated bronze handle. The significance of the reddish colour as well as the shimmering effect of the decoration of these mirrors has already been discussed in chapter 6, but there seems to be even further affinity with the colour red. The Birdlip mirror, the Old Warden I mirror and the Nijmegen mirror are all decorated with red hot glass. The decoration with red glass may not necessarily have any links to burials. A mirror handle found in Llanwnda in Wales and the Holcombe mirror (Figure 19d) also feature red glass studs, but neither was found in a burial context. [44]

The colour red is not restricted to just the mirrors. A large proportion of the mirror graves contain other grave goods which are either made out of a red or reddish material such as copper, bronze, reddish pottery,

decorated with enamel or red hot glass. The Colchester mirror grave contained *inter alia* a small bronze cup with a handle bearing a red glass boss and two red ware mica coated flagons (Fox 1948: 135-136), the Stamford Hill inhumation burial contained bracelets decorated with red glass (Smith 1907-09: 331), the cremated remains of the Latchmere Green mirror burial were found in a pale red pottery jar which may have been re-burnt (Fulford and Creighton 1998) and fragments of burnt red clay and charcoal were found alongside the mirror and two re-burnt pots in the mirror burial from Aston Hertfordshire (Rook *et al.* 1982: 19-20). Even though the charcoal is black, the imagery of red flames and glowing red charcoal springs to mind. Even the iron mirror found in Yorkshire in the grave of the so-called 'Wetwang chariot woman' was found with numerous red artefacts, as will be discussed in detail below. The prevalence of red grave goods appears to cross all burial rites, but seems most important in cremation burials. Out of 10 cremation burials nine contain grave goods which are either red or have associations with the colour red. Even outside a burial context there is evidence of mirrors connected to the colour red. The Glastonbury mirror was found with remains of antimony and rouge which was immediately interpreted as female make up (Smith 1907-09: 337). It can, however, not be ruled out, that the red and white colours of these substances had symbolic meaning as opposed to or in addition to merely beautifying qualities as will be discussed in further detail in chapter 10.

It is not the case that only red objects were placed in mirror burials. The Trelan Bahow mirror for example was found with a number of blue and yellow glass beads (Smith 1907-09: 330), and the Birdlip mirror burial contained allegedly a gold plated silver brooch and beads of amber, jet and grey marble (Smith 1907-09: 332). Yet, in contrast to the colour red, the use of other colours such as blue, black or silver seems inconsistent and negligible (Figure 7).

The colour red in mirror burials does not appear to be linked to gender. Prima facie it appears that mirror

---

[44] Johns suggested that the Holcombe mirror may have been from a burial context rather than a settlement context but does not give persuasive evidence for this suggestion (Johns 2002: 69).

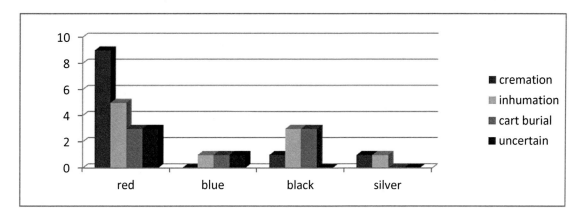

FIGURE 7: COLOUR OF GRAVE GOODS IN MIRROR BURIALS LINKED TO BURIAL RITE

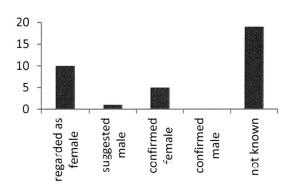

FIGURE 8: GENDER CONNOTATIONS OF MIRRORS

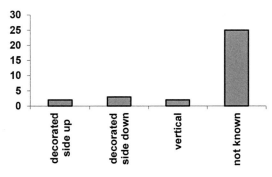

FIGURE 9: POSITION OF MIRROR

FIGURE 10: EVIDENCE OF CONTAINMENT OF MIRRORS

burials are gender specific and linked to female bodies. However, only the bodies found in the burial from Chilham Castle in Kent (Parfitt 1998: 348) and the Yorkshire mirror burials have been confirmed as female. Burials such as the Dorchester mirror burial (Fulford and Creighton 1998: 339) or the Birdlip mirror burial (Smith 1907-09: 332) have been interpreted as female because they are associated with mirrors. On the other hand, the Scilly Island mirror burial has been interpreted as male because it contains a sword (Johns 2002), but there is no conclusive evidence for gender (Figure 8). It is probable that mirror burials had female gender associations in Yorkshire, but there is not sufficient evidence to suggest that this is applicable elsewhere.

The link between mirrors and the colour red is therefore likely to have other symbolic meaning. As already discussed in chapter 6, the reflective quality of mirrors may have had symbolic connotations. Three of the decorated mirrors, the Dorton mirror (Farley 1993; Smith 1907-09: 337) the Chilham Castle mirror (Parfitt 1998: 345), and the Pegsdon mirror (Burleigh and Megaw 2007) were found beneath the human remains with the plain, undecorated side facing upwards (Figure 9). Jope suggested that the mirrors may have symbolized water as the reflective qualities of the plain side of the mirror may have been perceived as similar to that of water (Jope 2000: 140). As stated above, burials were often found in the vicinity of water, which may have been seen as a liminal zone, a boundary to the Otherworld. The laying of the corpse onto an upward facing mirror may have been a symbolic immersion into the boundary of the Otherworld. The liminality of this imagery may have been enhanced by the liminality and ambiguity of the colour red as a symbol of transformation, life and death as discussed above and in earlier chapters.

A further possible symbolic aspect of mirror burials is the wrapping or containment of mirrors. There is conclusive evidence that the Bryher mirror was wrapped in a cloth bag. However, if we take into account that brooches and pins on top of mirrors could be evidence for wrapping, and accept that boxing or placing inverted carts over mirrors are also a type of containment, then most of the mirror burials would fall into this category (Figure 10).

Concealment of mirrors is not limited to burial contexts. The Holcombe mirror found placed upside down in a pit within an Iron Age enclosure underlying a Roman villa may have been wrapped in organic material such as cloth or leather (Fox and Pollard 1973: 19) and the Balmaclellan mirror, which was found together with other objects in a Scottish bog had been wrapped in cloth (Smith 1907-1909: 334). If mirrors had been mere functional toiletry tools, the careful wrapping and manner of deposition does not make much sense. In terms of colour the wrapping or containing of mirrors is tantamount to a concealment and perhaps even preservation of the colour of the mirrors, but in any event would suggest that the colour of the mirror was sufficiently potent to warrant concealment. The symbolic meaning of containment will be further explored below in the context of cart burials, but in order to explain the symbolic use of the colour red in burial contexts, perhaps another group of red or red related grave goods can provide further insight.

Pots and vessels appear as grave goods all over Iron Age Britain and again, red seems to have been the predominant colour associated with them. The wooden buckets which appear as grave goods in cremation burials in Baldock, Herts and Aylesford, Kent are made out of yew (Stead 1971a: 258, 271), which has a striking red colour and which may have had magical connotations as discussed in chapters 6 and 8. The wood of a similar bucket found in a burial in Great Chesterford in Essex cannot be ascertained, but its bronze handles were decorated with red hot glass (Stead 1971a: 278). Although the function of these buckets is not certain, they did not contain any cremated remains, and Stead's (1971a: 276) suggestion that they were used as container for wine or water for mixing seems plausible.

Other vessels such as the amphorae and the cordoned pottery tazza found in the two main Welwyn cremation burial vaults were also of varying degrees of red (Smith 1912: 3) (Figure 20b). Interestingly, the urns containing the cremated bones in these burials were probably coated with black varnish (Smith 1912: 23) which does not only make an interesting contrast to the white bones but also sets the red vessels apart as containers of liquid. If the red vessels contained red liquid such as wine or, in the case of yew buckets, water which would have very quickly turned a reddish colour (as mentioned in chapter 6) there may have been a connotation with transformation and mediation on more than one level. Wine, especially the rather thick unmixed liquid which was imported from the Mediterranean, was coveted more than beer, perhaps because it resembled blood[45] and may have shared the

same ambiguous symbolic values, but perhaps also because it was very potent as a mind altering drug, used a mediating substance between this world and the Otherworld in burial rites (Arnold 2001: 12-19). The connotations between red and transformation might also have been enhanced by the fire dogs which were found in a number of the Welwyn rite cremation burials, such as the iron fire dog from Baldock, Herts (Tylecote 1986: 387). Whilst they are made of iron and are therefore black, they may have been mnemonic markers of the red flames of fire but perhaps also of the red glow of the very iron being worked. As already discussed, fire, is also an ambiguous element, being at the same time essential for technological advancement and thus the development of civilization, but also dangerous and life threatening. In addition, it has transformative qualities as discussed in chapter 4. Some cremation burials therefore echo the triplism of colours and associated connotations discussed above in relation to excarnation: The remnants of white brittle bones symbolize perhaps male ancestral notions. These are contained in a black pottery vessel which may have been perceived as female flesh[46] and buried alongside red vessels, containing red liquid and other grave goods evoking metaphorical suggestions of red flames. Not all vessels containing cremated bone are made out of black pottery. In Baldock, for example, the cremated remains were found near a bronze cauldron and may well have been placed in it. Interestingly, although the bronze contains 10% tin and virtually no zinc, which would have resulted in a reddish appearance, the cauldron also featured black iron strip rims (Lang 1986: 388).

Even though red may have been the predominant colour in burials, not only in East Yorkshire graves as stated by Stead (1979: 87), but throughout Iron Age Britain, there are too many inconsistencies in individual burials to conclude that the red white and black triplism and its associated symbolic connotations discussed earlier in this chapter are generally applicable throughout all of the British Iron Age. Each burial needs to be explored on its own merits in terms of colour, but perhaps against the wider background of the above mentioned symbolism.

Striking Colours – Case Studies

To give an example as to how the diversity of colours within a certain burial rite can nevertheless give useful information as to possible symbolic functions I will compare two burials from East Yorkshire with particularly striking colours; the burial of the so called 'Wetwang Chariot Woman' and the 'Queens Barrow' in Arras, Yorkshire.

---

[45] The use of wine as a symbol or actual transubstantiation of the blood of Christ in Christianity comes to mind.

[46] Not only is the shape of vessels such as amphorae reminiscent of the female form, but women are sometimes described as vessels and pottery is a material created out of soft clay, i.e. earth.

The Wetwang Chariot Woman

The discovery of a cart burial of a woman, dated to the middle Iron Age period, i.e. 400 to 100 BC, in Wetwang, Yorkshire in 2001 (Hill 2001: 2-3), presents a fascinating picture. The skeleton is that of an older woman who had given birth at least once and who had suffered from a dislocated shoulder. Her torso had been covered with pig bones, a single bronze strap union decorated with coral was found underneath her knees and an iron mirror had been placed across her lower legs. The mirror appears to have had a tassel of horse hair with tiny blue beads tied to the handle. The body of a cart was placed over her body, although the cart wheels were found separately at the north end of the grave. The horse bits found at the site appear to have had red glass or enamel inlays, and the terrets and trap unions were decorated with coral studs. Each terret has five red coral studs held in place by bronze pins, although in one case a red glass stud seems to have replaced or substituted a coral stud. The burial is particularly striking as it contains more coral than any other site in Iron Age Britain. The adhesive used for the harness fittings was made out of black birch bark tar mixed with another resin or tar from a coniferous plant, possibly pine. It is not certain if the pine material was combined with the birch before manufacture of the tar or if two separate tars were mixed together (Stacey 2004: 1-2). Wood tar in prehistory would have been used as a binding agent, a preservative or lubricant. In addition, its appearance in early prehistoric burials and its use, sometimes mixed with blood, in the decoration of early ceramics in mainland Europe would suggest certain magical qualities beyond mere functionality (Kośko and Langer, 1997: 26).

The skull of the chariot woman displays some slight distortion which according to some osteoarchaeologists might have been caused by a facial haemangioma, a growth of blood-vessels which would have given half her face a red lumpy appearance. Melanie Giles described her as 'enamelled by the gods' (Giles 2008: 73-74; 2012: 248). Although other colours are present in the burial site, the predominant colour scheme appears to be bright red against bronze and various black materials which would have been in stark contrast to the surrounding white chalk landscape.

The Queens Barrow in Arras

In comparison, the grave of another woman from the East Yorkshire area, the so called 'Queens Barrow' in Arras presents a very different picture: The site revealed the crouched skeleton of a female, also orientated North South and adorned with a necklace of over one hundred glass beads of which sixty six survive. The beads are blue with varying patterns of white or yellow, apart from a small number which are a translucent green decorated with white or yellow scrolls. The grave also contained an amber ring, a decorated bronze brooch, a bronze pendant, two bracelets, a toilet set consisting of a bronze nail cleaner and bronze tweezers and a gold finger ring (Stead 1979: 8, 78-79, 85, 86; Whimster 1981: 284). The prevalent colour in this grave appears to have been blue, although the bronze brooch was decorated with red coral and the amount of coral was according to Stead (1979: 66, 87) sufficiently significant to have made it a very costly item.

Discussion

So were these very different grave goods simply the personal possessions of two very different wealthy females? Barrett (1990: 186) believes that grave goods are an inefficient means to express status to a wider audience as they are usually only seen by the closest mourners who would be well aware of the deceased's status. He believes that the meaning of material culture could be transformed by specific ritual strategies (Barrett 1990: 187). Grave goods should perhaps be considered not so much as a reflection of the individual, but as a gift exchange or a symbol of social ties and relations between the living and the ancestral dead, as proposed by Fowler (2004: 73). If the grave goods are intact they will elicit a response from the world of the dead, but broken goods would not require reciprocity (Fowler 2004: 73). Fowler's argument, however, would not explain the fact that not all grave goods in a particular grave are broken or intact nor would it explain the diversity of grave goods on the one hand but certain similarities and patterns on the other hand.

If we assume that the grave goods in the two burials are not mere symbols of status or wealth or personal adornment, what explanation can be given? The occurrence of similar grave goods in other graves in East Yorkshire would suggest that they had meaning which transcended individuality. Another cart burial of a young woman in Wetwang has similar grave goods to that of the chariot woman. Both burials contained pig remains and inverted carts, iron tyres, bronze horse fittings, terrets decorated with beads of coral and undecorated iron mirrors. In addition, the young woman's burial also contained an unusual bronze container in the form of a closed cylinder made from sheet bronze with the ends crimped around the rim, decorated with roundels of red glass and curvilinear decoration, as well as the head of a broken iron and gold pin decorated with coral (Dent 1985: 88-89). Whilst the objects deposited in the grave were therefore not identical to those buried with the Wetwang chariot woman, there were significant similarities and again, red coral and red glass seems to have been important.

A female inhumation burial discovered in Garton Slack produced thirty five blue glass beads, making blue the dominant colour of the burial (Brewster 1971: 289, 1976) and suggests comparisons with the Queens Barrow.

One explanation for the use of certain coloured materials may be gender, perhaps coupled with maturity or other symbolic values. In East Yorkshire jet rings, amber beads and glass beads, predominantly blue, white or yellow, are generally associated with adult women's graves (Henderson 1982: 31; Stead 1991: 1967). Although some beads have also been found in temples such as Hayling Island, Hampshire (Henderson 1991:108) the main concentration of glass beads found in Yorkshire comes from burials sites and beads made out of pale or translucent glass with islands of dark brown glass are only known from burial contexts. Glass beads were found in graves in other geographical areas as well. To name a few examples, a Durotrigan inhumation burial in Whitcombe revealed a female skeleton with a yellow glass ring bead and an adolescent female with a necklace of glass paste and wooden beads (Whimster 1981: 261, 262). Glass beads were also discovered in cist burials in Trevorne, Cornwall (Dudley and Jope 1965: 18-21), a cist burial in the Scilly isles (Ashbee 1954: 11) and a translucent glass bead with an opaque yellow centre was found in Culverhole Cave, Llangenydd, Gower (Boon 1979a). In the last case it is not conclusive if the bead came from an Iron Age burial setting and gender could not be identified in either the Cornish or the Welsh burials.

The use of coloured beads as gender indicators exists in other cultural contexts. Among the Oromo tribe in Ethiopia, Kenya and Somalia beaded necklaces of red and yellow amber are worn on the birth of a child and are meant to represent blood, regeneration and the child's healthy waste matter, which is regarded as a fertility symbol by the Oromo. These beaded amulets are worn by women and children around the neck or upper left arm. The beads have multiple functions in society; they are symbols of spiritual and temporal power as well as authority, but they also represent fertility through the concept of gender and form ultimately part of a mystical cosmology (Kassam and Megersa 1989: 29-31).

There is evidence of gender connections in relation to amber in the works of Pliny. In his Natural History (37.34) he retells one of the myths of origin of amber. According to Demostratus amber is the solidified urine of lynx. Amber derived from the urine of the male of the species is red in colour, whereas that of the female is whiter in colour. In the same chapter Pliny also mentions that necklaces of amber were worn by women north of the river Po, but neither account is particularly helpful in terms of the British Iron Age. There is evidence of amber and glass beads in male burial contexts in the Iron Age. For example, an adult male in a sword burial context in Birdsall, North Grimstone had been buried with an amber and jet ring (Stead 1965: 110; Whimster 1981: 350). More significantly, a cremation burial from Welwyn Garden City, Hertfordshire revealed numerous amber beads, translucent brown and yellow glass beads

with opaque yellow on the surface, dark blue glass beads with eye fragments, segments of glass bracelets made out of brown glass with meandering tails of opaque yellow glass and a spectacular set of twenty four gaming pieces in four groups of six pieces, coloured opaque blue, opaque yellow, opaque white and translucent green respectively (Figure 20c). The pieces were decorated with eyes, i.e. spirals of opaque white glass in a translucent green or wine coloured ground. All pieces feature five eyes, apart from one blue piece which has seven eyes. The human remains found in the burial setting belonged to an adult male (Stead 1967: 14-19, 40). Gaming pieces seem to be an odd choice for grave goods. On the other hand gaming is dealing with uncertainty of fate, something outside the control of humans (Mallaby 2003: 1-31) and therefore akin to activities like divination. There is evidence of gaming pieces from other Iron Age burial contexts, e.g. a board game with black and white gaming pieces from the so called doctor's grave in Stanway, Essex which also contains iron and bronze divination rods, surgeons' tools and a straining bowl in which remains of the medicinal plant artemisia[47] were found (Aldhouse-Green and Aldhouse-Green 2005: 123). It is conceivable that the gaming pieces, like the divination rods were instruments of mediation between this world and the Otherworld, and the person who owned them and was ultimately interred with them may have been perceived to be a powerful, but also dangerous individual, perhaps a shaman. Considering that shamans in many societies display gender ambivalence and there is evidence of gender instability in a Romano-British context (Aldhouse-Green and Aldhouse Green 2005: 145, 162-170) it cannot be ruled out that the gaming pieces from the Welwyn Garden City cremation burial had indeed female connotations.

Whilst there may be a female gender element prevalent in the use of amber and coloured glass beads, the use of coral does not appear to be gender specific, although it is frequently related to warfare. One Wetwang burial of a young adult male which also featured the remains of a pig and possibly the remains of a cart inverted over his body, does not contain any coral or enamel. The body was buried with an iron sword, a scabbard with a bronze front plate and an iron chape and back plate, two iron cylinders which had perhaps been spine covers of a wooden shield and around and on top of the body seven iron spear heads which looked as if their shafts had been broken before they were put into the grave (Dent 1985: 86-88). However, a third Wetwang burial revealed the remains of a male body with an iron sword with a decorated bronze scabbard. Two cast bronze rings on either side of the sword's suspension loop had been decorated with red enamel (Dent 1985: 90-92). A warrior burial from Mill Hill in Deal, Kent, dated

---

[47] Artemisia was used in antiquity for abortions and to regulate menstrual bleeding (Hertling 2006: 173-174), but as already stated in chapter 8, it is also known as a hallucinogenic drug.

to about 200 BC revealed not only an iron sword and bronze scabbard, but also a suspension ring decorated with red coral, a bronze brooch also decorated with coral and the remains of a shield, also decorated with coral beads. The deceased had worn a unique headgear which would have been totally unsuitable as a warrior's helmet and is usually described as a crown (Parfitt 1991: 125, 1995: 19- 20) which would suggest that he was a person of some importance. The sword was placed up side down on the body and the shield, like the inverted carts in the cart burials described above, covered the body. Coral, and indeed red enamel, are therefore non gender specific decorations and although they appear in warrior graves, they are also evident in graves not related to warfare such as that of the chariot woman.

Another suggested explanation for use of certain materials for grave goods such as coral, amber, chalk and jet is a perceived link to geographical locations. Jones (2002: 163-166) argued in relation to the British Bronze Age that substances such as amber and jet are related to certain geographical regions and derive their meaning from these connections, whereas Shennan (1993: 63) suggested that the importance of amber was connected to the fact that it came from distant lands and its connotations to long distance travel and privileged access to strange and esoteric materials which may have carried magical powers or symbolic significance. The trade in coral and amber appears to have followed different exchange mechanisms than other goods imported from the Mediterranean. According to Collis (2001: 3-5) the trade in coral continued during the fourth century BC, a period where the trade in other goods from the Mediterranean had all but disappeared. On the other hand, as the trade in other goods resurfaced in the second century BC coral no longer featured as trade item.

Where coral and amber may have connotations with distant lands, jet, shale and chalk would have links to much closer geographical locations. For example, jet found in the East Yorkshire graves may well have come from nearby Whitby and the material therefore may have connotations with ancestral landscape or regional affinity. The geographical explanation is, however, neither sufficient for the prevalence of the colour red in graves, nor does it explain the use of blue and yellow glass beads.

Amber beads, according to Pydyn (1998: 103) may have had symbolic value derived from exposure to Greek influences, although Stjernquist (1993: 93) argued that amber as a material was believed to have magical qualities and was used for the manufacture of amulets much earlier than the Iron Age. Whether or not the belief in the symbolic meaning or magical value of amber was influenced by exposure to Greek culture or was handed down from earlier generations, it is possible that amber was believed to have magical or healing power

described later by Latin writers such as Pliny and Tacitus (Krumphanzlova 1993: 188). It is not clear, whether the supposed magical power of amber is connected to its colour, its fragrance, the fact that it is a valuable rare material or that it has electrostatic properties similar to jet, another material often associated with magic. One possible explanation may be found in philology. The Greek word for amber is 'elektron' which is also used to describe an alloy of gold and silver, a material of a similar colour and shining quality. On the other hand there may also be a connection to the old Greek word 'elektor' used by Homer, meaning 'beaming sun' and it is surely the case that the material's colour and its reflective and refractive qualities evoked such solar connotations (Causey 2004: 75).

Classical mythology connects amber with the sun and untimely deaths (Causey 2004, 76), but interestingly also water. One myth mentioned amongst others by Apollonius of Rhodes in his Argonautica (4.604-611) tells how Phaeton falls from the chariot of Helios into the opening of a deep lake. The daughters of Helios who are enclosed in tall poplar trees shed tears which are described as bright drops of amber. Interestingly, Apollonius interjects the story with a brief discourse that the Celts have attached the story to themselves, but that they refer to amber as the tears of Leto's son Apollo when he came to the 'sacred race of the Hyperboreans' and 'left shining heaven'.

Pliny retells a similar myth about Phaeton in his Natural History, but he also quotes Nicias who insisted that amber is a liquid produced by the rays of the sun, effectively liquid sunshine. However, he also gives a more scientific explanation of amber as a gum of trees in which one can see winged creatures (Pliny Natural History 37.34-42). It is possible that the symbolic meaning of amber travelled with the material (Hughes-Brock 1993: 223–224) and, that British Iron Age communities knew that amber was indeed a preserved and preserving liquid with mythical and symbolical connotation to both sun and water. The preserved reflection of sunshine in water would have been a very powerful symbolic image. The reflective quality of water may have been seen as a means of communication with the Otherworld which may have been perceived as more important than water itself. In addition, the connection between water and the dead appears to be part of a fertility rite which links the dead to seasonality and agricultural cycles, especially in areas where water flow follows seasonal patterns such as the Yorkshire Gypsey Race (Bevan 1999c: 90).

It has been suggested that the magical qualities of certain materials are imbued in the materials themselves and thus artificial imitation products such as glass would not have the same magical properties (Graefin Schwerin von Krosigk 2005: 132). The archaeology of coloured materials would, however, suggest otherwise. The yellow and blue beads found in the Queens Barrow and numerous burials in Iron Age may have had similar symbolic properties as amber. The link between the sun's reflected rays on water and the blue and yellow beads is suggested by the wave like patterns found on numerous blue beads. A line from the early Irish poem 'The Voyage of Bran', which is a description of a mythical passage full of colour references and possibly contained druidic codes, describes this imagery beautifully: 'the brightness of the sea pours forth yellow and blue' (Green and O'Connor 1967: 46).

The blue and yellow beads may however have had a further function as healing agents. Colour therapists believe that blue soothes inflammation and eases high blood pressure, and exposure to ultraviolet (blue) light has been found to be a successful treatment for jaundice in babies (Holtzschue 2002: 38: Pavey 1980: 46-47). Interestingly, blue and yellow are the colours normally 'seen' in modern shamanic healing by the shaman during a healing trance.[48] Although we have no indication that colour therapy was practised by British Iron Age communities, it is not inconceivable, especially if we consider that this form of therapy relies on empirical evidence and Iron Age healers would have been astute observers of nature. One further clue to the association of blue and yellow glass and healing, although geographically removed from Iron Age Britain, lies in the blue and yellow striped miniature glass dog dated to the second century BC and found in Wallertheim in Germany. The association of dogs with healing is well known from British Iron Age sites such as Lydney and was probably based on the perception of self healing powers of dogs (Green 1989: 144). The little dog may therefore have been used as a healing amulet and perhaps its blue and yellow stripes, and indeed blue and yellow glass beads and armlets re-enforced such healing qualities.

Similarly, as already discussed in chapter 7 any magical or symbolic qualities of coral may have been imitated by other red materials. In the East Yorkshire region alone, grave goods in Arras, Burton Fleming and Danes Graves have inlays not only in coral, but also red glass, red porphyry, red pebbles, red chalk, blocks and beads made of polished sandstone coated in red resin and a clay paste mixed with haematite, which would have been used as a red colorant (Stead 1965: 64, 1979: 87). It seems that the resin coated paste and sandstone was used to imitate coral prior to the introduction of red enamel (Stead 1965: 64-65). Clearly, the colour of the material must have played a more important role than the actual material if imitation was used so readily. As suggested in Chapter 7 the colour red in coral and red hot glass may well have

had connotations to life blood, perhaps with apotropaic qualities due to its durability, lustre and preservation.

Returning to the two female Yorkshire burials, even though they are at first glance very different, they display perhaps similar symbolic themes. Both women must have been clearly important persons to have warranted the expense and complexity of their funerary rites and grave goods. One burial appears to feature mainly black and red together with a small amount of blue and bronze, and the other mainly blue and yellow with some bronze, red and gold, but there are parallels. Both share elements of preservation and containment and both include colours or coloured objects with symbolic values which may have operated as agents or mediators between this world and the next world.

There are however also significant differences concerning the coloured materials. Water and sun are external elements and the effect of a necklace of beads with such metaphorical connotations could be perceived as the submersion of the body into water hit by sunrays. There may be parallels with mirror burials, where the placing of a body onto the shiny surface may also symbolize submerging the body into water,[49] but it is also reminiscent of the ritual sacrifice of objects in lakes such as in Llyn Cerrig Bach or human victims such as Lindow man II (Figure 20d). If this line of thought is followed, it cannot be ruled out that this burial is perhaps evidence of a ritual sacrifice, perhaps a symbolic drowning, rather than just the burial of a woman of importance.[50]

Red, on the other hand, if it indeed symbolized blood, is a bodily fluid with multifaceted meaning as discussed above and in chapter 7. Red glass and coral are often found on objects which are either connected to violence and warfare or piercing, such as swords, scabbards, shields, horse gear or brooches. Red is possibly also part of a symbolic triadism of red white and black. Whereas the dyadism of white and black suggests connotations of opposites such as day and night, life and death, light and dark, positive and negative, the addition of red creates a tension between these two opposites, but perhaps also refers to a crossing of boundaries (Green 1998a: 225-226). In British Iron Age iconography, triplism such as the addition of a third horn on cattle or triple penises or teats on horses may have been interpreted as a deliberate act of disturbing the natural order of life, yet at the same time the creation of a symbolic link between

---

[48] Personal comment from Mary Madhavi, initiate of the shamanic star maiden circle and healer.

[49] The symbolic interpretation of mirrors as metaphor for water might have been reinforced in the Wetwang Chariot burial by the addition of blue beads.
[50] There is evidence of violent deaths and humans being buried alive in the East Yorkshire Iron Age burials. One burial site discovered in nearby Garton Slack revealed the remains of a 30 year old woman and a young man in his late teens together with that of a six month old foetus. The bodies of the man and woman had been pinned down with a wooden stake. It has been suggested that the couple had been buried alive and the child was born in the grave as a result of the trauma (Brewster 1976: 115).

opposites (Green 1998a: 224-225). The addition of red in the context of burials could therefore have been a very powerful intervention into the natural order of death. In excarnation burials the deceased's bodies would have been allowed to disintegrate naturally into distinctive parts of white ancestral bones and black earth and their spirits may have passed on to the Otherworld. However, the addition of a huge quantity of red in an inhumation burial might have symbolized an artificial preservation of blood, thereby preventing the body from decomposition and disintegration and ultimately from leaving the world of the living. At the same time the body is contained within the ancestral earth at the edge of but still close to the community of the living. The elements of containment such as placing the body of a cart over the body, and dismantling the wheels, thereby preventing actual and symbolic movement, may strengthen this argument. The body of the chariot woman, and perhaps to a lesser extent also the woman in the Queen's Barrow, would therefore have remained symbolically in a stasis between the world of the dead and the world of the living. She would not have been allowed to come back and haunt the living, nor would she have been allowed to move on, but perhaps had to act as a mediary between the world of the dead and the world of the living. Again, it cannot be ruled out that the chariot woman had been sacrificed.[51]

The deposition of human bodies in bogs may have been perceived to have had a similar effect of keeping the deceased in a form of stasis as the preservative qualities of bogs may have been well known (Chamberlain and Parker Pearson 2001: 46). The features of triplism found in the context of the remains of the body referred to as Lindow Man II (Figure 20d) may strengthen the argument for such interpretation. This well groomed, well nourished male who had clearly been of some status, was killed in an elaborate ritual. He was struck twice on the head with such force that pieces of bone were driven into his cranium, then he was garrotted and his throat was cut before he was finally placed face down into a shallow pool within a bog in Lindow Moss, Cheshire (Stead and Turner 1985: 26-29).

This trifold killing, however, has further elements of triplism. The blow to the head was a killing of the skull, the garrotting took away the man's breath, perhaps perceived to be his life force or an element of soul and the cutting of his throat would have spilled his blood, a

further medium of life force, thus dealing with a triple aspect of personhood. If we look at the colour context, the blow to the skull might have evoked images of white bone, the naked body may have looked pale against the backdrop of the blackish bog water, yet on the assumption that the preservative qualities of the bog were known, the preservation of flesh as a black substance may already have been in the minds of those carrying out the sacrifice. In addition to this dualism of black and white, red as a third colour is added by the cutting of the man's throat, which would have had the effect of huge quantities of red blood spurting out, had it been carried out at the same time as the garrotting (Chamberlain and Parker Pearson 2001: 66). Interestingly, the body had been naked but for an armlet of red fox fur, worn on his left upper arm (Stead and Turner 1985: 26). Perhaps the red colour meant to echo the colour of his blood and was perhaps also deliberately introduced to complete the triad of colours, thus creating a deliberate symbolic intervention into the natural order of things.

Whatever the circumstances of the two women's death or their function and role in life, the survivors must have had reasons to keep both bodies in a controlled stasis between the world of the living and the world of the dead and colours acted as powerful agents in a multilayered and multifaceted symbolism to keep them preserved in this liminal place.

Pit Burials

Pit burials appear mainly in the chalk lands of Wessex in sites such as Danebury, Hampshire or Gussage All Saints, Dorset and are dated to the early and middle Iron Age. The remains found in pits are the results of both primary and secondary burials, and depositions of whole bodies or mere body parts, all during the same period and in the same settlements. Cunliffe's (1995a: 85-88) suggestion of a seasonal 'life cycle' of pits and a 'pit belief system' was contradicted by Hill (1995: 125-128), who argued convincingly that the deposits in pits were a distinct, irregular social practice involving a specific range of deposits and carried out according to site specific rules and sequences (Hill 1995: 75).

Colour Implications of Pits and Infill

On the most superficial visual level, the mere contrast between the white chalklands of Wessex and the darkness of the pits dug into them would have been quite striking.

The shape of the pits, the chthonic associations linked to dark caves and holes, but perhaps also the associations between community, landscape and female goddesses found in later Irish myth such as the Irish goddess of Tara, Meadhbh (Ó hÓgáin 1999: 133-134) evoke suggestions of life and death symbolism, but also metaphors of womblike spaces and of white bone.

---

[51] If the two female bodies in Yorkshire had indeed been sacrificed, it cannot be assumed that they had gone to their deaths unwillingly, that they were from outside the community or perceived to be dangerous whilst living. Amongst the African Dinka tribe, spiritual leaders called masters of the fishing spear are sometimes buried alive of their own volition in order to give the tribe life and ensure that they are not perturbed by evil. The body is placed on a platform in a hollow in the ground and covered by a second platform which is covered with dung and after a period of time he becomes part of the earth (Lienhardt 2004: 123).

In addition, the infill depositions themselves may have had their own specific colour associations. The interpretation of such infill is of course hampered by the fact that the archaeological record only reveals part of what was originally deposited and as such offers a biased picture (Hill 1995: 3). Evidence of materials such as leather, wood, fabric or flowers would have all but disappeared, but this does not mean that the remaining objects should not be examined for certain trends and patterns. Even though we do not have the full picture of the infill, we are still able to draw certain conclusions from the remaining archaeology. The three objects mostly found with human remains were fragmented quern stones, iron implements and worked bone or antler (Hill 1995: 55). The quern stones, made out of light coloured stone, the white antler and bone tools such as spindle whorls or loom weights and equally white chalk moulds were predominantly found in the lower and middle fill of pits (Hill 1995: 47). The middle and upper thirds of the pits contained iron implements and material such as grain and plant remains which had often been deliberately charred before deposition (Hill 1995: 74).[52] Whilst the charring would have made the grains useless as seed grain or for the production of foodstuffs, it would also have rendered them black. According to Cynthia Poole (1995: 260) timbers, grain and charcoal layers were deliberately burnt in situ in the Danebury pits, as indicated by the discoloration of the chalk to a blue/grey colour. This brings a further colour element into the picture. The burning would have resulted in a transformation from green or brown to black through the medium of red flames. Equally, the iron implements would have been of a black-ish colour, perhaps showing some red rust.

Many pits containing human remains contained pottery sherds, possibly deliberately broken, which were usually burnished and often also decorated (Hill 1995: 68). Surface treatments like the application of crushed iron oxide and other forms of burnishing achieved a glossy red or black surface on the ceramics (Cunliffe 1984: 308-308, 2003: 127-130; Cunliffe and Poole 1991a: 300).

The remains of a large variety of wild animals were found in pit burials, but depositions of corvicaes, kittiwakes and badgers, all of which are either black or black and white in colour, are more frequently encountered. According to Wait ravens were much more common in the context of ritual deposits during the Iron Age than the bird population would suggest (Wait 1985: 138). At Winklebury in Hampshire a unique assemblage of a red deer and twelve foxes were found in a pit context. The adult, probably male red deer was well articulated which would indicate that it entered the pit with its skin intact.

There was some indication of gnawing on the antlers and bones of the deer and also the bones of the foxes (Green 1992: 125; Smith 1977: 64-65; Wait 1985: 138), but it is possible that all thirteen animals or at least the foxes were still alive when deposited in the pit, but the fact that the deer was found in a complete and articulated state would indicate that infill followed very quickly after its death (Smith 1977: 64) and it is possible that the animals were deposited because of their specific colour.

Human Remains

Human remains were at least in the middle Iron Age deposited after quern stones and metal working moulds (Hill 1995: 47) and appear to belong to three different groups. The first group consists of the articulated remains of children, often neonatal; the second group is made up of the articulated bodies of adults. Bodies belonging to either group would have been deposited soon after death or perhaps while they were still alive, but before decay had begun. According to Cunliffe (1995a: 73-75) most of the articulated whole burials in Danebury show indication that bodies may have been bound, perhaps even buried alive. The presence of slingshot in some of the pits and may be a further indication of a violent, and perhaps bloody, death for some of the human remains. For example, the remains of a young adult male found in a pit in Gussage All Saints, shows severe cuts on the tibia and left clavicle which were inflicted just before or after death, probably by a sword or axe. Keepax believes that the injuries are consistent with slicing rather than chopping and suggests that the wounds may have been caused by combat (Keepax 1979: 164, 167, 169). It is possible that the body may have been covered in fresh red blood and may have been still bleeding, when it was deposited in the pit. The striking image of flowing red blood on those bodies which died violently in the pits or immediately before deposition may have been perceived as a temporary medium of transformation from one stage to another, very much like the red flames which charred plant and wood material.

The third group consists of deposited body parts, which had either been deliberately dismembered prior to deposition or deposited after any connecting tissue had decayed (Cunliffe 1995: 47) suggesting perhaps ancestral connotations linked to the white colour of bone.

Other than evidence of binding on some of the bodies, we do not have any evidence of specifically coloured clothing or shrouds used for deposition, although the absence of fibulas might indicate that the bodies were deposited naked (Cunliffe 1984: 450). There are only very few objects found in pits which are made out of strikingly different colours, such as blue or yellow glass beads. Only three blue glass beads were found in Gussage All Saints and they were not found in the context of human remains (Wainwright 1979: 187). In

---

[52] Pollard (1996: 111) noted that the deposited wood in the riverside pits in the late Iron Age pits in St Ives, Cambridgeshire seemed to have been made up of boundary features such as hedges and fences, thus re-inforceing boundary symbolism and was also often charred.

Danebury only eight blue glass beads, some of which were decorated with yellow or white, were found. Only three of them were found in pits and only one of these was found together with human remains.It was buried in the neck of a female body (Cunliffe 1984: 396; 2003: 141), perhaps as a gender specific decoration.

I would therefore suggest that the emphasis on the triad of red black and white in pit burials was deliberate and reminiscent of the colours found in other burial contexts, even though pit burials are not burials in the same sense as cremation burials or other inhumation burials.

Conclusion

Colours employed in the context of burial have polyvalent meaning. There appears to be geographical divergence, and localised symbolism. Colours may be indicators of gender or at least gender related roles, perhaps as part of a multilevel symbolism which also takes into account connotations of healing and environmentally salient colour associations. Colours are used in metaphorical representations of cosmological tiers, but they are also expressions and manifestations of transformative processes, both natural and manipulated, dealing with diverse symbolic values such as memory, personhood, ancestrality, regeneration, fertility, preservation, community, death and afterlife.

Chapter 10

Transforming Skin – Body Decoration in the British Iron Age

*'Do you still in your madness imitate the painted Britons
and play the wanton with foreign dyes upon your head?'*

(Propertius Elegies 2.18 D, 1-4)

Introduction

The idea of the woad painted savage Celtic warrior which has been firmly implanted in our minds through imagery such as the 16th century engraving of a tattooed headhunter by Theodore De Bry or Henry Ford's illustration in a children's book written in the early 20th century by Fletcher and Kipling, which shows clean shaven, pale Roman officers opposing dark skinned, tattooed and wild haired Britons. Hingley believes that the imagery in this particular book is typical of British imperialism, in as much as the Romans are likened to British officers and the wild Britons to Indian natives (Aldhouse-Green 2006: 3-4; Hingley 2000: 65). More recently Hollywood has used the opposite imagery in embracing the notion of the noble savage in films like the notoriously inaccurate Braveheart, which played on the 'Celtic heritage' of the Scottish freedom fighter William Wallace by showing him as a woad painted, blood splattered and wild haired warrior, or the film King Arthur, set during the later Roman British occupation, where the indigenous freedom fighting tribes living north of Hadrian's wall are referred to as 'woads' and decorated with swirling blue 'Celtic designs'. The archaeological and historical evidence for body decoration in the British Iron Age is, however, limited and does not necessarily support such imagery. In this chapter I will discuss the evidence for body art as well as its function and meaning.

Evidence for Body Decoration

Written Sources

The numerous classical sources which refer to body decoration practised by indigenous British tribes are listed both in the original Greek or Latin and in translation in Appendix 4. These sources are, however, inconsistent and less than conclusive.

As far as body paint or decoration is concerned, the sources date from the first century BC to the fourth century AD and whilst the earlier texts refer to British tribes, the later ones clearly refer to Northern tribes and specifically the Picts. There is an unresolved debate as to whether the people referred to as Picts were related to Iron Age Britons. The word Pretani or Briteni and the old Irish version of the people of Britain, Cruthen or Cruithni derive possibly both from P Celtic Priteni, meaning tattooed people or people of designs (Pyatt *et al.* 1995: 71; Sutherland 1994: 40). The Picts were referred to as Cruithni in early Irish sources and this has led to an argument that these were the same people as the Priteni, but this could be simly an eliptic interpretation of the classical sources based on the translation of the name as linked to tattooes and body painting. According to Dunbavin the earliest reference to Cruithni was to a tribe in Ireland, mentioned in myths, sagas and annals, but there is no indication in either that these people tattooed their bodies (Dunbavin 1998: 2-3). Some sources such as Bede or Nennius suggest that the Picts were invaders, related to the Scythians and therefore not linked to the earlier Irish tribe at all.

Secondly, the earlier writers such as Caesar, Pliny, Martial, Propertius and Ovid who were temporally much closer to the British Iron Age period, do not refer to actual designs, but rather to body colour and staining. Only later writers such as Herodian, Solinus and possibly Bede, who, as already stated, may have written about people who were unrelated to the British Iron Age tribes, refer to tattoos or scarring and actual designs such as animals. Whether tattoos were widespread amongst the Picts or post Roman Northern British tribes is not certain, as the Classical written sources are sparse, and there are no clear references to such customs in early Welsh and Irish myth (MacQuarrie 2000: 44-45). If Caesar had personally seen figurative body decoration on Iron Age Britons, he would surely have described such an alien and in the eyes of the Roman beholder doubtless barbarian custom. Thomas (1963: 89) referred to a passage in Tacitus' Agricola as possible evidence for tattooing. However, Tacitus not only writes specifically about the Caledonians, but the interpretation of the wording 'decora gestantes', usually translated as 'decorations he had earned', as 'tattoos' is far fetched. Elsewhere, Tacitus makes an unambiguous reference to body painting in his description of the Eastern Germanic Tribe of the Harii, using the words 'tincta corpora' (Tacitus Germania 43). He would surely have been more specific in his description of the Caledonians, had he wanted to describe the custom of tattooing.

Gillian Carr (2005: 278) suggested that the word 'inficere' in the relevant passage of Caesar's De Bello Gallico, should be translated as the Britons 'infecting' themselves with glass, thereby implying tattoos or scarification. However, the word 'inficere' is usually translated as 'to stain' or 'to dye' rather than 'to infect' and it is also unlikely that tattoos or scars would have been cut with glass.[53] Instead needles or metal implements such as knives[54] would have been used, and such a procedure would not have resulted in a sky blue colour unless some other agent had been introduced. In Greek and Roman antiquity branding and tattooing was not practised save as a penalty for slaves and prisoners or as a marker for Roman lower class professions such as undertakers (Jones 2000: 7; Bodel 2000: 142)[55] and the Greek word 'stigma' was used for such body decoration (Jones 1987, 2000: 2). Tattoos or branding would have been perceived as barbarian (Jones 1987: 155) and Caesar would not have left out the opportunity to imply the barbaric nature of the Britons by using the word 'stigma' in his description.

Thirdly, the description of material used for body painting or staining and the resulting colour is inconclusive. Caesar, who is often quoted as the main source of evidence of the woad stained British warrior, used the word 'vitrum'. Pomponius Mela, who may have used Caesar as a source, also refers to 'vitrum'. 'Vitrum' has been sometimes translated as woad, but it possibly refers to a copper mineral pigment such as azurite or malachite (Pyatt et al. 1991: 69) rather than a plant derived dye. However, to add to the confusion, Carr (2005: 278) correctly argues that the word 'vitrum' has been used to describe woad by Vitruvius in his Architectura (7.14, 2). He claims that 'vitrum' is called 'isatis' by the Greeks. 'Isatis' is referred to by Pliny as a dye plant and is more than likely to be woad, which is still called 'isatis tinctoria' by botanists. Pliny classes woad, i.e. 'isatis tinctoria' (Natural History 20.59), amongst the lettuce plants and describes its use as a dye of wools. He accurately describes its leaves as similar to those of wild sorrel and also remarks on its healing properties. 'Isatis tinctoria' does not only contain indigo, the same dying chemical as 'indigofera tinctoria', albeit in far smaller concentration, but it is in fact still used in modern homoepathy for its anti viral properties (Bernd Hertling, pers. comment).

Pliny is the only writer who specifically refers to the use of a vegetable dye as basis for body staining in Iron Age Britain (Pliny Natural History 22.2). However, he states that the wives of the Britons and their daughters-in-law use a Gaulish plant called 'glastum' to dye their bodies, which makes them look like Ethiopians. He likens the plant to the plantain, which looks very different from woad. Glastum may be woad, but it has also been translated as greenweed or 'genista tinctoria'. However, that particular plant does not look like plantain either and would in any event produce a green or yellow stain (Cardon 2007: 180), which would be difficult to reconcile with Pliny's reference to the British women looking like Ethiopians. Moreover, it is not certain what colour Pliny actually meant when he referred to Ethiopians. The colour references used by classical writers are inconsistent. Caesar, Propertius and Martial use the term for 'sky blue', Ovid's use of the word 'virides ' may hint at a green colour and Propertius refers also to 'Belgic colour'. The latter, however, may be a term used to describe the cosmetic nature of body paint in general rather than a specific colour. Pliny's reference to British women staining themselves and looking like Ethiopians may describe a hue similar to a naturally dark tanned colouring. But it is also possible that Pliny refers generally to a darker skin coloration without a specific colour association, or, as he is not the most reliable source, perhaps he is reminded of the nearly blue black skin colour of other African tribes. There is also a further intriguing possibility. Elsewhere in his Natural History (6.190) Pliny writes about the Ethiopian tribe of the Mesaches who are ashamed of their black colour and smear their whole body with red clay. This is reminiscent of a passage in Herodotus (7.69) who described the Ethiopian warriors in the Persian campaign of Xerxes thus: 'when they went to war they painted half their bodies with white chalk and the other half with vermilion'. Perhaps the association in Pliny's account of British women hints at a red body stain or paint.

Finally, with the exception of Caesar none of the earlier sources refers to warriors or war paint, and even Caesar refers the custom of body painting being practised by all Britons, not just the men. And whilst he states that the blue colour gives the Britons a terrifying appearance in battle, he does not specify that the paint is applied for that particular reason. He merely describes the effect it would have on a civilised Roman. Martial, Propertius and especially Pliny emphasize that body paint was practised by British women only. The poets look at the custom as a mere cosmetic decoration, but Pliny hints at religious reasons for body decoration and specifies that it is only married women who stain themselves. It is also worth noting that apart from the extremely doubtful reference mention above, neither Tacitus nor Cassius Dio who, whilst also biased, are perhaps more reliable sources for Iron Age Britain, mention the practice of body decoration. As already stated above, Tacitus does

---

[53] Propertius also uses the word '*inficere*' and in the context of his poem which deals with women using colour as cosmetics it is even less plausible to accept the translation as tattooing or scarring. Bradley (2009:175) argues that the terms simply infers that the colour does not naturally belong to the body and is a disguise of the natural colour.

[54] Carr herself (2005: 282) alludes to a green stained needle found in Dragonby as material evidence for tattooing. Solinus, who clearly refers to scarification, uses the words 'designs marked out with iron'.

[55] It appears, however, that tattooing of corpse bearers cited by Martial was a localised custom. In Puteoli, undertakers were expressly forbidden to employ tattooed workmen, perhaps with the specific intention to exclude criminals and slaves from the profession (Bodel 2000: 143).

refer to such a custom in his description of a Germanic tribe.

We have to take into account that Caesar's De Bello Gallico is an attempt at picturing the Britons as barbarians and his description may be based on hearsay (Pyatt et al. 1991: 66-67) although Caesar's own sources would have been able to verify his accounts. Pliny is often unreliable and Martial, Ovid and Propertius wrote poetry and therefore cannot be relied on as accurate ethnographic writers. Nevertheless, there must have been a readily recognizable imagery of painted Britons in the minds of cultured Romans; otherwise the poetic references would not have been understood by the poets' audiences.

The temporally closer references refer to staining rather than figurative design or tattooing and suggest female gender connotations and perhaps ritual contexts rather than war paint. The colour may be blue, green or even dark brown or red, but it can of course not be ruled out that various colours and even various materials may have been used.

In this context reference should also be made to the custom of lime washed hair. Diodorus Siculus gives an account of this practice which would have resulted in yellow spiky hair and would have been an interesting contrast to painted or stained bodies, especially if they were blue. The yellow spikes might have evoked connotations not only with horses, as suggested by Diodorus Siculus himself, but perhaps also the sun's rays or the spirit world (Aldhouse-Green 2004b: 305,306). But there is no evidence that this custom was practiced by Iron Age Britons. Diodorus Siculus mentions it in relation to the Gauls which he distinguishes from the inhabitants of Britain and none of the sources referring to body decoration of the British tribes mention lime washed or spiky hair. Strabo tells us in his Geography that the Britons were less blond than the Gauls. Whether this refers to the difference in natural hair colour or the difference between lime washed hair and naturally blond hair is uncertain, but it would strengthen the argument that the Britons did not treat their hair with lime.

Archaeological Evidence

Bog Bodies

There is very little and inconclusive archaeological evidence for body decoration. Examinations on Lindow Man II and in particular Lindow Man III suggested that there may have been some evidence of body paint. In Lindow Man III the copper levels found in the skin were elevated in comparison to the average composition of minerals in the skin and it was suggested that this could neither be explained as normal skin tissue nor by the influence of the surrounding peat. Although diet could be an explanation, in this particular context there were

inconsistencies which would cast doubt on such an interpretation. It was therefore suggested as a possible conclusion that this elevated copper content was the result of a foreign substance on the skin, possibly a clay paste mixed with copper pigment which could have been intensely red, black, bright green or blue. Although attempts to find remnants of body paint on Lindow II were restricted to a search for evidence of vegetable rather than mineral dyes, it has been suggested that the green fluorescence found around Lindow II's hair and beard under examination in UV Light (Priston 1986: 71) might also be an indication of copper enrichment (Pyatt et al. 1991: 64-65, 1995: 69-70). Pyatt et al. (1995: 73) concluded that Lindow man II and III had a different nature of body painting rather than different diet and that they may have been natives of different areas and therefore differently decorated.

However, Cowell and Craddock (1995: 75) cast doubt on these conclusions. In their view, whilst the copper content on the torso of Lindow man III is higher than that of other skin samples on this particular bog body, the evidence is not of sufficient magnitude to provide convincing evidence for copper paint, especially as the original epidermis is lost. It is not clear if copper had moved from the body to bog or from bog to body, but moderately higher levels of copper can be explained by factors other than deliberate application. None of the other Iron Age bog bodies found in Britain or elsewhere in Northern Europe appear to have had traces of body paint or tattoos and the evidence for body paint from the Lindow bodies, whether vegetable or mineral based, remains therefore inconclusive.

Gaulish Coinage

It has been argued that some Iron Age coins found in Gaul are archaeological evidence of body decoration. Thomas (1963: 120) lists these coins which show male faces decorated with stars, eyes, plants, triskeles, scrolls, or waves. One face in particular displays wave and eye decoration similar to that found on glass beads. Again, the evidence is less than conclusive. The faces are not necessarily those of warriors, but arguably men rather than women. The decoration is figurative, but it is impossible to ascertain if the depictions are meant to be realistic renditions of painted or otherwise decorated faces or if the iconography of the coinage is merely symbolic or metaphorical and their meaning would have been readily understood by those minting or dealing with such coins. Even if the depictions were realistic portrayals of actual body decoration, we do not know if it would have been painted, and if so, what colour the paint would have been. Alternatively the decoration might have been the result of scarring or tattooing. Thomas likens the imagery to tattoos and in particular refers to the tattoos found on the frozen bodies of the Siberian ice bodies dated to about 500 BC excavated by Sergei

Rudenko in 1924 and 1947 in the Altai mountains on the border between the Soviet Union, China and Mongolia (Chamberlain and Parker Pearson 2001: 133; Thomas 1963: 91).

Tattoos are not unknown in European prehistory. The Neolithic frozen body found in the Tyrolean Alps, nicknamed Oetzi, displayed a series of tattoos of a bluish colour which was probably achieved by the use of powdered charcoal as pigment (Fleckinger 2003: 41-42; Spindler 1994: 169-171). These tattoos are however not representations of animals but rather simplistic patterns and, as will be discussed below, may have had functional rather than decorative purposes. The tattoos on one of the Siberian Ice men in particular showed elaborate depictions of animals such as horses, deer and mythical animals like dragons or winged lions which seem to wind themselves round the body (Chamberlain and Parker Pearson 2001: 135-136) and it is easy to imagine that any movement of the body would have had the effect of making these creatures come to life. Such pictorial depiction is very reminiscent of the descriptions of decorated northern British tribes by Solinus and Herodian, but the iconography of the Belgian coinage looks nothing like the creatures tattooed on the Siberian bodies. Indeed, none of them show any depiction of animals at all. And even though Solinus, Herodian and Claudian refer to the marking with iron and drinking in the dye which can be interpreted as scarification or tattooing, they do not describe people contemporaneous with or even geographically close to those shown on the Belgian coins.

Carr (2005: 282) suggested that needles such as the blue green stained bone needle found in Dragonby, North Lincolnshire (Greep 1996: 347), are evidence of tattooing. She claims that the razors found at the same site were also tools used in the process as may be necessary to remove hair prior to tattooing. However, Caesar mentions in De Bello Gallico 5.14 that the Britons shaved their whole bodies apart from the head and upper lip, and razors would have been used for shaving on a regular basis without any connection to tattooing. The blue green stain on the needle may be a colour, but could perhaps have been the result of oxidation of a bronze object. The report by Greep is silent as to the origin of the stain. However, Greep does state that such stained needles are usually a feature of the early Roman period (Greep 1996: 347) which would contradict the suggestion of tattooing native British warriors. Furthermore, the assumption by Carr that the needle may have been used for tattooing was presumably based on the evidence of woad at Dragonby, but woad as a pigment is not a good tattooing agent and would not have resulted in blue colour. On the contrary, as it is caustic, it would leave scars but no traces of colours as the account of the tattooist Pat Fish's experiment as published on an internet webpage demonstrated (hippy.com).

Finally, as Thomas admitted (1963: 92), there are no equivalent coins in Britain and apart from the reference to Belgian colour by Propertius in his Elegiae, all references to body decoration, whether to blue staining or painting or tattooing, specify Britain.

Woad

The use of woad as material for body paint had been questioned, as woad is not an indigenous plant to Britain and no archaeological evidence of woad had been recovered from British Iron Age sites (Pyatt et al. 1991, 61). However, this changed when the Iron Age and Romano British site at Dragonby revealed samples of woad. 18 plant fragments stemming from the central part of the plant fruit were found in the lower levels of a waterlogged pit. There is no evidence for the use of the pit, but the remains were found together with other seed remains which represent species usually found in the context of human occupation. Although no remnants of other dye plants were found in the pit, there is evidence of weld, a dye plant producing a yellow colour, at other find spots in Dragonby. The pit has been dated to the late Iron Age before the advent of the Roman army (Van der Veen et al. 1993: 367-368; Van der Veen 1996: 199-202) and the presence of woad would therefore correspond with Caesar's account. Carr argues convincingly that woad may well have been present but overlooked at other sites (Carr 2005: 279) and that in any event traces of woad leaves would only survive in exceptional circumstances. Also, it is impossible to distinguish woad pollen from the pollen of other members of the cruciferae plants (Carr 2005: 280).

In any event, it appears that woad had been introduced to Britain sometime during or even before the Iron Age. This must have happened for a specific reason and the most likely reason is its purpose as a dye plant. The process of obtaining dye as known from the context of medieval dye vats is a complex sequence of fermentation. The leaves of the plant were pulped and formed into balls for a first period of fermentation, then ground and re-fermented in a woad bath with the addition of other materials such as bran, madder or dung. Lime was added to maintain an alkaline environment and the bath would have to be kept at 50° Celsius for a few days (Edmonds 1998: 7; Van der Veen et al. 1993: 368-370; Van der Veen 1996: 211). This method was used for dying fabrics rather than obtaining pigment, but there are relatively straightforward processes to obtain the actual indigo pigment from the plant. One method is to steep the leaves in boiling water, strain the liquid, mix it with ammonia such as urine and then leave it to dry in a container (Robertson 1973: 80). When the water has evaporated, small particles of the blue indigo pigment remain on the bottom of the container and can then be scraped off. Alternatively, the woad leaves can be crushed and reduced to a paste, then moulded into a hand sized ball and dried. The dry, hard woad balls can then be broken or ground up for the pigments to be released (Cardon 2007: 369; Edmonds 1998: 7). It is therefore possible that blue pigments derived from woad were known and used in the Iron Age in Britain, but in order to ascertain whether they were used for body paint other evidence needs to be taken into account.

Cosmetic grinders

Further archaeological evidence which may shed some light on the use of body paint comes from the little cosmetic grinder sets catalogued by Jackson (1985; 2010). Jackson originally listed 99 pestle and mortar sets, increased to 625 in his more recent publication and suggested that these were used for cosmetics on the basis that any substance ground in them would have had to be very small. Possible other uses may have been the grinding of salt, spices, flavourings or medicaments (Jackson 1985: 171; 1993: 166; 2010: 12-14).

A large number of these sets were found in temple sites, graves and cemeteries (Jackson 1985: 172). They are mostly found in Britain and were probably in use during the first and second century AD, possibly even prior to the Roman conquest, although dating the sets is difficult (Carr 2005: 274; Jackson 1993: 167). It appears that they were in use at the same time as Roman cosmetic paraphernalia such as stone palettes, bronze spatulae and ligulae (Jackson 1985: 172, 175, 1993: 167; 2010: 12) and Jackson queried the reasons for this co-existence. Perhaps he thought of the sets too much in terms of mere cosmetic accessories. The use of the grinders in the context of body decoration may have had ritual connotations as suggested by Pliny, as well as or instead of merely beautifying functions. This would also explain their deposition in temples and cemeteries. If these sets were indeed used for grinding cosmetic pigments, the paint would have been unlikely to have been a fat based unguent, but possibly mineral based (Jackson 1985: 1172, 2010: 13). Carr argued that the grinders could have been used in the last stages of grinding up dried indigo pigments (Carr 2005: 274). However, as the pigments would either have to be scraped off the bottom of a container, which would result in a pigment powder, or derived from the grinding of a hard woad ball, it is unlikely that the small grinders were used for this process. Jackson demonstrated in experiments that small minerals could be ground very efficiently (Jackson 2010: 13, 14). If woad was indeed used, the grinders could have been used for grinding small parts and then mixing and binding the dried powdery pigments.

Gillian Carr suggested that the iconography shown on the grinders such as ducks, bovine or phallic designs may bear a relation to the mixing agents such as eggs, fat or semen (Carr 2005: 276). She experimented with woad pigments and several binding agents ranging from milk, beef dripping, semen, saliva, water to egg white and yolk. The colours derived vary from grey to midnight blue and the consistency ranges from watery to grease paint, but it appears that whatever mixing agent is used the paint either rubs off, flakes off easily or stays waxy, none of which would lend itself to figurative design (Carr 2005: 276). Woad as a pigment is not suitable for painting elaborate Celtic designs on faces or bodies as it smudges and rubs off (Edmonds 1998: 7). It is therefore more likely that woad was used as a stain or block body paint, but this stands in contradiction to the small scale of the grinders and would point more towards the use of a woad vat. Although there is no archaeological evidence for woad vats in an Iron Age context, not only would it make sense as much less plant material would be required[56] to stain bodies in a vat than applying pigment, and it is entirely possible that cloth or wool was stained using such a process. Also, the process of fermentation in the vat creates a pigmented scum, which stains skin after repeated contact to a nearly black lasting colour (Edmonds 1998: 7). Woad vats were known in Hellenistic Egypt (Cardon 2007: 374; Halleux 1981: 138-140) and there is a possible reference to a woad vat in early Irish myth. In the tale of Cuchulainn's boyhood deeds, the hero is dipped in three vats of water and is afterwards given a blue cloak by Queen Mugain (Kinsella 1970: 92). Even though the story does not refer to woad or dyeing as such, the triple dipping is reminiscent of the repeated dipping of cloth in a woad vat during the dyeing process (Cardon 2007: 346, 373) in order to achieve the correct colour. The colour blue is referred to in the colour of the cloak which would have been the result of such repeated dipping.

If Iron Age Britons used the woad vat or a similar process to stain their skin, the argument that the grinders were used for body paint seems less convincing. However, there is evidence of different mineral pigments from a late Bronze Age site at Runnymede. A blue bead, which had initially been taken to be blue glass, has since been identified as a mineral compound made of a mixture of silica, lime, copper mineral and a small amount of alkali, known as Egyptian Blue (Needham and Bimson 1988). The beads would have been ground to powder and used as pigment or made into a paste. The little pestle and mortar sets would have been ideally suited for this task. Smith refers to remains of antimony and rouge found with the Glastonbury mirror in his report (Smith 1907-09: 337).

---

[56] In order to obtain 1kg of pigment, 1tonne of fresh leaves is required (Cardon 2007: 371) which, if indeed all Britons used paint derived from the indigo pigment on a daily basis, would have meant substantial cultivation of the woad plant. For dyeing the same vat might have been used as in medieval times for a period of six months (Cardon 2007: 371) which makes it much more economical. Woad vats however require fermentation and the smell of fermenting woad is so unpleasant that Queen Elizabeth I forbade cultivation and preparation of woad within an 8 mile radius of her residences (Cardon 2007: 369). It is therefore possible that dyeing and staining may have been carried out away from settlements, perhaps as a seasonal activity, or even as part of a ritual such as the procession described by Pliny.

Although there is no surviving material evidence for this, it is an intriguing thought that face paint may have been red and white, instead of blue, whether merely for cosmetic purposes as Smith averred, or for other reasons. Some of the little grinder sets are decorated with either red glass or blue enamel. Perhaps the colours on the grinders relate to the colour of the substance processed in them in a similar way as the iconography relates to the binding medium as suggested by Carr. Red decorated grinders may have been used for red paint whereas blue decorated grinders may have contained blue pigments. Unfortunately, scientific analysis of the surface of the grinders has been inconclusive and no specific pigments or materials have been identified (Jackson 2010:13)

Meaning of Body Colouring

If one were to assume, despite the inconclusive evidence in written and material sources, that body decoration was practised by Iron Age Britons, the reasons for such decoration need to be explored. There are numerous explanations for body art and sometimes the people practising it are not even consciously aware as to why they are doing it. Sillitoe (1988: 314) stated that the Wola in Subsaharan Africa are unable to explain the structural social exchanges in relation to body decoration amongst themselves, but it features prominently in their lives. One of the tribe members said: 'When not decorated we are non entities, when we decorate ourselves we are big men. Women's thoughts are excited – there are notions of belonging, of status, of sexuality'.

Body decoration, whether applied in the form of paint or tattoos or even scarification, involves a transformation of the body from its natural state to a deliberately created artificial state, although the effect can vary widely. All forms of body decoration or adornments create specific impression of the adorned's self, either reflexively or to others (Treherne 1995: 127) or both. They can express creativity, individuality, or belonging, both in terms of social standing or kinship. Body decoration can be uniform or individual, abstract or descriptive, it can confirm social orders or demonstrate rebellion against them, it can form a narrative and it can be used as a form of magic. It can change significantly through contact with other cultures as differences between tattooing practices and artforms in Tahiti prior and post contact with Western society demonstrates (Kuwahara 2005: 44-59). Whatever format, however, it is a means of an expression of self awareness, identity and communication of the interrelationship between the individual and its place within society or cosmic order (Groening 2001; Svendsen 2006: 77).

Sometimes body paint is used to accentuate certain features of the face or the body and has purely beautifying functions, such as make up in the modern Western world or the face paint used by the Wodabe men in Niger once a year for the Geerewol festival where they make themselves as attractive as possible to women in a bridegroom parade dance by accentuating the whiteness of their eyes and teeth by black rims or narrowing the appearance of the nose by drawing lines (Groening 2001: 125). Hannah (2004: 100-104) argued that red ochre may have been used as body paint in Classical Athens as a cosmetic and to create the impression of a healthy tan.

Body art can also symbolize tribal, clan or family membership or indicate social standing. The Mangbetu tribe in the north east of Zaire used abstract patterns of paint made out of redwood and palm oil to indicate social superiority (Groening 2001: 158). The beautiful tattoos or 'Moko' of the Maori in New Zealand symbolise in addition to other meanings a state of freedom and nobility. Slaves were not allowed to wear any tattoos (Robley 1896: 23). Body art can have symbolic, magical, ritual or religious functions. The women of the Loma tribe in Guinea paint black pigments in the style of abstract plants on the bodies of girls during their rite of passage rituals. The paint symbolizes the transition from the natural state to a cultured grown up state. When the colours fade the girls are regarded as adults (Groening 2001: 169). Sometimes several layers of paint all meaning different things are applied. The paints and designs are not always evident, neither are they readily understood apart from by those initiates who applied them.

Protection and health, both literally and symbolically, can be another reason for body art. The Andamanese in the Gulf of Bengal apply paint made of white clay or red ochre for different reasons. They believe that only painted bodies are healthy bodies. Red ochre is perceived to be medicinally important and used internally as well as externally. Red is understood to give warmth, energy, vitality and excitement. White, on the other hand, is associated with light, good weather and therefore general well being. The clay paint is however, also a proven protection against insects (Groening 2001: 191,192). On the other hand, body paint can also have the opposite effect of poisoning.

Body paint can be in the form of block staining, abstract design, figurative depictions or may emulate animal skins. Sometimes more than one form is used simultaneously as demonstrated by the Nuba tribe in Sudan where scarification applied to women reflects the role they play in society, whereas the shade of clay with which they paint themselves is indicative of kinship (Groening 2001: 146).

The body decoration of the Iron Age Britons is generally interpreted as war paint, purely based on Caesar's account. Treherne (1995) argued in relation to Bronze Age toilet sets that any grooming utensils and therefore also any body decoration was an aesthetic celebration of the male warrior's body, both in life and death and it is tempting to interpret Iron Age body paint in this manner. Attempts to replicate Iron Age body decoration usually result in the depictions of either animals or Celtic symbols such as triskeles. However, assuming that the Roman sources carry some truth, body decoration was not an exclusively male prerogative, it was practised by either all Britons or perhaps just married women. Carr (2005: 277) suggested that the colour achieved by mixing woad with beef dripping is similar to camouflage paint. Not only would this presuppose a certain style of warfare which is difficult to reconcile with the highly visible red decoration on military paraphernalia such as swords, scabbards and horse gear, but it would also contradict the ritual use of body staining by married women as alluded to by Pliny.

Carr's argument that body staining in vats practised by both genders in the earlier Iron Age was replaced by painting and tattooing in the later Iron Age/Roman conquest period, that cosmetic grinders were rare and the grinding of pigments therefore a controlled activity involving esoteric knowledge (Carr 2005: 283) is doubtful. By 2005 more than 600 grinders had been found in Iron Age Britain (Carr 2005: 284), yet the sources dating to the later Iron Age and Roman conquest do not mention tattoos or indeed figurative decoration and refer to a practice carried out by either all Britons or all British women. There is no persuasive archaeological evidence for tattooing in Iron Age Britain and if, as Carr suggests, tattooing was a badge of courage during the Roman conquest (Carr 2005: 285) it would surely have been mentioned by some of the contemporary historians.

Furthermore her argument that body painting becomes a wholly cosmetic procedure practiced by women (Carr 2005: 286,287) does not hold true either, because later writers refer to tattoos and body decoration on men. Also, the grinders with their undoubtedly symbolic iconography exist alongside Roman cosmetic sets and must therefore have had a different and perhaps ritual function.

Figurative decoration is not mentioned by the earlier sources. Given, that figurative decoration on metal or stone usually has the effect to make inanimate materials animate, it would not make sense to paint decorations such as triskeles on moving features. The idea of staining or block painting a particular colour makes more sense, but the use of the colour blue would contradict the use of red as the principal colour used in military contexts.

In Irish myth, blue seems to have had connotations with water and cooling, possibly even healing. As mentioned above, in the tale of Cuchulainn's boyhood deeds, the hero is in such a rage that the only way to cool him down is to put him in three vats of water and the blue cloak given to him provides the colour association. The potential healing symbolism of the colour blue may have

precedents in the Tyrolean Iceman's blue tattoos. They were found mainly on those parts of his body where he would have had pain due to stresses and strains on his body and where modern acupuncturists would place needles to relieve pain. It is therefore highly likely that the function of the tattoo was one of pain relief rather than, or perhaps as well as, body decoration (Dorfner et al. 1998; Spindler 1994: 169-171). Due to its antiviral and antibacterial properties woad may well have been used as a protective measure which over time perhaps evolved into a ritual. This interpretation would not even rule out its use in a military context. Perhaps the intention was not so much one of instilling fear into the enemy, but to protect the body and encourage quick healing of wounds. Another explanation of the colour blue as a protective and life preserving colour is the appearance of blood. Blood flowing from the body is red, turning ultimately black, but blood flowing in veins appears blue, suggesting therefore perhaps a connotation between a healthy, injury free body and the colour blue (personal comment Alison Brookes).

Conclusion

It is possible that some form of body decoration was practised in the British Iron Age, but the common perception of blue, figurative, woad based war paint or tattoo is very unlikely. It is more probable that woad vats or similar procedures were used as a stain, perhaps as part of a religious ceremony or for reasons of protection. The use of woad was perhaps not gender restricted or, if it was, it is more likely that it was practised by women, possibly only married ones, rather than men. Woad staining would suggest that body decoration was not used to express individuality or difference from the norm, but perhaps rather belonging to a certain group. This could be a community, an age group, or perhaps a symbolic group playing a particular role during a religious festival or at certain times. However, this kind of decoration does not rule out that other methods, such as ground up mineral based pigments were used to apply body decoration. It is also entirely possible that a variety of colours and perhaps even different forms of decoration were used, perhaps for different purposes or to express different symbolic values. If the associations discussed in relation to decorated metal ware, especially weaponry, in chapter 7 are accepted, it is suggested that that any decoration to incite aggression or express ambiguity or transformation should have been red, rather than blue. On the other hand, blue might have been used to express protection or healing. Whilst we currently do not have any conclusive evidence from chemical analysis, it is to be hoped that future finds and development in technology might shed further light on the pigments and colours used.

Chapter 11

Conclusion

The Function of Colour in the Iron Age

In the introductory chapter of a relatively recent publication on Celtic art, Chris Gosden and J.D. Hill (2008: 12-13) made the point that any attempt to understand Iron Age art, even the examination of the sensory and cultural impact of Iron Age objects, is to a large extent still tantamount to 'chasing a ghost'. The same can be said about any attempt to understand colours in the Iron Age. The paucity of material evidence is just one of the many factors which make an examination of colour in the Iron Age problematic. But even though we may never fully understand the language of British Iron Age art and iconography, its study continues to give us valuable insights into British Iron Age culture. The same must be said for colour. Colour is as important a part of the visual language of material culture as shape or form and is equally useful for the interpretation of archaeological remains.

It would be naïve to expect a simple classification of colours with a corresponding symbolic meaning. Colours can have multilayered meanings and any interpretation must be made in the light of contextual associations. Even within a given context, certain symbolic meanings may be personal and will always elude anybody unfamiliar with such highly subjective signals. But this should not deter from taking colour into account during any examination of material objects. Even though we have no knowledge of colour perception or colour terms used in the British Iron Age, I have sought to demonstrate that we can make certain colour related observations and that there are certain recurring patterns in relation to the use of colour, which can assist in the interpretation of material objects and ultimately help us to gain a better understanding of Iron Age cosmologies and belief systems.

The close relationship – predominantly in the earlier Iron Age - between certain materials such as chalk, coral or amber, their symbolic values and their inate colours discussed in chapters 5, 7 and 9 leads me to believe that colour was not seen in isolation but was very much perceived as an important part of the material. There must also have been an acute awareness of changes in colour during transformative processes (whether human made or naturally occurring) as discussed in chapters 4, 6 and 9 such as decay, cremation, metal making or manipulation of objects, which might suggest that basic colour terms may not have been as important as the expression of change or temporary status of colour, or the connection between colour and certain values which is probably best served by using descriptive adjectives. It appears that colour may not have been looked at in isolation from its underlying material until the Roman occupation. Luminosity may have been of equal importance as hue, as outlined in chapter 6 and may have been used as a signifier of numinosity.

Colour clearly played an important role as a tool, but also in communicating values, relationships and social constructs. On a very obvious level colour operated as a marking, identifying and gauging tool in the British Iron Age. As outlined in chapter 4, the identification of metallic ore would have been based primarily on colour recognition. The awareness of the colour changes in metal during the smelting and forging processes correlating to the malleability of the material, as well as the colour of flames as an indicator of temperature would have been an important, colour related, technical skill in the metal making process.

Colour may have been a marker for gender and perhaps even social groups. It might have set certain people apart from the rest of the community, e.g. miners whose hair or skin might have been coloured by copper oxide particles, married women who wore blue glass beads and perhaps stained their bodies, or ritualists who wore white or black garments as discussed in chapters 4, 8 and 10. Perhaps there was even a social difference between those who controlled with colour and those who were controlled by colour. Whilst blue may have been an indicator for gender, it may also have had connotations with maturity or healing and may even have been used to communicate gender bending as suggested in relation to the Welwyn Garden City cremation burial in chapter 9.

Colours were used as external communication tools for example in the dazzling displays created by the brilliant, red decorated horse gear discussed in chapter 7. Yet at the same time the same red decoration may also have had internal meaning such as protection and survival.

The colour white appears to have bound the community to its actual as well as a metaphorical and perhaps ancestral landscape, as evidenced by the Uffington White Horse, the Yorkshire figurines discussed in chapter 5 and also burials in chalk lands as discussed in chapter 9. White chalk was an inherent part of the real and symbolic landscape for numerous Iron Age communities, and this may have imbued artefacts made out of chalk with corresponding symbolic meaning. It was also an important factor in community affirming rituals such as the scouring of the Uffington Horse and other rituals such as the cutting of mistletoe. Other colours, combined with their underlying materials may have had apotropaic or healing qualities. Finally, colours would also have been part of a symbolic language dealing with concepts such as seasonality, fertility, life and death, day and night and this world and the Otherworld. They may have been used in constructing and deconstructing notions of personhood and individuality in funerary rites and pit burials. It appears that colours were an important feature in a multitiered cosmology where white and gold belong to the upper astral or ancestral sphere, black and iron to the lower or chthonic sphere and red and copper alloys lie in between.

Developments in the Later Iron Age

During the Early Iron Age any symbolic qualities of colour were perhaps intrinsically linked to the underlying natural material of the objects. Their colour may even have been of secondary relevance, but the fact that, for example, amber and coral were perceived as petrified liquids seems to have been interwoven with their respective colours and the symbolic values attached to them. It would appear, however, that in the Later Iron Age colour became the primary signifier of such symbolic values. Amber and coral were replaced by other materials such as yellow and red coloured glass. They even shared certain biographical qualities, i.e. the solidification of a liquid, as well as colour and symbolic values, with the materials they sought to replace. But the most important distinction of glass as a replacement material is that it is human made.

Advances in technology during the Iron Age period, especially in the metal making process, may have been perceived as increasing control and power over the natural environment and perhaps led to a fascination with the results of such technological advancements. This might explain the prevalence of bronze and copper alloys over gold and the alloying of pure gold. But I would suggest that this is just an outward signifier of an underlying shift in belief systems and socio-political changes. The development of La Tène art with its characteristic swirling, shape shifting and ambiguous iconography goes hand in hand with an emphasis on red hot glass decoration, primarily on weapons and horse gear, the creation of shimmering and irredescent effects such as cross hatching, and the controlled disposal of the dead in cremation burials all of which indicate a concern with, control over and negotiation of boundaries, liminality, transgression and transformation and an increased emphasis on human made materials.

New Colours – New Cosmologies?

The Later Iron Age is marked by a radical change in defining landscape and the negotiation of settlements (Haselgrove and Moore 2007: 5). As Simon James and Melanie Giles have argued, the later Iron Age was not a pacified rural idyll, but marked by violence; perhaps as a result of conflict over people, land and stock, but perhaps also as a means of gaining power and personal status (Giles 2008: 66-67: James 2007).

Hill (2007: 21) argued that Later Iron Age communities were perhaps not so much ruled by a warrior elite as suggested by Cunliffe (1997: 107), but that they were corporate communities or segmentary societies of farmer warriors led by a number of competing leading individuals or families. In his view power rested with the community and required constant negotiation.

A society marked by such violent conflicts would explain the prevalence of the colour red as signifier of blood. But on a different level, conflicts concerning the material world and human power plays, whether such power was political or religious, led perhaps to increased creativity, following the principle of Heraclitus of Ephesus (Fragments 25) as stated in the fifth century BC: 'War is the father and king of all'. Yet conflict coupled with creativity, increased control and domestication of landscape and animals as well as advanced technology may have also been the source of a construct of the human self as a powerful negotiator in a world, which is no longer perceived as a simplistic model of polar opposites such as good and evil, white and black, life and death, astral divinities and dark chthonic realms. Instead we are faced with a cosmology where fatalistic belief in the total control by divine or supernatural forces had been replaced by a world in which boundaries are fluid, where risks and actions are more important than reflection or devotion, where tension, disharmony and conflict is resolved by human intervention, negotiation, agency and movement, a society where control over the material world leads ultimately to political and religious control.

It is not suggested that Iron Age societies were secular, or that political and religious power battles were new developments in the Iron Age. Perhaps an analogy with Homer's epoi can best illustrate the suggested concept. In the Iliad the gods have absolute control over the fate of humans, who pray and make sacrifices to them but are ultimately helpless against the will of the sometimes arbitrary divine powers. In the later Odyssey the hero still believes in the same divine forces, but there is a distinct shift of power at play. He negotiates with the gods and even outwits them. By his very actions he becomes powerful and godlike himself.

The existence of the divine is not negated, but dealing with it is no longer merely an act of passive supplication or devotion. It is instead characterised by negotiation, bargaining and action. Later Iron Age cosmology was still based on a multi-tiered universe, perhaps a shamanic world, where each metal (and its attributed colour) seemed to have had its place in a hierarchy of materials and colours, and where certain constant symbolic values have been ascribed to each of them. However, the visual language of transformation or the controlled negation of such changes seems to have outweighed the importance of innate colour. Creative processes such as metal making or deconstructive processes such as cremation may have been perceived to be acts of magic. The colours employed were possibly not just outward manifestations of such processes, but also added to and were probably deliberately used in the creation of the visible effects of such 'enchantment' or magic. Similarly, the effects of certain manipulation of material and colour, such as the creation of shimmering effects, brilliance or luminosity were perhaps used to dazzle and entrance the spectator, to give agency and perhaps even life to inanimate objects.

The concepts of polarity, conflict, transformation and ambiguity in Later Iron Age art and iconography are not an expression of devotion or a depiction of the pale stillness of ancestral divinity, but an articulation of the subjective experiences of powerful humans, reflecting their status as persons who transgress boundaries and undergo risks to derive power, but at the same time they are a means of dazzling, enchanting and influencing others. It makes sense that such messages are realised in materials which are not only human-made, but which have colours that share the symbolic language of ambiguity, transformation and thresholds like red hot glass or bronze. Colours are controlled by humans, but they are also used by humans to control others.

Roman influence appears to have created an interest in a new form of decorated metal ware which stands in sharp contrast to such cosmology. The geometrical and symmetrical decoration in blue and yellow as well as red glass on yellow brass suggests a further shift in cosmology in parallel to existing symbolic notions, which lacks the tension, violence and ambiguity of the red hot glass decoration. Instead it may have had connotations with healing and harmony, but it is perhaps also an embrace of Roman aesthetics[57], Roman values or a belief in a regulated world with rigid social boundaries. Perhaps it is even an overt defiance of traditional values and social structures.

The shape of Iron Age pits, the chthonic associations linked to dark caves and holes, but perhaps also the associations between community, landscape and female goddesses found in later Irish myth such as the Irish goddess of Tara, Meadhbh (Ó hÓgáin 1999: 133-134) evoke suggestions of life and death symbolism, but also metaphors of womblike spaces and of white bone.

Outlook and Further Research

For reasons outlined in chapter 1 my conclusions are primarily suggestive and further research is necessary to gain a fuller understanding of the intricacy of correlations between material, colour and symbolic meaning. Yet even at this stage correlations between colour, technology, art, belief systems and socio-political constructs emerge.

I have sought to demonstrate that colour needs to be taken into account in the examination and discussion of each and every archaeological object. Further and detailed analysis of areas which I have largely left out or treated in a discursory fashion is required. Improved technological analysis of metals and other materials will lead to a better determination of the actual colours of such materials and should also provide further insight into techniques such as alloying and patination. The colour implications in the manufacture and use of pottery and possible parallels to metalworking would provide a further interesting topic for study. A detailed examination of decorative colours used in Romano-British sites and a comparison between purely Roman and indigenous colours might shed further light on aesthetic influences or resistance. The examination of colours in a post Roman context might provide insights into areas such as retro-ideology. Another area of research would be a comparison with developments in Continental Europe to ascertain if there were common symbolic values of colours and coloured materials.

Any further research in this area, however, should not look at colour in isolation, but, in accordance with the findings of the Iron Age working party referred to in chapter 1 (Champion et al. 2001) colour must be treated as part of a holistic approach, taking into account not only the object per se, but its biography, effect, geographical, historical and multi-sensory context.

---

[57] The deliberate use of Roman colour schemes to enforce support for Rome is known from examples such as the colour scheme in Herod's Palace (Rozenberg 2004: 28).

FIGURE 11A: CARL ANDRE, 32 BAR SQUARE FUGUE ON 4 ANCIENT METALS
—MUNICH MUSEUM BRANDHORST
(PHOTOGRAPH AND © COPYRIGHT RAY FUGE)

FIGURE 11B: UFFINGTON WHITE HORSE FROM GROUND LEVEL
(PHOTOGRAPH AND © COPYRIGHT RAY FUGE)

FIGURE 11C: CHALK FIGURINE WITH SUSPENDED SWORD
(PHOTOGRAPH RAY FUGE, © COPYRIGHT HULL AND EAST
RIDING MUSEUM: HULL MUSEUMS)

FIGURE 11D: CHALK FIGURINE WITH BELT
(PHOTOGRAPH RAY FUGE, © COPYRIGHT HULL AND
EAST RIDING MUSEUM: HULL MUSEUMS)

FIGURE 12A: CHALK FIGURINE WITH HOODED CLOAK
(PHOTOGRAPH RAY FUGE, © COPYRIGHT HULL AND EAST RIDING
MUSEUM: HULL MUSEUMS)

FIGURE 12B: CHALK FIGURINE RAISING ARM
(PHOTOGRAPH RAY FUGE, © HULL AND EAST RIDING MUSEUM:
HULL MUSEUMS)

FIGURE 12C: DEAL KENT MAN
(PHOTOGRAPH AND © COPYRIGHT DOVER MUSEUM AND BRONZE
AGE GALLERY)

FIGURE 12D: BATTERSEA HEAD
(PHOTOGRAPH AND © COPYRIGHT MUSEUM OF LONDON)

FIGURE 13A: ROOS CARR FIGURINES
(PHOTOGRAPH RAY FUGE, © COPYRIGHT HULL AND EAST RIDING MUSEUM: HULL MUSEUMS)

FIGURE 13B: ROOS CARR FIGURINES
(PHOTOGRAPH RAY FUGE, © COPYRIGHT HULL AND EAST RIDING MUSEUM: HULL MUSEUMS)

FIGURE 13C: BALLACHULISH WOMAN
(© COPYRIGHT NATIONAL MUSEUMS SCOTLAND)

FIGURE 13D: KINGSTEIGNTON IDOL
(© COPYRIGHT ROYAL ALBERT MEMORIAL MUSEUM AND ART GALLERY EXETER CITY COUNCIL)

FIGURE 14A: LLYN CERRIG BACH PLAQUE
(PHOTOGRAPH AND © COPYRIGHT NATIONAL MUSEUM OF WALES CARDIFF)

FIGURE 14B: SNETTISHAM GOLD TORQUES
(PHOTOGRAPH AND © COPYRIGHT TRUSTEES OF THE BRITISH MUSEUM)

FIGURE 14C: DESBOROUGH MIRROR
(PHOTOGRAPH AND © COPYRIGHT TRUSTEES OF THE BRITISH MUSEUM)

FIGURE 14D: MONASTEREVIN DISC
(PHOTOGRAPH AND © COPYRIGHT TRUSTEES OF THE BRITISH MUSEUM)

FIGURE 15A: IRON SPEAR WITH CROSSHATCHED BRONZE DECORATION FROM RIVER THAMES
(PHOTOGRAPH AND © COPYRIGHT TRUSTEES OF THE BRITISH MUSEUM)

FIGURE 15B: BRONZE SWORD SCABBARD WITH CROSSHATCHED BRONZE DECORATION FROM
BUGHTORPE, YORKSHIRE
(PHOTOGRAPH AND © COPYRIGHT TRUSTEES OF THE BRITISH MUSEUM)

FIGURE 15C: GOLD TORCS FROM THE IPSWICH HOARD
(PHOTOGRAPH AND COPYRIGHT TRUSTEES OF THE BRITISH MUSEUM)

Figure 15d: Witham Shield
(photograph and © copyright Trustees of the British Museum)

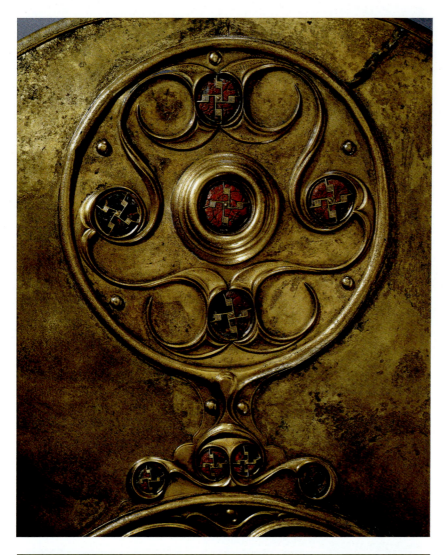

FIGURE 16A: BATTERSEA SHIELD
(PHOTOGRAPH AND © COPYRIGHT
TRUSTEES OF THE BRITISH MUSEUM)

FIGURE 16B: STRAP FITTING FROM
WESTHALL IN SUFFOLK
(PHOTOGRAPH AND © COPYRIGHT
TRUSTEES OF THE BRITISH MUSEUM)

FIGURE 16C: TERRET FROM WHITTON
(PHOTOGRAPH AND © COPYRIGHT
NATIONAL MUSEUM OF WALES)

FIGURE 16D: HARNESS FITTINGS INCLUDING HARNESS FITTING FROM POLDEN HILL, EARED MOUNT FROM
WESTHALL, SUFFOLK, BRIDLE BIT FROM SAHAM TONEY
(PHOTOGRAPH AND © COPYRIGHT TRUSTEES OF THE BRITISH MUSEUM)

Figure 17a: Cat on Patera from Snowdon
(photograph and © copyright National Museum of Wales Cardiff)

Figure 17b: Saham Toney Terret
(photograph and © copyright Norwich Castle Museum)

FIGURE 17C: KIRKBURN SWORD
(PHOTOGRAPH AND © COPYRIGHT TRUSTEES OF THE BRITISH MUSEUM)

FIGURE 17D: PART OF SANTON EARED MOUNT
(PAINTING AND © COPYRIGHT MARLIES HOECHERL)

FIGURE 18A: PART OF SANTON EARED MOUNT VARIATION OF COLOUR
(PAINTING AND © COPYRIGHT MARLIES HOECHERL)

FIGURE 18B: MISTLETOE
(PHOTOGRAPH AND © COPYRIGHT RAY FUGE)

Figure 18c: Yew wood
(photograph and © copyright Ray Fuge)

Figure 18d: Water coloured by Yew
(photograph and © copyright Marlies Hoecherl)

FIGURE 19A: PIECES OF YEW OAK AND ALDER
(PHOTOGRAPH AND © COPYRIGHT MARLIES HOECHERL)

FIGURE 19B: YEW OAK AND ALDER IMMERSED IN WATER
(PHOTOGRAPH AND © COPYRIGHT MARLIES HOECHERL)

FIGURE 19C: YEW OAK AND ALDER EXPOSED TO ELEMENTS
(PHOTOGRAPH AND © COPYRIGHT MARLIES HOECHERL)

FIGURE 19D: HOLCOMBE MIRROR handle with red glass decoration
(PHOTOGRAPH AND © © COPYRIGHT TRUSTEES OF THE BRITISH MUSEUM)

FIGURE 20A: DRAWING OF HISPANIC VASE FRAGMENT EXCARNATION BY SCAVENGER
(DRAWING AND © COPYRIGHT MARLIES HOECHERL)

FIGURE 20B: WELWYN BURIAL
(PHOTOGRAPH AND © COPYRIGHT TRUSTEES OF THE BRITISH MUSEUM)

116

Figure 20c: Welwyn Garden burial gaming pieces
(photograph and © copyright Trustees of the British Museum)

Figure 20d: Lindow Man II
(photograph and © copyright copyright Trustees of the British Museum)

Bibliography

Alexander, M. 1982. *British Folklore, Myths and Legends*. London, Weidenfeld and Nicolson.

Aldhouse-Green, M. J. 2001. Cosmovision and metaphors: Monsters and shamans in Gallo-British cult expressions. *European Journal of Archaeology* 4(2): 203-232.

Aldhouse-Green, M. J. 2001a. Pagan Celtic iconography and the concept of sacral kingship. *Zeitschrift fuer Celtische Philology* 52: 102-117.

Aldhouse-Green, M. J. 2004. *Beyond the Gods: biographies, values and cosmologies in 'Celtic' Iconography*. Amsterdam, Zesentwintigste Kroon-Voordracht, Amsterdams Archeologisch Centrum van de Universiteit van Amsterdam.

Aldhouse-Green, M. J. 2004a. *An Archaeology of Images*. London, Routledge.

Aldhouse-Green, M .J. 2004b. Crowning glories: languages of hair in later prehistoric Europe. *Proceedings of the Prehistoric Society* 70: 299-325.

Aldhouse-Green, M .J. 2006. *Boudica Britannia*. London, Pearson Longman.

Aldhouse-Green, M. J. and S. H .R. 2005. *The Quest for the Shaman*. London, Thames and Hudson.

Aldhouse-Green, S. H. R. (ed.) 2000. *Paviland Cave and the 'Red Lady': A Definite Report*. Bristol, Academic and Specialist Press.

Aldhouse-Green, S. H .R. 2000a. Climate, ceremony, pilgrimage and Paviland: the 'Red Lady' in his palaeoecological and technoetic context. In S. H. R. Aldhouse-Green (ed.), *Paviland Cave and the 'Red Lady': A Definite Report*: 227-246. Bristol, Academic and Specialist Press.

Armstrong, E. C. R. 1923. The La Tène Period in Ireland. *Journal of the Royal Society of Antiquaries Ireland* 53: 1-33.

Arnold, B. 2001. Power drinking in Iron Age Europe. *British Archaeology* 57: 12-19.

Ashbee, P. 1954. The excavations of a cist-grave cemetery and associated structures near Hughtown, St Mary's, Isles of Scilly, 1949-50. *Archaeological Journal* 111: 1-25.

AustralianMuseum. 2003, *Decomposition*. www.deathonline.net/decomposition/decomposition.

Bahn, P. G. 2001. Save the last trance for me: an assessment of the misuse of Shamanism in rock art studies. In H. P. Francfort and R. N. Hamayon (eds.), *The Concept of Shamanism: Uses and Abuses*: 51-94. Budapest, Akadémiai Kíado.

Bailey, D. (ed.) 1998. *The Archaeology of Value*. Oxford, British Archaeological Reports International Series 730.

Bailey, D. 2005. *Prehistoric Figurines: Representation and corporeality in the Neolithic*. London, Routledge.

Banck-Burgess, J. 1999. *Hochdorf IV, Die Textilfunde aus dem spaethallstattzeitlichen Fuerstengrab von Eberdingen-Hochdorf (Kreis Ludwigsburg) und weitere Grabtextilien aus hallstatt- und latènezeitlichen Kulturgruppen*. Stuttgart, Konrad Theiss Verlag.

Bancroft-Hunt, N. 1981. *The Indians of the Great Plains*. London, Little Brown and Company (UK) Limited.

Barber, E. J. W. 1991. *Prehistoric Textiles: The Development of Cloth in the Neolithic and Bronze Ages*. Princeton, Princeton University Press.

Barber, E. J. W. 1995, *Women's Work, The First 20,000 Years: Women, Cloth, and Society in Early Times*. New York, W.W. Norton and Company.

Barrett, J. C. and Kinnes, I. A. (eds.) 1988. *The Archaeology of Context in the Neolithic and Bronze Age: Recent Trends*. Sheffield, John R. Collis.

Barrett, J. C. 1988. The living, the dead and the ancestors: Neolithic and early Bronze Age mortuary practices. In J. C. Barrett and I. A. Kinnes (eds.), *The Archaeology of Context in the Neolithic and Bronze Age: Recent Trends*: 30-41. Sheffield, John R. Collis.

Barrett, J .C. 1990. The monumentality of death; the character of early Bronze Age mortuary mounds in Southern Britain. *World Archaeology* 22: 179-189.

Bateson, J. D. 1981. *Enamel-working in Iron Age, Roman and Sub-Roman Britain; The Products and Techniques*. Oxford, British Archaeological Reports British Series 93.

Bateson, J. D. 1987. Enamels from Britain to A.D. 1500, in From Pinheads to Hanging Bowls, the Identification, Deterioration and Conservation of Applied Enamel and Glass Decoration on Archaeological Artefacts. Occasional Papers 7. The United Kingdom Institute for Conservation. 1987: 3-6.

Bauer, B. S., and Stanish, Ch. 2001. *Ritual and Pilgrimage in the Ancient Andes: The Islands of the Sun and the Moon*. Austin, University of Texas Press.

Bayley, J., Crossley, D. and Ponting, M. 2008. *Metals and Metalworking: A Research Framework for Archaeometallurgy*. London, The Historical Metallurgy Society.

Bell, M. 2000. *Prehistoric Intertidal Archaeology in the Welsh Severn Estuary*. Council for British Archaeology Research Report 120. York, Council for British Archaeology.

Betz, O. 1995. Considerations on the real and the symbolic value of gold. In G. Morteani and P. J. Northover (eds.), *Prehistoric Gold in Europe: Mines, Metallurgy and Manufacture*: 19-28. Dordrecht, Kluwer Academic Publishers.

Berlin, B. and Kay, P. 1969. *Basic Colour Terms: Their Universality and Evolution.* Berkeley, University of California Press.

Bevan, B. (ed.) 1999. *Northern Exposure: Interpretative Devolution and the Iron Ages in Britain.* Leicester Archaeology Monographs No 4. Leicester, University of Leicester.

Bevan, B. 1999a. Northern exposure: interpretative devolution and the Iron Ages in Britain. In Bevan, B. (ed.), *Northern Exposure: Interpretative Devolution and the Iron Ages in Britain:* 1-20. Leicester, University of Leicester.

Bevan B. 1999b. Land, life, death, regeneration; interpreting a middle Iron Age landscape in eastern Yorkshire In Bevan, B. (ed.), *Northern Exposure: Interpretative Devolution and the Iron Ages in Britain:*123-148. Leicester, University of Leicester.

Bevan B, 1999c. The landscape context of the Iron Age square barrow burials, East Yorkshire. In Downes, J. and Pollard, T. (eds.), *The Loved Body's Corruption*: 69-93. Glasgow, Cruithne Press.

Bevan-Jones, R. 2002. *The Ancient Yew.* Macclesfield, Windgather Press.

Bick, D. E. 1990. Observations on Ancient Mining in Wales. *Early Mining in the British Isles.* Plas Tan Y Bwlch Occasional Paper No 1. Blaenau Festiniog, Plas Tan Y Bwlch, Snowdonia National Park Study Centre: 75-77.

Biek, L. and Bayley, J. 1979. Glass and other vitreous materials. *World Archaeology,* 11: 1-26.

Bird, J., Hassall, M. and Sheldon, H. (eds.) 1996. Interpreting Roman London. Oxbow Monograph 5. Oxford, Oxbow Books.

Birkhan, H. 1997. *Kelten: Versuch einer Gesamtdarstellung ihrer Kultur.* Wien, Verlag der Oesterreichischen Akademie der Wissenschaften.

Birren, F. (ed.) 1969. *Munsell: A Grammar of Colour.* New York, Van Nostrand Reinhold Company.

Blakely-Westover, S. 1999. Smelting and sacrifice: comparative analysis of Greek and Near Eastern cult sites from the late Bronze Age through Classical Periods. In S. M. M. Young, A. M. Pollard, P. Budd and R. A. Ixer (eds.), *Metals in Antiquity.* British Archaeological Reports 792: 86- 90. Oxford, Archaeopress.

Blakolmer, F. 2004. Colour in the Aegean Bronze Age: from monochromy to polychromy. In L. Cleland and K. Stears (eds.), *Colour in the Ancient Mediterranean World.* British Archaeological Reports International Series 1267: 61-67. Oxford, John and Erica Hedges Limited.

Bodel, J. 2000. Dealing with the dead: undertakers, executioners and potter's fields in ancient Rome. In V. Hope and E. Marshall (eds.), *Death and Disease in the Ancient City*: 128-151. London and New York, Routledge.

Boon, G. C. 1979. A neglected late-Celtic mirror-handle from Llanwnda near Fishguard. Bulletin of the Board of Celtic Studies 28: 743-744.

Boon, G. C. 1979a. Two Iron Age glass beads in the National Museum. Bulletin of the Board of Celtic Studies 28: 745-746.

Boon, G. C. 1975. A silver trumpet brooch with relief decoration, parcel-gilt, from Carmarthen and a note on the development of the type. Antiquaries Journal 55: 41-62.

Boon G. C. and Lewis, J. M. (eds.) 1976. *Welsh Antiquity: Essays mainly on Prehistoric Topics Presented to H. N. Savory upon his Retirement as Keeper of Archaeology.* Cardiff, National Museum of Wales.

Boriç, D. 2002. Apotropaism and Temporality of Colours. In A. Jones and G. MacGregor (eds.), *Colouring the Past*: 23-43. Oxford, Berg.

Born, H. 2004. Auch die Bronzen waren bunt. In V. Brinkmann and R. Wuensche (eds.), *Bunte Goetter: Die Farbigkeit Antiker Skulptur*: 126-132. Munich, Glyptothek.

Boyd, C. E. and Dering, P. J. 1996. Medicinal and hallucinogenic plants identified in the sediment and pictographs of the Lower Pecos Texas Archaic. *Antiquity* 70: 256-275.

Bradley, M. 2004. The colour 'blush' in ancient Rome. In L. Cleland and K. Stears (eds.), *Colour in the Ancient Mediterranean World.* British Archaeological Reports International Series 1267: 117-121.Oxford, John and Erica Hedges Limited.

Bradley, R. 1988. Hoarding, recycling and the consumption of prehistoric metalwork; technological change in Western Europe. *World Archaeology* 20 (2): 249-260.

Bradley, R. 1990. *The Passage of Arms.* Cambridge, Cambridge University Press.

Bradley, R. 2002. *The Past in Prehistoric Societies.* London, Routledge.

Brailsford, J. and Stapley, J. E. 1972. The Ipswich Torcs. *Proceedings of the Prehistoric Society* 38: 219-234.

Brailsford, J. 1975. *Early Celtic Masterpieces from Britain in the British Museum.* London, British Museum Publications.

Brailsford, J. 1975a. The Polden Hill Hoard. Somerset. *Proceedings of the Prehistoric Society* 41: 222-234.

Breathnach, M. 1982. The sovereignty goddess as a goddess of death. *Zeitschrift fuer Celtische Philology* 39: 243-260.

Brewster, T. C. M. 1971. The Garton Slack chariot burial, East Yorkshire. *Antiquity*, XLV: 289-292.

Brewster, T. C. M. 1976. Garton Slack. *Current Archaeology* 51: 104-116.

Brinkmann, V. and Wuensche R. (eds.) 2004. *Bunte Goetter: Die Farbigkeit Antiker Skulptur.* Munich, Glyptothek.

Brinkmann, V. 2004. Einfuehrung in die Ausstellung. In V. Brinkmann and R. Wuensche R. (eds.), *Bunte*

Goetter: Die Farbigkeit Antiker Skulptur: 24-69. Munich, Glyptothek.

Brookes, A. 2004. *The Visible Dead: A New Approach to the Study of Late Iron Age Mortuary Practice in South Eastern Britain.* Unpublished PHD University of Wales College, Newport.

Brooks, J. A. 1987. *Ghosts and Legends of Wales.* Norwich, Jarrold Colour Publications.

Brueck, J. 1995. A place for the dead: the role of human remains in Late Bronze Age Britain. *Proceedings of the Prehistoric Society* 61: 245-277.

Brueck, J. 1999. Ritual and rationality; some problems of interpretation in European archaeology. *European Journal of Archaeology* 2(3): 313-344.

Brysbaert, A. 2004. Take it or leave it: Towards more non-destructive approaches in Aegean and Eastern Mediterranean Bronze Age Painted Plaster Studies. In L. Cleland and K. Stears (eds.), *Colour in the Ancient Mediterranean World,* British Archaeological Reports International Series 1267: 9-15. Oxford, John and Erica Hedges Limited.

Brzeziński, W. and Piotrowski, W. (eds.) 1997. *Proceedings of the First International Symposium on Wood Tar and Pitch.* Warsaw, State Archaeological Museum.

Budd, P. and Taylor, T. 1995. The faerie smith meets the bronze industry: magic versus science in the interpretation of prehistoric metal making. *World Archaeology* 27: 133-143.

Burleigh, G. and Megaw, V, 2007. The Iron Age mirror burial at Pegsdon, Shillington, Bedfordshire. *The Antiquities Journal* 87: 109-140.

Butler, R. M. (ed.) 1971. *Soldier and Civilian in Roman Yorkshire.* Leicester, Leicester University Press.

Butt Colson, A. 2001. Itoto (Kanaimà) as death and anti structure. in L. Rival and N. L. Whitehead (eds.), *Beyond the Visible and the Material: The Amerinianization of Society in the Work of Peter Rivière*: 221-234. Oxford, Oxford University Press.

Cain, H. U. and Rieckhoff, S. (eds.) 2002. *Fromm Fremd Barbarisch: Die Religion der Kelten.* Mainz, Von Zabern Verlag.

Caplan, J. (ed.) 2000. *Written on the Body; The Tattoo in European and American History.* London, Reaktion Books Limited.

Cardon, D. 2007. *Natural Dyes: Sources, Tradition, Technology and Science.* London, Archteype Publications.

Carr, G. and Knuesel, C. 1997. The ritual framework of excarnation by exposure as the mortuary practice of the early and middle Iron Ages of central southern Britain. In A. Gwilt and C. Haselgrove (eds.), *Reconstructing Iron Age Societies,* Oxbow Monograph 71: 167-173. Oxford, Oxford Books.

Carr, G. 2005. Woad, tattooing and identity in later Iron Age and early Roman Britain. *Oxford Journal of Archaeology* 24 (3): 273-292.

Carr, G. 2007. Excarnation to cremation: continuity or change? In C. Haselgrove and T. Moore (eds.), *The Later Iron Age in Britain and Beyond*: 444-453. Oxford, Oxbow Books.

Causey, F. with Shepherd, J. 2004. Amber. In L. Cleland and K. Stears (eds.), *Colour in the Ancient Mediterranean World.* British Archaeological Reports International Series 1267: 74-77. Oxford, John and Erica Hedges Limited.

Chamberlain, A .T. 2003. Lunar eclipses, Saros cycles and the construction of the Causeway. In N. Field and M. Parker Pearson. *Fiskerton: An Iron Age Timber Causeway with Iron Age and Roman Votive Offerings*: 136-143. Oxford, Oxbow Books.

Chamberlain, A. T., and Parker Pearson, M. 2001. *Earthly Remains: The History and Science of Preserved Human Bodies.* London, The British Museum Press.

Chamberlain, A. T. and Parker Pearson, M. 2003. Social implications of lunar eclipse measuremens for caldendrical knowledge and archaeoastronomy. In In N. Field and M. Parker Pearson. Fiskerton: An Iron Age Timber Causeway with Iron Age and Roman Votive Offerings: 144-148. Oxford, Oxbow Books.

Champion, S. 1976. Coral in Europe: Commerce and Celtic Ornament. In P. M. Duval and Ch. Hawkes (eds.), Celtic Art in Ancient Europe: Five Protohistoric Centuries, Proceedings of the Colloquy held 1972 at Oxford Maison Francaise: 29-37. London, Seminar Press.

Champion, S. 1995. Jewellery and adornment. In M. J. Green (ed.), *The Celtic World*: 411-419. London, Routledge.

Champion, T. C. and Collis, J. R. (eds.) 1996. *The Iron Age in Britain and Ireland: Recent Trends.* Sheffield, J. R. Collis Publications.

Champion, T. C., Haselgrove, C., Armit, I., Creighton, J. and Gwilt, A. 2001. *Understanding the British Iron Age: an agenda for action. A Report for the Iron Age Research Seminar and the Council of the Prehistoric Society.* Salisbury, Trust for Wessex Archaeology

Chandler, D. 2002. *Semiotics; the Basics.* London, Routledge.

Chapman, J. 2002. Colourful Prehistories: The Problem with the Berlin and Kay Colour Paradigm. In A. Jones and G. MacGregor (eds.), *Colouring the Past*: 45-72. Oxford, Berg.

Chapman, M. 1995. 'Freezing the Frame': Dress and ethnicity in Brittany and Gaelic Scotland. In J. B. Eicher (ed.), *Dress and Ethnicity*: 7-28. Oxford, Berg.

Charles, J. A. 1980. The coming of copper and copper-base alloys and iron. In T. A. Wertime and J. D. Muhly (eds.), *The Coming of Age of Iron:* 151-182. New Haven and London, Yale University Press.

Clarke, J. 2004. Colour sequences in Catullus' long poems. In L. Cleland and K. Stears, (eds.), *Colour in the Ancient Mediterranean World,* British Archaeological Reports International Series 1267: 122-125. Oxford, John and Erica Hedges Limited.

Clarke, M. 2004. The semantics of colour in the early Greek word-hoard. In L. Cleland and K. Stears, (eds.), *Colour in the Ancient Mediterranean World*, British Archaeological Reports International Series 1267: 131-139. Oxford, John and Erica Hedges Limited.

Cleland, L. 2004. Introduction. In L. Cleland and K. Stears, (eds.), *Colour in the Ancient Mediterranean World*, British Archaeological Reports International Series 1267: v-vii. Oxford, John and Erica Hedges Limited.

Cleland, L. 2004a. Colour in antiquity. In L. Cleland and K. Stears, (eds.), *Colour in the Ancient Mediterranean World*, British Archaeological Reports International Series 1267: 140-146. Oxford, John and Erica Hedges Limited.

Cleland, L. and Stears, K. (eds.) 2004. *Colour in the Ancient Mediterranean World*, British Archaeological Reports International Series 1267. Oxford, John and Erica Hedges Limited.

Coles, B. 1990. Anthropomorphic wooden figures from Britain and Ireland. *Proceedings of the Prehistoric Society* 56: 315-333.

Coles, B. 1998. Wood Species for Wooden Figures: A Glimpse of a Pattern. In A. Gibson and D. Simpson (eds.), *Prehistoric Ritual and Religion*: 163-175. Stroud, Sutton Publishing Limited.

Coles, J., Heal, S. V. E. and Orme, B. J. 1978. The use and character of wood in prehistoric Britain and Ireland. Proceedings of the Prehistoric Society 44: 1-46.

Coles, J., Orme, J. and Rouillard, S. E. (eds.) 1985. Somerset Levels Papers 11, Exeter.

Coles, J. and Orme, J. 1985. Prehistoric woodworking from the Somerset Levels: 2, Species selection and prehistoric woodlands. In J. Coles, J. Orme and S. E. Rouillard (eds.), *Somerset Levels Papers* 11: 7-24. Exeter.

Collis, J. R. 1973. Burials with weapons in Iron Age Britain. *Germania* 51: 121-133.

Collis, J. 2001. Coral, amber and cockle shells: trade in the middle La Tène period. *Past* 38: 3-5.

Conckey, M. W., Soffer, O., Stratmann, D. and Jablonski, N. (eds.) 1997. *Beyond Art: Pleistocence Image and Symbol*. Wattis Symposium Series in Anthropology. Memoirs of the California Academy of Sciences 23. San Francisco, University of California Press.

Conckey, M. W. 1997. Beyond art and between the caves: Thinking about context in the interpretative process. In M. W. Conckey, O. Soffer, D. Stratmann and N. Jablonski (eds.), *Beyond Art: Pleistocence Image and Symbol*. Wattis Symposium Series in Anthropology. Memoirs of the California Academy of Sciences 23: 343-368. San Francisco, University of California Press.

Condren, M. 1989. *The Serpent and the Goddess: Women, Religion and Power*. San Francisco, Harper & Row.

Coote, J. and Shelton, A. (eds.) 1992. *Anthropology Art and Aesthetics*. Oxford, Clarendon Press.

Coote, J. 1992. Marvels of everyday vision: The anthropology of aesthetics and the cattle-keeping Nilotes. In J. Coote and A. Shelton (eds.), *Anthropology Art and Aesthetics*: 245-273. Oxford, Clarendon Press.

Cooney, G. 2002. So many shades of rock: Colour symbolism and Irish stone axeheads. In A. Jones and G. MacGregor (eds.), *Colouring the Past*: 93-108. Oxford, Berg.

Corder, P. and Hawkes, C. F. C. 1940. A panel of Celtic ornament from Elsmwell, East Yorkshire. *Antiquaries Journal* 20: 338-357.

Cotton, J. 1996. A miniature chalk head from the Thames at Battersea and the 'cult of the head'. In J. Bird, M. Hassall and H. Sheldon (eds.), Interpreting Roman London. Oxbow Monograph 5: 85-96. Oxford, Oxbow Books.

Cowell, R. and Craddock, P. T. 1995. Addendum: Copper in the skin of Lindow Man. In R. C. Turner and R. G. Scaife (eds.), *Bog Bodies: New Discoveries and New Perspectives*:74-75. London, British Museum Press.

Craddock, P. T. 1995. *Early Metal Mining and Production*. Edinburgh, Edinburgh University Press.

Craddock, P., Cowell, M. and Stead, I. 2004. Britain's first brass. *The Antiquaries Journal* 84: 339-346.

Creighton, J. 2000. *Coins and Power in late Iron Age Britain*. Cambridge, Cambridge University Press.

Crew, P. 1991. The experimental production of prehistoric bar iron. *Historical Metallurgy* 25: 21-36.

Cunliffe, B. 1979. *The Celtic World*. London, The Bodley Head Limited .

Cunliffe, B. 1984. *Danebury, An Iron Age Hillfort in Hampshire, Vol 2*. Council for British Archaeology research report 52. London, Council for British Archaeology.

Cunliffe, B. 1987. Hengistbury Head, Dorset. Oxford University Committee for Archaeology, Monograph Nr 13. Oxford, Oxford University Institute for Archaeology.

Cunliffe, B. 1988. *Mount Batten Plymouth: A Prehistoric and Roman Fort*. Oxford University Committee for Archaeology Monograph 26. Oxford, Oxford University Institute for Archaeology.

Cunliffe, B. 1991. *Iron Age Communities in Britain*. London and New York, Routledge.

Cunliffe, B. 1995. *Iron Age Britain*. London, B.T. Batsford/English Heritage.

Cunliffe, B. 1995a. *Danebury, An Iron Age Hillfort in Hampshire, Vol 6*. Council for British Archaeology research report 102. York, Council for British Archaeology.

Cunliffe, B. 1997. *The Ancient Celts*. London, Penguin Books.

Cunliffe, B. 2003. *Danebury Hillfort*. Stroud, Tempus Publishing.

Cunliffe, B. and Poole C. 1991. *Danebury, An Iron Age Hillfort in Hampshire, Vol 4*, Council for British Archaeology research report 73. London, Council for British Archaeology.

Cunliffe, B., and Poole C., 1991a, *Danebury, An Iron Age Hillfort in Hampshire, Vol 5*, Council for British Archaeology research report 73. London, Council for British Archaeology.

Cunliffe B. and Poole, C. 2000. *The Danebury Environs Programme: The Prehistory of a Wessex Landscape, Volume 2 – part 3, Suddern Farm, Middle Wallop Hants, 1991 and 1996*. English Heritage and Oxford University Committee for Archaeology. Monograph 49. Oxford, Institute for Archaeology.

Cunnington, E. 1884. On a hoard of bronze, iron and other objects found in Bulbury Camp, Dorset. *Archaeologica* 84: 115-120.

D'Andrade, R. 1990. Some propositions about the relations between culture and human cognition. In J. W. Stigler, R. A. Shweder and G. Hendt (eds.), *Cultural Psychology; Essays – Comparative Human Development*:65-129. Cambridge, Cambridge University Press.

Darvill, T. 2002. White on Blonde: Quartz pebbles and the use of quartz at neolithic monuments in the Isle of Man and beyond. In A. Jones and G. MacGregor (eds.), *Colouring the Past*: 73-92. Oxford, Berg.

Davies, S. and James, N. A. (eds.) 1997. *The Horse in Celtic Culture*. Cardiff, University of Wales Press.

Davies, S. 1997. Horses in the Mabinogion. In S. Davies and N. A. James (eds.), *The Horse in Celtic Culture*: 121-140. Cardiff, University of Wales Press.

Davies, J. L. and Spratling, M. 1976. The Seven Sisters hoard: a centenary study. In G. C. Boon and J. M Lewis (eds.), *Welsh Antiquity: Essays mainly on Prehistoric Topics Presented to H. N. Savory upon his Retirement as Keeper of Archaeology*: 121-147. Cardiff, National Museum of Wales.

Davidovits F. 2004. Notes on the nature of Creta Anularia and Vitruvius' recipe for Egyptian Blue. In L. Cleland and K. Stears, (eds.), *Colour in the Ancient Mediterranean World*, British Archaeological Reports International Series 1267: 16-21. Oxford, John and Erica Hedges Limited.

Davis, F. 1992. *Fashion, Culture and Identity*. London, The University of Chicago Press.

Davis, O. 2002. *Localities, Localities, Localities: A Re-Interpretation of the Danebury Evidence*. Unpublished MA dissertation, School of History and Archaeology Cardiff University.

Davis, M. and Gwilt, A. 2008. Material, style and identity in first century AD metalwork, with particular reference to the Seven Sisters hoard. In D. Garrow, D. Ch. Gosden and J. D. Hill (eds.), *Rethinking Celtic Art:* 146-184. Oxford, Oxbow Books.

Deacy S. and Villing, A. 2004. Athena blues? Colour and divinity in ancient Greece. In L. Cleland and K. Stears, (eds.), *Colour in the Ancient Mediterranean*

World, British Archaeological Reports International Series 1267: 85-90. Oxford, John and Erica Hedges Limited.

De Coppet, D. (ed.) 1992. *Understanding Rituals*. London, Routledge.

De Grandis, L. 1986. *Theory and Use of Colour*. Poole Dorset, Blandford Press.

Dent, J. 1978. Wetwang Slack. *Current Archaeology* 61: 46-50.

Dent, J. 1982. Cemeteries and settlement patterns on the Yorkshire wolds. *Proceedings of the Prehistoric Society* 48: 437-457.

Dent, J. 1983. Weapons, wounds and war in the Iron Age. *Archaeological Journal* 140: 120-128.

Dent, J. 1984. Danes Graves Iron Age cemetery. *Archaeological Journal* 141: 30-31.

Dent, J. 1985. Three cart burials from Wetwang, Yorkshire. *Antiquity* LIX: 85-92.

Diepeveen-Jansen, M. 2001. *People, Ideas and Goods*. Amsterdam, Amsterdam University Press.

Diinhoff, S. 1997. The custom of sacrifice in Early Iron Age burial tradition. In C. K. Jensen and K. H. Nielsen (eds.), *Burial & Society: The Chronological and Social Analysis of Archaeological Burial Data*: 111-116. Aarhus, Aarhus University Press.

Djarvoskin, S. 2003. How Sereptie Djarvoskin of the Ngansasans (Tavgi Samoyeds) became a shaman. In G. Harvey G. (ed.), *Shamanism: A Reader*: 31-40. London, Routledge.

Dobney, K. and Ervynck, A. 2007. To fish or not to fish; evidence for the possible avoidance of fish consumption during the IronAge around the North Sea. In C. Haselgrove and T. Moore (eds.), *The Later Iron Age in Britain and Beyond*: 403-418. Oxford, Oxbow Books.

Dorfner, L., Moser, M., Spindler, K., Bahr, F., Egarter-Vigl, E., and Dohr, G. 1998. 5200 year old acupuncture in Central Europe? *Science* 28: 239.

Downes, J. and Pollard, T. (eds.) 1999. *The Loved Body's Corruption*. Glasgow, Cruithne Press.

Downes, J. 1999. Cremation: a spectacle and journey. In J. Downes and T. Pollard (eds.), *The Loved Body's Corruption*: 19-29. Glasgow, Cruithne Press.

Dronfield, J. 1995. Subjective vision and the source of Irish megalithic art. *Antiquity* 65: 539-549.

Dronfield, J. 1995a. Migraine, light and hallucinogens: the neurocognitive basis of Irish megalithic art. *Oxford Journal of Archaeology* 14(3): 261-275.

Dronfield, J. 1996. The vision thing: diagnosis of endogenous derivation in abstract arts, in *Current Anthropology*. 37(2): 373-391.

Dudley, D. and Jope, E. M. 1965. An Iron Age cists burial with two brooches from Trevone, North Cornwall. *Cornish Archaeology* 4: 18-23.

Duigan, M. 2004. Colour and the deceptive gift. In L. Cleland and K. Stears (eds.), *Colour in the Ancient Mediterranean World*, British Archaeological

Reports International Series 1267: 78-84. Oxford, John and Erica Hedges Limited.

Dunbavin, P. 1999. *Picts and Ancient Britons: An Exploration of Pictish Origins. Nottingham*, Third Millenium Publishing.

Dungworth, D. 1996. The production of copper alloys in Iron Age Britain. *Proceedings of the Prehistoric Society* 62: 399-421.

Dungworth, D. 1997. Copper metallurgy in Iron Age Britain: some recent research. In A. Gwilt and C. Haselgrove (eds.), *Reconstructing Iron Age Societies*. Oxbow Monograph 71:46-50. Oxford, Oxford Books.

Dunning, G. C. 1928. An engraved bronze mirror fom Nijmegen, Holland. *Archaeological Journal* 85, 69-70.

Duval, P. M. and Hawkes, Ch. (eds.) 1976. *Celtic Art in Ancient Europe: Five Protohistoric Centuries, Proceedings of the Colloquy held 1972 at Oxford Maison Francaise*. London, Seminar Press.

Eaverly M. A. 2004. Colours of Power: Brown Men and Brown Women in the Art of Akhenaten. In L. Cleland and K. Stears (eds.), *Colour in the Ancient Mediterranean World*, British Archaeological Reports International Series 1267: 53-55. Oxford, John and Erica Hedges Limited.

Eco, U. 1976. *A Theory of Semiotics*. London, Macmillan.

Edmonds, J. 1998. *The History of Woad and the Medieval Woad Vat*. Little Chalfont, John Edmunds Publisher.

Ehrenreich, R. M. 1999. Archaeometallurgy: Helping archaeology bridge the gap between science and anthropology. In S. M. M. Young, A. M. Pollard, P. Budd and R. A. Ixer, (eds.), *Metals in Antiquity*, British Archaeological Reports 792:218-226. Oxford, Archaeopress.

Eicher, J. B. (ed.) 1995. *Dress and Ethnicity*. Oxford, Berg.

Eldar, R. 2005. Tibetan Sky burial in China. www.travelblog.org/Asia/China/blog-7890.html.

Eliade, M. 1989. *Shamanism: Archaic Techniques of Ecstacy*. London, Arkana Penguin.

Ellison, A. and Drewett, P. 1971. Pits and postholes in British early Iron Age; some alternative explanations. *Proceedings of the Prehistoric Society* 37: 183-194.

Eluere, C. 1995. Gold and society in Prehistoric Europe. In G. Morteani and P. J. Northover (eds.), *Prehistoric Gold in Europe: Mines, Metallurgy and Manufacture*: 29-31. Dordrecht, Kluwer Academic Publishers.

Endicott, K. M. 1970. *An Analysis of Malay Magic*. Oxford, Clarendon Press.

Eremin, K., Quye, A., Edwards, H., Villar S. J. and Manley, B. 2004. Colours of Ancient Egyptian Funerary Artefacts in the National Museum of Scotland. In L. Cleland and K. Stears (eds.), *Colour in the Ancient Mediterranean World*, British Archaeological Reports International Series 1267: 1-8. Oxford, John and Erica Hedges Limited.

Evans, C. 1989. Perishables and wordly goods – artefact decoration and classification in the light of wetlands

research. *Oxford Journal of Archaeology* 8 (2): 179-201.

Evans-Pritchard, E. E. 2004. Witchcraft, oracles and magic among the Azande. In A. C. G. M. Robben (ed.), *Death, Mourning and Burial, A Cross Cultural Reader*: 115-121. Oxford, Blackwell Publishing.

Fairbanks, A. 1931. *Philostratus Imagines Callistratus Descriptions*.Translation. London, William Heinemann Ltd.

Favre, J. P. and November, A. 1979. *Colour and Communication*. Zurich, ABC Edition.

Farley, M. 1983. A mirror burial at Dorton, Buckinghamshire. *Proceedings of the Prehistoric Society* 49: 269-302.

Fenton-Thomas, Ch. 2003. *Late Prehistoric and Early Historic Landscapes on the Yorkshire Chalk*. Oxford, British Archaeological Reports, British Series 350, Archaeopress.

Field, N. and Parker Pearson, M. 2003. *Fiskerton: An Iron Age Timber Causeway with Iron Age and Roman Votive Offerings*. Oxford, Oxbow Books.

Finnegan, R. 1992. *Oral Traditions and Verbal Arts*. London, Routledge.

Firth, R. 1992. Art and Anthropology. In J Coote and A. Shelton (eds.), *Anthropology Art and Aesthetics*: 15-39. Oxford, Clarendon Press.

Fisher, J. A. 2002. Tattoing the body, marking culture. *Body and Society* 8(4): 91-107.

Fitzpatrick A. P. and Morris, E. L. (eds.) 1994. *The Iron Age in Wessex: Recent Work*. Salisbury, Trust for Wessex Archaeology Ltd.

Fitzpatrick, A. P. 1994. The Late Iron Age Cremation Cemetary at Westhampnett, West Sussex. In A. P. Fitzpatrick and E. L. Morris (eds.), *The Iron Age in Wessex: Recent Work*: 31-32. Salisbury, Trust for Wessex Archaeology Ltd.

Fitzpatrick, A. P. 1996. Night and day: the symbolism of astral signs on later Iron Age anthropomorphic short swords. *Proceedings of the Prehistoric Society* 62: 373-398.

Fitzpatrick, A. P. 1996a. A 1st century AD 'Durotrigan' inhumation burial with a decorated Iron Age mirror from Portesham Dorset. Dorset Natural History and Archaeological Society 118: 51-70.

Fitzpatrick, A. P. 1997. Archaeological Excavations on the Route of the A27Westhampnett Bypass, West Sussex, 1992, Vol.2 The Late Iron Age, Romano-British and Anglo-Saxon Cemeteries. Wessex Archaeology Report 12, Salisbury.

Fitzpatrick, A. P. 1997a. Everyday life in Iron Age Wessex, in A. Gwilt and C. Haselgrove, (eds.), *Reconstructing Iron Age Societies*. Oxbow Monograph 71: 73-86. Oxford, Oxford Books.

Fitzpatrick, A. P. 2007. Dancing with dragons: fantastic animals in the earlier Celtic art of Iron Age Britain. In C. Haselgrove and T. Moore (eds.), *The Later Iron Age in Britain and Beyond*:339-357. Oxford, Oxbow Books.

Fleckinger, A. 2003. *Ötzi, the Iceman: The Full Facts at a Glance*. Vienna/ Bolzano, Folioverlag.

Foster, J. 1995. Metalworking in the British Iron Age: The evidence from Weelsby Avenue, Grimsby. In B. Raftery, V. Megaw and V. Rigby (eds.), *Sites and Sights of the Iron Age*, Oxbow Monograph 56: 49-61. Oxford, Oxbow Books.

Foster, I. L. L. and Alcock, L. (eds.) 1963. *Culture and Environment: Essays in Honour of Sir Cyril Fox*. London, Routledge & Kegan Paul.

Founoulakis, A. 2004. The colours of desire and death: colour terms in Bion's epitaph on Adonis. In L. Cleland and K. Stears (eds.), *Colour in the Ancient Mediterranean World*, British Archaeological Reports International Series 1267:110-116. Oxford, John and Erica Hedges Limited.

Fowler, C. 2004. *The Archaeology of Personhood; An Anthropological Approach*. London, Routledge.

Fox, A. and Pollard, S. 1973. A decorated bronze mirror from Holcombe. *The Antiquaries Journal* 53: 16-41.

Fox, C. 1925. A late Celtic bronze mirror from Wales. *The Antiquaries Journal* 5: 254-257.

Fox, C. 1948. The incised ornament on the Celtic mirror from Colchester, Essex. *The Antiquaries Journal* 28: 123-137.

Fox, C. 1958. *Pattern and Purpose, A Survey of Early Celtic Art in Britain*. Cardiff, National Museum of Wales.

Fox, C. 1960. A Celtic mirror from Great Chesterford. *Antiquity* 34: 207-210.

Francfort, H. P. and Hamayon, R .N. (eds.) 2001. *The Concept of Shamanism: Uses and Abuses*. Budapest, Akadémiai Kíado.

Francfort, H. P. 2001. Prehistoric section: and introduction, in H. P. Francfort and R. N. Hamayon (eds.), *The Concept of Shamanism: Uses and Abuses*: 31-50. Budapest, Akadémiai Kíado.

Freud, S. 1999. *Die Traumdeutung*. Frankfurt am Main, Fischerverlag.

Fulford, M. and Creighton, J. 1998. A late Iron Age mirror burial from Latchmere Green near Silchestere, Hampshire. *Proceedings of the Prehistoric Society* 64: 331-342.

Gansum, T. 2004. Role the bones - from iron to steel. Norwegian Archaeological Review 37(1): 41-57.

Gantz, J. (translator) 1976. *The Mabinogion*. London, Penguin.

Gage, J. 1993. *Colour and Culture*. London, Thames and Hudson.

Garrow, D. Gosden, Ch. and Hill, J. D. (eds.) 2008. *Rethinking Celtic Art*. Oxford, Oxbow Books.

Gazin-Schwartz, A. and Holtorf, C. J. (eds.) 1999. *Archaeology and Folklore*. London, Routledge.

Gell, A. 1992. The technology of enchantment and the enchantment of technology. In J. Coote and A. Shelton (eds.), *Anthropology Art and Aesthetics*: 40-63. Oxford, Clarendon Press.

Gibson, A. and Simpson, D. (eds.) 1998. *Prehistoric Ritual and Religion*. Stroud, Sutton Publishing Limited.

Giles, M. 2000. *Open-weave, Close-knit: Archaeologies of Identity in the Later Prehistoric Landscape of East Yorkshire*. Unpublished PhD thesis, University of Sheffield.

Giles, M. 2007. Making metal and forging relations; Ironworking in the British Iron Age. *Oxford Journal of Archaeology* 26(4): 395-413.

Giles, M. 2007a. Good fences make good neighbours. In C. Haselgrove and T. Moore (eds.), *The Later Iron Age in Britain and Beyond*: 235-249. Oxford, Oxbow Books.

Giles, M. 2008. Seeing red: the aesthetics of martial objects in the British and Irish Iron Age. In D. Garrow, Ch. Gosden and J. D. Hill (eds.), *Rethinking Celtic Art*: 59-77. Oxford, Oxbow Books.

Gillis, C. 1999. The economic value and colour symbolism of tin. In S. M. M. Young, A. M. Pollard, P. Budd and R. A. Ixer (eds.), *Metals in Antiquity*. British Archaeological Reports 792: 140-145. Oxford, Archaeopress.

Gillis, C. 2004. The use of colour in the Aegean Bronze Age. In L. Cleland and K. Stears (eds.), *Colour in the Ancient Mediterranean World*, British Archaeological Reports International Series 1267: 56-60. Oxford, John and Erica Hedges Limited.

Goethe, J. W. v. 1840. *Theory of Colours*. London, John Murray. Reproduced in 1979. Cambridge, MIT Press.

Goody, J. 1962. *Death, Property and the Ancestors*. London, Tavistock Publications.

Gosden, Ch. and Hill, J. D. 2008. Introduction: reintegrating 'Celtic' art. In D. Garrow, Ch. Gosden and J. D. Hill, (eds.), *Rethinking Celtic Art*: 1-14. Oxford, Oxbow Books.

Gosden, Ch. and Lock, G. 2007. The aesthetics of landscape. In C. Haselgrove and R. Pope (eds.), *The Earlier Iron Age in Britain and the near Continent*: 279-292. Oxford, Oxbow Books.

Graefin Schwerin von Krosigk, H. 2005. Ueber magische Schwertperlen by Sarmaten, Alanen und Abchasen. *Prehistorische Zeitschrift* 80: 110-133.

Graeslund, B. 1994. Prehistoric soul beliefs in Northern Europe. *Proceedings of the Prehistoric Society* 60: 15-26.

Graves-Brown, P. M. 1995. Fearful symmetry. *World Archaeology* XXVII: 88-99.

Green, B. 1972. Three Iron Age bronze terrets from Norfolk. *The Antiquaries Journal* 52: 346.

Green, C. 1949. The Birdlip Iron Age burials: a report. *Proceedings of the Prehistoric Society* 15: 188-190.

Green, D. and O'Connor, F. 1967. *A Golden Treasury of Irish Poetry AD 600 – 1200*. Dingle Co. Kerry, Brandon Ireland and UK Limited.

Green, M. J. 1986. *The Gods of the Celts*. Stroud, Alan Sutton Publishing Limited.

Green, M. J. 1989. *Symbol and Image in Celtic Religious Art*. London and New York, Routledge.

Green, M. J. 1991. *The Sun-Gods of Ancient Europe*. London, B.T. Batsford Ltd.

Green, M. J. 1992. *Animals in Celtic Life and Myth*. London and New York, Routledge.

Green, M. J. 1992a. *Dictionary of Celtic Myth and Legend*. London, Thames & Hudson.

Green, M. J. 1993. *Celtic Myths*. London, British Museum Press.

Green, M. J. 1995. *Celtic Godesses*. London, British Museum Press.

Green, M. J. (ed.) 1995. *The Celtic World*. London, Routledge.

Green, M. J. 1997. *Exploring the World of the Druids*. London, Thames & Hudson.

Green, M. J. 1997a. The Symbolic Horse in Pagan Celtic Europe. In S. Davies and N. A. James (eds.), *The Horse in Celtic Culture*: 1-22. Cardiff, University of Wales Press.

Green, M. J. 1998. The Time Lords: Ritual Calendars, Druids and the Sacred Year. In A. Gibson and D. Simpson (eds.), *Prehistoric Ritual and Religion*: 190-202. Stroud, Sutton Publishing Limited.

Green, M. J. 1998a. Crossing the boundaries: triple horns and emblematic transference. *European Journal of Archaeology* 1(2): 219-240.

Green, M. J. 1999. Back to the Future: Resonances of the Past in Myth and Material Culture. In A. Gazin-Schwartz and C. J. Holtorf (eds.), *Archaeology and Folklore*: 48-66. London, Routledge.

Greep, S. J. 1996. Hair pins and needles. In J. May, *Dragonby: Report on Excavations at an Iron Age and Romano-British Settlement in North Lincolnshire*. Volume 1: 345-348. Oxford, Oxbow Books.

Grimes, W. F. 1939. *Guide to Collections Illustrating the Prehistory of Wales*. Cardiff, National Museum of Wales Press.

Groening, K. 2001. *Decorated Skin: A World Survey of Body Art*. London, Thames and Hudson.

Grose, D. F. 1997. The Origins and Early History of Glass. In D. Klein and W. Lloyd (eds.), *The History of Glass*: 9-38. London, Tiger International Books.

Guido, M. 1978. *The Glass Beads of the Prehistoric and Roman Periods in Britain and Ireland*. London, Thames and Hudson Ltd.

Gwilt, A. and Haselgrove, C. (eds.) 1997. *Reconstructing Iron Age Societies*. Oxbow Monograph 71. Oxford, Oxford Books.

Haaland, R. 2004. Technology, transformation and symbolism; ethnographic perspectives on European iron working. *Norwegian Archaeological Review* 37(1): 1-19.

Hageneder, F. 2007. *Yew; A History*. Stroud, Sutton Publishing.

Haley, S. 1999. Death and after death. In J. Downes and T. Pollard (eds.), *The Loved Body's Corruption*: 1-8. Glasgow, Cruithne Press.

Halleux, R. 1981. *Les Alchimistes Grecs – Papyrus de Leyde – Papyrus de Stockholm – Recettes*. Paris, Les Belles Lettres.

Hannah, P. 2004. The cosmetic use of red ochre (miltos). In L. Cleland and K. Stears (eds.), *Colour in the Ancient Mediterranean World*, British Archaeological Reports International Series 1267: 100-105. Oxford, John and Erica Hedges Limited.

Harding, A. F. 2000. *European Societies in the Bronze Age*. Cambridge, Cambridge University Press.

Harner, M. 2003. Discovering the way. In G. Harvey (ed.), *Shamanism: A Reader*: 41-56. London, Routledge.

Hartmann, H. 1952. *Der Totenkult in Irland*. Heidelberg, Carl Winter Universitaetsverlag.

Hartmann H. 2001. Was ist Wahrheit (2). *Zeitschrift fuer Celtische Philologie* 52: 1-101.

Harvey, G. (ed.) 2003. *Shamanism: A Reader*. London, Routledge.

Harvey, G. 2006. *Animism: Respecting the Living World*. New York, Columbia University Press.

Haselgrove, C. and Moore T. (eds.) 2007. *The Later Iron Age in Britain and Beyond*. Oxford, Oxbow Books.

Haselgrove, C. and Moore T. 2007. New narratives of the Later Iron Age. In C. Haselgrove and T. Moore (eds.), *The Later Iron Age in Britain and Beyond*: 1-15. Oxford, Oxbow Books.

Haselgrove, C. and Pope, R. (eds.) 2007. *The Earlier Iron Age in Britain and the near Continent*. Oxford, Oxbow Books.

Härke, H. 1997a. Final comments: Ritual, symbolism and social interference. In C. K. Jensen and K. H. Nielsen (eds.), *Burial & Society: The Chronological and Social Analysis of Archaeological Burial Data*: 191-195. Aarhus, Aarhus University Press.

Hauptmann, A., Pernicka, E. and Wagner, G. A. (eds.) 1989. *Archaeometallurgie der Alten Welt*. Bochum, Selbstverlag des Deutschen Bergbau Museums.

Hawkes, C. F. C. and Clarke, R. R. 1963. Gahlstord and Caister-on-Sea: Two finds of Late Bronze Age Irish gold. In I. L. L. Foster and L. Alcock (eds.), *Culture and Environment: Essays in Honour of Sir Cyril Fox*: 193-250. London, Routledge & Kegan Paul.

Hedeager, L. 1992. *Iron Age Societies, From Tribe to State in Northern Europe, 500BC to AD700*. Oxford, Blackwell Publishers.

Helvenston, P. A and Bahn, P. G. 2003. Testing the 'three stages of trance model'. *Cambridge Journal of Archaeology* 13 (2): 213-224.

Henderson, J. 1982. *X-ray fluorescence analysis of Iron Age Glass*. Unpublished PhD thesis, University of Bradford.

Henderson, J. 1985. The raw materials of early glass production. *Oxford Journal of Archaeology* 4(3): 267-292.

Henderson, J. 1987. Glass working. In B. Cunliffe. Hengistbury Head, Dorset. Oxford University

Committee for Archaeology, Monograph Nr 13: 180-185. Oxford, Oxford University Institute for Archaeology.

Henderson, J. 1991. Industrial specialization in late Iron Age Britain and Europe. Archaeological Journal 148: 104-148.

Henry, F. 1933. Émailleurs D'Occident. *Préhistoire* 2: 65-143.

Herbert, E. 1993. *Iron, Gender and Power; Rituals of Transformation in African Societies*. Bloomington and Indianapolis, Indiana University Press.

Hertling, B. 2006. *Wie aus dem Zankapfel die Einbeere wurde: (Heil-)pflanzen im griechischen Mythos*. Augsburg, Fotzick Verlag.

Hertz, R. 1960. *Death and the Right Hand*. Translation by Rodney and Claudia Needham. London, Cohen & West.

Hey, G., Bayliss, A. and Boyle, A. 1999. Iron Age inhumation burials at Yarnton, Oxfordshire. *Antiquity* 73: 551-562.

Hill, J. D. 1995. *Ritual and Rubbish*. British Archaeological Reports Series 242. Oxford, Tempvs Reparatvm, Archaeological and Historical Associates Limited.

Hill, J. D. 1997. The end of one kind of body and the beginning of another kind of body? 'Toilet Instruments' and 'Romanization' in Southern England during the First Century AD. In A. Gwilt and C. Haselgrove (eds.), *Reconstructing Iron Age Societies*. Oxbow Monograph 71: 96-107. Oxford, Oxford Books.

Hill, J. D. 2001. A new cart chariot burial from Wetwang, East Yorkshire. *PAST* 38: 2-3.

Hill, J. D. 2007. The dynamics of social change in Later Iron Age eastern and south-eastern England. In C. Haselgrove and T. Moore (eds.), *The Later Iron Age in Britain and Beyond*: 16-40. Oxford, Oxbow Books.

Hingley, R. 1997. Iron, ironworking and regeneration: a study of the symbolic meaning of metal working in Iron Age Britain. In A. Gwilt and C. Haselgrove (eds.), *Reconstructing Iron Age Societies*. Oxbow Monograph 71: 9-18. Oxford, Oxford Books.

Hingley, R. 2000. *Roman Officers and British Gentlemen: The Imperial Origins of Roman Archaeology*. London, Routledge.

Hingley, R. 2009. Esoteric knowledge? Ancient Bronze artefacts from Iron Age contexts. *Proceedings of the Prehistoric Society* 75: 143-166.

Hodder, I. 1982. *Symbols in Action*. Cambridge, Cambridge University Press.

Hodder, I. (ed.) 1989. *The Meaning of Things: Material Culture and Symbolic Expression*. London, Unwin Hyman.

Hodder, I. 1989a. Post-modernism, post-structuralism and post-processual archaeology. In I. Hodder (ed.), *The Meaning of Things: Material Culture and Symbolic Expression*:64-78. London, Unwin Hyman.

Hodge, R. and Kress, G. 1988. *Social Semiotics*. Cambridge, Polity Press.

Hodson, F. R. 1994. A Muensingen fibula. In B. Raftery, V. Megaw and V. Rigby (eds.), *Sites and Sights of the Iron Age*. Oxbow Monograph 56: 62-66. Oxford, Oxbow Books.

Holtzschue, L. 2002. *Understanding Colour: an Introduction for Designers*. New York, John Wiley & Sons.

Hope, V. and Marshall, E. (eds.) 2000. *Death and Disease in the Ancient City*. London and New York, Routledge.

Hosler, D. 1995. Sound, colour and meaning in the metallurgy of Ancient West Mexico. World Archaeology 27: 100-115.

Hovers, E., Ilani, S., Bar-Yosef, O. and Vandermeersch, B. 2003. An early case of colour symbolism; ochre use by modern humans in Qafzeh cave. *Current Anthropology* 44: 491-522.

Howell, R. 2006. *Searching for the Silures: An Iron Age Tribe in South-East Wales*. Stroud, Tempus Publishing Limited.

Hughes, M. J. 1972. A technical study of opaque red glass of the Iron Age in Britain. *Proceedings of the Prehistoric Society* 38: 98-105.

Hughes, M. J. 1987. Enamels: Materials, Deterioration and Analysis, in From Pinheads to Hanging Bowls, the Identification, Deterioration and Conservation of Applied Enamel and Glass Decoration on Archaeological Artefacts. Occasional Papers 7. The United Kingdom Institute for Conservation: 10-12.

Hughes-Brock, H.. 1993. Amber in the Aegean in the Late Bronze Age: Some problems and perspectives. Amber in Archaeology. Proceedings of the Second International Conference of Amber in Archaeology, Liblice 1990. Praha, Institute of Archaeology: 219-229.

Humphrey, J. (ed.) 2003. Re-searching the Iron Age: Selected Papers from the Proceedings of the Iron Age Research Student Seminars, 1999 and 2000. Leicester Archaeology Monographs No 11. Leicester, School of Archaeology and Ancient History University of Leicester.

Huntington, R. and Metcalf, P. 1979. *Celebrations of Death: The Anthropology of Mortuary Ritual*. Cambridge, Cambridge University Press.

Hutcheson, N. 2003. Material culture in the landscape: a new approach to the Snettisham hoards. In J. Humphrey (ed.), Re-searching the Iron Age: Selected Papers from the Proceedings of the Iron Age Research Student Seminars, 1999 and 2000. Leicester Archaeology Monographs 11:87-97. Leicester, School of Archaeology and Ancient History University of Leicester.

Ierodiakonou, K. 2004. Empedocles and the ancient painters. In L. Cleland and K. Stears (eds.), *Colour in the Ancient Mediterranean World*, British

Archaeological Reports International Series 1267: 91-95. Oxford, John and Erica Hedges Limited.

Jackson, K. H. 1961. *The International Popular Tale and Early Welsh Tradition*. Cardiff, University of Wales Press.

Jackson, R. 1985. Cosmetic sets from Late Iron Age and Roman Britain. *Britannia* 16: 165-192.

Jackson, R. 1993. The function and manufacture of Romano-British cosmetic grinders; two important new finds from London. *The Antiquaries Journal* 73: 165-169.

Jackson, R. 2010. *Cosmetic Sets of Late Iron Age and Roman Britain*. London, The British Museum.

Jacobsthal, P. 1944. *Early Celtic Art*. Oxford, Clarendon Press.

James, D. 1990. Prehistoric Copper Mining on the Great Orme's Head. *Early Mining in the British Isles*. Plas Tan Y Bwlch Occasional Paper 1. Blaenau Festiniog, Plas Tan Y Bwlch, Snowdonia National Park Study Centre: 1-4.

James, S. 2007. A bloodless past. In C. Haselgrove and R. Pope. (eds.), *The Earlier Iron Age in Britain and the near Continent*: 160-173. Oxford, Oxbow Books.

Jensen, C. K. and Nielsen, K. H. (eds.) 1997. *Burial & Society: The Chronological and Social Analysis of Archaeological Burial Data*. Aarhus, Aarhus University Press.

Johns C. 2002. Iron Age sword and mirror cist burial from Bryher, Isles of Scilly. *Cornish Archaeology* 41(2): 1-80.

Jones, A. 1999. Local colour: megalithic architecture and colour symbolism in Neolithic Arran. *Oxford Journal of Archaeology* 18(4): 339-350.

Jones, A. and MacGregor, G. (eds.) 2002. *Colouring the Past*. Oxford, Berg.

Jones, A. and MacGregor, G. 2002a. Introduction: Wonderful things – colour studies in Archaeology from Munsell to materiality. In A. Jones and G. MacGregor (eds.), *Colouring the Past*: 1-21. Oxford, Berg.

Jones, A. 2002. A Biography of Colour: Colour, Material Histories and Personhood in the Early Bronze Age of Britain and Ireland. In A. Jones and G. MacGregor (eds.), *Colouring the Past*: 159-174. Oxford, Berg.

Jones, C. P. 1987. Stigma: tattooing and branding in Graeco-Roman antiquity. *Journal of Roman Studies* 77: 139-155.

Jones, C. P. 2000. Stigma and tattoo. In J. Caplan (ed.), *Written on the Body; The Tattoo in European and American History*: 1-16. London, Reaktion Books Limited.

Jones, R. 1977. The Animal Bones. In K Smith 1977. The excavation of Winklebury Camp, Basingstoke, Hampshire. *Proceedings of the Prehistoric Society* 43: 58-66.

Jones O'Day, S., Van Neer, W. And Ervynk, A. (eds.) 2004. *Behaviour behind Bones: The Zooarchaeology of Ritual, Religion, Status and Identity*. Oxford, Oxbow Books.

Jope, M. 2000. *Early Celtic Art*. Oxford, Oxford University Press.

Jope Rogers, J. 1873. Romano-British, or late Celtic, remains at Trelan Bahow, St. Keverne, Cornwall. Archaeological Journal XXX: 267-272.

Joy, J. 2007. *Reflections on the Iron Age: Biographies of Mirrors*. Unpublished PhD thesis, University of Southampton.

Joy, J. 2008. Reflections on Celtic art: a re-examination of mirror decoration. In D. Garrow, Ch. Gosden and J. D. Hill (eds.), *Rethinking Celtic Art*: 78-99. Oxford, Oxbow Books.

Judd, D. B. 1970. Introduction to Goethe, J. W. v. Theory of Colours. Cambrigde, MIT Press: v-xvi.

Jung, C. G. 1992. *Die Archetypen und das kollektive Unbewusste. Gesammelte Werke* 9(1). Olten, Walter Verlag.

Kassam, A. and Megersa, G. 1989. Iron and beads: male and female symbols of creation. A study of ornament among Booran Orono. In I. Hodder (ed.), *The Meaning of Things: Material Culture and Symbolic Expression*: 23-32. London, Unwin Hyman.

Keates, S. 2002. The Flashing Blade: Copper, Colour and Luminosity in North Italian Copper Age Society. In A. Jones and G. MacGregor (eds.), *Colouring the Past*: 109-126. Oxford, Berg.

Keller C. M. and Keller, J. D. 1996. *Cognition and Tool Use; The Blacksmith at Work*. Cambridge, Cambridge University Press.

Kelly, P. 1997. The earliest words for 'horse' in the Celtic languages. In S. Davies and N. A. James (eds.), *The Horse in Celtic Culture*: 43-63. Cardiff, University of Wales Press.

Keepax, C. 1979. The Human Bones. In G. J. Wainwright, *Gussage All Saints: An Iron Age Settlement in Dorset*. Department of the Environment Archaeological Reports 10: 161-171. London, Her Majesty's Stationery Office.

Kinsella, T. 1970. *The Taín: Translated From the Irish Epic 'Taín Bo Cuailnge'*. London, Oxford University Press.

Klein, D. and Lloyd, W. (eds.) 1997. *The History of Glass*. London, Tiger International Books.

Koch, J. T. (ed.) 1995. *The Celtic Heroic Age*. Malden Massachusetts, Celtic Studies Publications.

Kośko, A. and Langer, J. J. 1997. Wood tar in the culture of early agrarian communities in Europe. In W. Brzeziński and W. Piotrowski (eds.) *Proceedings of the First International Symposium on Wood Tar and Pitch*: 25-28. Warsaw, State Archaeological Museum.

Krumphanzlova, Z. 1993. Burgwallzeitliche Bernsteinfunde auf den Graeberfeldern in Boehmen. Amber in Archaeology, Proceedings of the Second International Conference of Amber in Archaeology. Liblice 1990: 187-190. Praha, Institute of Archaeology.

Kuechler, S. 1992. Malangan and the idiom of kinship in Northern New Ireland. In J. Coote and A. Shelton (eds.), *Anthropology Art and Aesthetics*: 94-112. Oxford, Clarendon Press.

Kuehni, R. G. 1983. *Colour: Essence and Logic*. New York, Van Nostrand Reinhold Company.

Kuehni, R. G. 2005. *Colour: An Introduction to Practice and Principles*. New York, John Wiley & Sons Inc.

Kuwahara, M. 2005. *Tattoo: An Anthropology*. Oxford, Berg.

Lahiri, N. 1995. Indian metal and metal-related artefacts as cultural signifiers: an ethnographic perspective. *World Archaeology* 27: 116-132.

Lang, J. 1986. Cauldron from burial 1. In I. M. Stead and V. Rigby, *Baldock, The Excavation of a Roman and Pre-Roman Settlement, 1968-72*. Britannia Monograph Series No 7: 388. London, Society for the Promotion of Roman Studies.

La Niece, S., Hook, C. and Craddock, P. (eds.) 2007. *Metals and Mining: Studies in Archaeometallurgy*. London, Archetype Publications.

Letherbridge, T. C. 1953. Burial of an Iron Age warrior at Snailwell. *Proceedings of the Cambridgeshire Antiquarian Society* XLVII: 25-37.

Lewis, A. 1990. Underground exploration of the Great Orme Copper Mines. *Early Mining in the British Isles*. Plas Tan Y Bwlch Occasional Paper No 1: 5-10. Blaenau Festiniog, Plas Tan Y Bwlch, Snowdonia National Park Study Centre.

Lewis-Williams, J. D. 1997. Harnessing the Brain: Vision and Shamanism in Upper Palaeolithic Western Europe. In M. W. Conckey, O. Soffer, D. Stratmann and N. Jablonski (eds.), *Beyond Art: Pleistocence Image and Symbol*. Wattis Symposium Series in Anthropology. Memoirs of the California Academy of Sciences 23: 321-342. San Francisco, University of California Press.

Lewis-Williams, J. D., Dowson, T. A. *et al.* 1988. The signs of all times: entoptic phenomena in Upper Palaeolithic art. *Current Anthropology* 29(2): 201-245.

Lienhardt, G. 2004. Burial alive. In A. C. G. M. Robben (ed.), *Death, Mourning and Burial, A Cross Cultural Reader*: 122-133. Oxford, Blackwell Publishing.

Locher, A. 1998. Ist Bergbau boese? Antikes und Aktuelles zur Moral der Metallkultur. In T. Rehren, A. Hauptmann and J. D. Muhly, (eds.), *Metallurgica Antiqua, in Honour of Hans Gert Bachmann and Robert Maddin*: 93-98. Bochum, Deutsches Bergbau Museum.

Lock, M. 2004. Displacing suffering; the reconstruction of death in North America and Japan. In A. C. G. M. Robben (ed.), *Death, Mourning and Burial, A Cross Cultural Reader*: 91-111.Oxford, Blackwell Publishing.

Loebner, S. 2002. *Understanding Semantics*. London, Arnold.

Loney, H. L. and Hoaen, A. W. 2005. Landscape, memory, material culture: diversity in the Iron Age. *Proceedings of the Prehistoric Society* 71: 361-378.

Longworth, I., Herne, A., Varndell, G. and Needham, S. 1991. *Excavations at Grimes Graves Norfolk, 1972 – 1976, Fascicule 3 Shaft X: Bronze Age Flint, Chalk and Metal Working*. London, British Museum Press.

Lynch, F. 1998. Colour in Prehistoric Architecture. In A. Gibson and D. Simpson (eds.), *Prehistoric Ritual and Religion*: 62-67. Stroud, Sutton Publishing Limited.

Macdonald, P. 2007. *Llyn Cerrig Bach: A Study of the Copper Alloy Artefacts from the Insular La Tène Assemblage*. Cardiff, University of Wales Press.

MacDonell, A. A. 1968. *A History of Sanskrit Literature*. New York, Haskell House Publishers Limited.

MacGregor, G. 2002. Making Monuments Out of Mountains: The Role of Colour and Texture in the Constitution of Meaning and Identity at Recumbent Stone Circles. In A. Jones and G. MacGregor (eds.), *Colouring the Past*: 141-158. Oxford, Berg.

MacGregor, M. 1976. *Early Celtic Art in North Britain, volume 1*. Leicester, Leicester University Press.

MacQuarrie, C. W. 2000. Insular Celtic tattooing: history, myth and metaphor. In J. Caplan (ed.), *Written on the Body; The Tattoo in European and American History*: 32-45. London, Reaktion Books Limited.

Mallaby, T. 2003. *Gambling Life: Dealing in Contingency in a Greek City*. Chicago, University of Illinois Press.

Manning, W. H. 1972. Ironwork hoards in Iron Age and Roman Britain. Britannia 3: 224-250.

Marshack, A. 1981. On paleolithic ochre and the early uses of colour and symbol. *Current Anthropology* 22: 188-192.

Martin, E. A. 1978. A new Iron Age terret from Weybread. *Suffolk Institute of Archaeology and History* 34: 137-140.

Maryon, H. 1971. *Metalwork and Enamelling; a Practical Treatise on Gold and Silversmiths' Work and their Allied Crafts*. New York, Dover Publications.

Maschio, T. 1994. *To Remember the Faces of the Dead: The Plenitude of Memory in Southwestern New Britain*. Madison, The University of Wisconsin Press.

May, J. 1976. *History of Lincolnshire, I, Prehistoric Lincolnshire*. Licoln, Cox and Wyman.

May, J. 1996. *Dragonby: Report on Excavations at an Iron Age and Romano-British Settlement in North Lincolnshire*. Volume 1. Oxford, Oxbow Books.

Mays, S. 1998. *The Archaeology of Human Bones*. London, Routledge .

McGrail, S. (ed.) 1982. *Woodworking Techniques before A.D.1500*. British Archaeological Reports International Series 129. Oxford, British Archaeological Reports.

McKerrell, H. and Tylecote, R. F. 1972. The working of copper arsenic alloys. *Proceedings of the Prehistoric Society* 38: 209-218.

McKinlay, J. 1994. A pyre and grave goods in British cremation burials; have we missed something? *Antiquity* 68: 132-134.

Megaw, R. and Megaw, V. 1986. *Early Celtic Art in Britain and Ireland*. Princes Risborough, Shire Publications.

Megaw, R. and Megaw, V. 1989. *Celtic Art: From its Beginnings to the Book of Kells*. London, Thames & Hudson.

Megaw, V. and Megaw, R. 1995. The Nature and Function of Celtic Art. In M. J. Green (ed.), The Celtic World: 345 – 375. London, Routledge.

Melas, E. M. 1989. Etics, emics and empathy in archaeological theory. In I. Hodder (ed.), *The Meaning of Things: Material Culture and Symbolic Expression*: 137-155. London, Unwin Hyman.

Miles, D. and Palmer, S. 1995. White Horse Hill. *Current Archaeology* 142: 372-378.

Miles, D., Palmer, S., Lock, G., Gosden, C. and Cromarty, A. M. 2003. *Uffington White Horse and Its Landscape: Investigations at White Horse Hill, Uffington, 1989 – 1995, and Tower Hill, Ashbury, 1993-4*. Oxford, Oxford Archaeological Unit Limited.

Miller, H. M. 2009. *Archaeological Approaches to Technology*. Walnut Creek, Left Coast Press.

Moore, C. N. 1973. Two examples of late Celtic and early Roman metalwork from South Lincolnshire. Britannia 4: 154-159.

Moreno García, M. 2004. Hunting practices and consumption patterns. In S. Jones O'Day, W. Van Neer and A. Ervynk (eds.), *Behaviour behind Bones: The Zooarchaeology of Ritual, Religion, Status and Identity*: 327-334. Oxford, Oxbow Books.

Morris, I. 1987. *Burial and Ancient Society*. Cambridge, Cambridge University Press.

Morteani, G. and Northover, P. J. (eds.) 1995. *Prehistoric Gold in Europe: Mines, Metallurgy and Manufacture*, Dordrecht, Kluwer Academic Publishers.

Mortimer, J. R. 1905. *Forty Years' Researches in British and Saxon Burial Mounds of East Yorkshire*. London, A. Brown and Sons.

Moscati, S. *et al.* (eds.) 1991. *The Celts*. Milan, Gruppo Editoriale Fabbri SPA.

Muhly, J. D. 1980. The Bronze Age setting. In T. A. Wertime and J. D. Muhly (eds.), *The Coming of Age of Iron*: 25-68. New Haven and London, Yale University Press.

Muir, R. J. and Driver, J. S. 2004. Identifying ritual use of animals in the northern American Southwest. In S. Jones O'Day, W. Van Neer and A. Ervynk (eds.), *Behaviour behind Bones: The Zooarchaeology of Ritual, Religion, Status and Identity*: 128-143. Oxford, Oxbow Books.

Mulville, J. and Outram, A. K. (eds.). 2005. *The Zooarchaeology of Fats, Oils, Milk and Dairying*. Oxford, Oxbow Books.

Murphy, H. 1992. From dull to brilliant: the aesthetics of spiritual power among the Yolngu. In J. Coote and A. Shelton (eds.), *Anthropology Art and Aesthetics*: 181-208. Oxford, Clarendon Press.

Muskett, G. 2004. Colour coding and the representation of costumes in Mycenaean wall painting. In L. Cleland and K. Stears (eds.), *Colour in the Ancient Mediterranean World*. British Archaeological Reports International Series 1267: 68-73. Oxford, John and Erica Hedges Limited.

Nassau, K. 1983. *The Physics and Chemistry of Colour*. New York, Wiley.

Neal, T. 2006. Blood and hunger in the Illiad. *Classical Philology* 101: 15-33.

Needham, S. P. 1990. *The Potters Late Bronze Age Metalwork – An analytical study of Thames Valley Metalwork in its settlement context*. British Museum Occasional Paper 70. London, British Museum.

Needham, S. P. and Bimson, M. 1988. Late Bronze Age Egyptian blue at Runnymede. *The Antiquaries Journal* 68: 314-315.

Niblett, R. 1999. *The Excavation of a Ceremonial Site at Folly Lane, Verulamium*. Britannia Monograph series 14. London, Society for the Promotion of Roman Studies.

Nosch, M. L. 2004. Red coloured textiles in the Linear B inscriptions. In L. and K. Stears (eds.), *Colour in the Ancient Mediterranean World*. British Archaeological Reports International Series 1267: 32-39. Oxford, John and Erica Hedges Limited.

Northover, P. J. 1989. Properties and use of arsenic-copper alloys. In A. Hauptmann, E. Pernicka and G. A. Wagner (eds.), *Archaeometallurgie der Alten Welt*: 111-118. Bochum, Selbstverlag des Deutschen Bergbau Museums.

Northover, P. J. 1994, Bronze, silver and gold in Iron Age Wessex. In A. P. Fitzpatrick and E. L. Morris (eds.), *The Iron Age in Wessex: Recent Work: 22-26*. Salisbury, Trust for Wessex Archaeology Ltd.

Northover, P. J. 1995. Bronze Age gold in Britain. In G. Morteani and P. J. Northover, (eds.), *Prehistoric Gold in Europe: Mines, Metallurgy and Manufacture*: 515-531. Dordrecht, Kluwer Academic Publishers.

Northover, P. J. 1998. Exotic alloys in antiquity. In T. Rehren, A. Hauptmann and J. D. Muhly, (eds.), *Metallurgica Antiqua, in Honour of Hans Gert Bachmann and Robert Maddin*: 113-121. Bochum, Deutsches Bergbau Museum.

Novalis (Friedrich Leopold Baron von Hardenberg). 1798. Aphorismen und Fragmente. *Athenaeum*, 1.1.

O'Brien, W. 2004. *Ross Island, Mining, Metal and Society in Early Ireland, Bronze Age Studies 6*. Galway, Department of Archaeology, National University of Ireland.

Ó hÓgáin, D. 1999. *The Sacred Isle: Belief and Religion in Pre-christian Ireland*. Woodbridge, Boydell Press.

Orme, B. J. 1982. Prehistoric woodlands and woodworking in the Somerset Levels. In S. McGrail, (ed.), *Woodworking Techniques before A.D.1500*. British Archaeological Reports International Series 129: 79-94. Oxford, British Archaeological Reports.

Ottaway, B. S. 1994. *Praehistorische Archaeometallurgie*. Espelkamp, Verlag Marie L. Leidorf.

Owoc, M. A. 2002. Munselling the Mound: The Use of Soil Colour as Metaphor in British Bronze Age Funerary Ritual. In A. Jones and G. MacGregor (eds.), *Colouring the Past*: 127-140. Oxford, Berg.

Palk, N. A. 1991. Metal Horse Harness of the British and Irish Iron Ages. Unpublished PhD thesis, Oxford.

Parfitt, K. 1986. The Deal man. *Current Archaeology* 101: 166-168.

Parfitt, K. and Green, M. 1987. A chalk figurine from Upper Deal, Kent. Britannia 18: 295-298.

Parfitt, K. 1991. Deal. *Current Archaeology* 125: 215-220.

Parfitt, K. 1995. *Iron Age Burials from Mill Hill, Deal*. London, British Museum Press.

Parfitt, K. 1998. A Late Iron Age burial from Chilham Castle, Nr Canterbury, Kent. *Proceedings of the Prehistoric Society* 64: 353-351.

Parker Pearson, M. 1993. The powerful dead: archaeological relationships between the living and the dead. *Cambridge Archaeological Journal* 3: 203-229.

Parker Pearson, M. 1996. Food, fertility and front doors in the first millennium B.C. In T. C. Champion and J. R. Collis (eds.), *The Iron Age in Britain and Ireland: Recent Trends*: 117-132. Sheffield, J. R. Collis Publications.

Parker Pearson, M. 1999. Food, sex and death: cosmologies in the British Iron Age with particular reference to East Yorkshire. *Cambridge Archaeological Journal* 9(1): 43-69.

Parker Pearson, M. 1999a. *The Archaeology of Death and Burial*. Stroud, Sutton Publishing Limited.

Parker Pearson, M. 1999b. Fearing and celebrating the dead in Madagascar. In Downes, J. and Pollard, T. (eds.), *The Loved Body's Corruption*: 9-18. Glasgow, Cruithne Press.

Parkin, D. 1992. Ritual as Spatial Direction and Bodily Diversion. In D. De Coppet (ed.), *Understanding Rituals*: 11-25. London, Routledge.

Parkinson, J. 2002. The gift/curse of "second sight". *History of Religions* 42(1): 19-58.

Pavey, D. *et al*. 1980. *Colour*. London, Marshall Editions Limited.

Paynter, S. 2007. Innovations in bloomery smelting in Iron Age and Romano-British England. In S. La Niece, C. Hook and P. Craddock (eds.), *Metals and Mining: Studies in Archaeometallurgy*: 202-210. London, Archetype Publications.

Pearce, J. 1997. Death and time: the structure of late Iron Age mortuary ritual. In A. Gwilt and C. Haselgrove (eds.), *Reconstructing Iron Age Societies*, Oxbow Monograph 71: 174-180. Oxford, Oxford Books.

Pearce, M. and Tosi, M. (eds.) 1998. *Papers from the EAA Third Annual Meeting at Ravenna, 1997*. Volume I: Pre-and Protohistory, British Archaeological Reports International Series 717. Oxford, Archaeopress.

Perrin, F. 2002. Die Mistel. In H. U. Cain and S. Rieckhoff (eds.), *Fromm Fremd Barbarisch: Die Religion der Kelten*: 15-16. Mainz, Von Zabern Verlag.

Pingel, V. 1995. Technical aspects of prehistoric gold objects on the basis of material analysis. In G. Morteani and P. J. Northover, (eds.), *Prehistoric Gold in Europe: Mines, Metallurgy and Manufacture*: 385-398. Dordrecht, Kluwer Academic Publishers.

Pleiner, R. 200. *Iron in Archaeology: The European Bloomery Smelters*. Prague, Archeologický Ústav AV ČR.

Pollard, J. 1996. Iron Age riverside pit alignments at St Ives, Cambridgeshire. Proceedings of the Prehistoric Society 62: 93-115.

Polomé, E. C. 1997. Zu keltischen Goetternamen. *Zeitschrift fuer Celtische Philology* 49/50: 737-748.

Poole, C. 1995. Pits and propitiation. In B. Cunliffe. *Danebury, An Iron Age Hillfort in Hampshire, Vol 6*. Council for British Archaeology research report 102: 249-275. York, Council for British Archaeology.

Pope, R. 2007. Ritual and the roundhouse. In C. Haselgrove and R. Pope (eds.), *The Earlier Iron Age in Britain and the near Continent*: 204-228. Oxford, Oxbow Books.

Price, N. (ed.) 2001. *The Archaeology of Shamanism*. London and New York, Routledge.

Price, N. 2001a, An archaeology of altered states. In N. Price (ed.), *The Archaeology of Shamanism*: 3-16. London and New York, Routledge.

Priston, A. V.. 1986. The hair. In I. M. Stead, J. B. Bourke and D. Brothwell (eds.), *Lindow Man, The Body in the Bog*: 71 London, Trustees of the British Museum.

Pyatt, F. B., Beaumont, E. H., Lacy, D., Magilton, J. R. and Buckland, P. C. 1991. Non isatis sed vitrium or, the colour of Lindow man. *Oxford Journal of Archaeology* 10(1): 61-73.

Pyatt, F. B., Beaumont, E. H., Buckland, D. C., Lacy, D., Magilton, J. R. and Storey, M. C. 1995. Mobilisation of elements from the bog bodies Lindow Man II and III, and some observations on body painting. In R. C. Turner and R. G. Scaife (eds.), *Bog Bodies: New Discoveries and New Perspectives*: 62-73. London, British Museum Press.

Pydyn, A. 1998. Universal or relative: Social economic and symbolic values in central Europe in the transition from Bronze Age to the Iron Age. In D. Bailey (ed.), *The Archaeology of Value*: 97-104. Oxford, British Archaeological Reports International Series 730.

Radford, C. A. R. 1936. The Roman Villa at Ditchley, Oxon. *Oxoniensa* 1: 24-69.

Raftery, B. 1994. *Pagan Celtic Ireland*. London, Thames & Hudson.

Raftery, B., Megaw, V. and Rigby, V. (eds.) 1995. *Sites and Sights of the Iron Age*. Oxbow Monograph 56. Oxford, Oxbow Books.

Rehren, T., Hauptmann, A. and Muhly, J. D. (eds.) 1998. *Metallurgica Antiqua, in Honour of Hans Gert Bachmann and Robert Maddin*. Bochum, Deutsches Bergbau Museum.

Reid, A. and MacLean, R. 1995. Symbolism and the social contexts of iron production in Karagwe. *World Archaeology* 27: 144-161.

Reynolds, P. J. 1974. Experimental Iron Age storage pits: an interim report. *Proceedings of the Prehistoric Society* 40: 118-131.

Rhys, J. 1980. *Celtic Folklore: Welsh and Manx, Volume I*. London, Wildwood House.

Rieckhoff, S. 2002. Die Religion der Kelten. In H. U. Cain and S. Rieckhoff (eds.), *Fromm Fremd Barbarisch: Die Religion der Kelten*: 129-179. Mainz, Von Zabern Verlag.

Rival, L. and Whitehead, N. L. (eds.) 2001. *Beyond the Visible and the Material: The Amerinianization of Society in the Work of Peter Rivière*. Oxford, Oxford University Press.

Robben, A. C. G. M. (ed.) 2004. *Death, Mourning and Burial, A Cross Cultural Reader*. Oxford, Blackwell Publishing.

Robertson, S. 1973. *Dyes from Plants*. New York, Van Nostrand Reinhold Company.

Robley, H. 189., *Moko or Maori Tattooing*. London, Chapman and Hall.

Rook, T., Lowery, P. R., Savage, R. D. A. and Wilkins, R. L. 1982. An Iron Age bronze mirror from Aston Hertsfordshire. *Antiquaries Journal* 62: 18-34.

Rozenberg, S. 2004. The role of colour in Herod's palace at Jericho. In L. Cleland and K. Stears (eds.), *Colour in the Ancient Mediterranean World*. British Archaeological Reports International Series 1267: 22-31. Oxford, John and Erica Hedges Limited.

Saint-Germain, C. 2005. Animal fat in the cultural world of the native people of Neartheastern America. In J. Mulville and A. K. Outram (eds.), *The Zooarchaeology of Fats, Oils, Milk and Dairying*: 107-113. Oxford, Oxbow Books.

Sands, R. 1997. *Prehistoric Woodworking*. London, Institute of Archaeology.

Saunders, N. J. 1999. Biographies of brilliance: pearls, transformations of matter and being, ca AD1492. *World Archaeology* 31(2): 243-257.

Saunders, N. J. 2002. The colours of light: materiality and chromatic cultures of the Americas. In A. Jones and G. MacGregor (eds.), *Colouring the Past*: 209-225. Oxford, Berg.

Saunders, N. J., and Gray, D. 1996. Zemís, trees, and symbolic landscapes: three Taíno carvings from Jamaica. *Antiquity* 70: 801-812.

Savory, H. N. 1964. A new hoard of La Tène Metalwork from Merionethshire. *Bulletin of the Board of Celtic Studies* XX(IV): 449-475.

Savory, H. N. 1964a. The Tal-Y-Llyn hoard. *Antiquity* 38: 18-31.

Savory, H. N. 1966. A find or early Iron Age metalworkfrom the Lesser Garth, Pentyrch, Glam. *Archaeologia Cambrensis* 115: 27-44.

Savory, H. N. 1976. *A Guide Catalogue of the Early Iron Age Collections*. Cardiff, National Museum of Wales Press.

Scarre, Ch. 2002. Epilogue: colour and materiality in prehistoric society. In A. Jones and G. MacGregor (eds.), *Colouring the Past*: 227-242. Oxford, Berg.

Schopenhauer, A. (transl. Payne, E. F. J.) (ed. Cartwright D. E.) 1994. *On Vision and Colours*. Oxford, Berg Publishers.

Schrijver, P. 1999. Henbane and early European narcotics. *Zeitschrift fuer Celtische Philologie* 61: 17-46.

Scott, B. G. 1990. *Early Irish Iron Working*. Belfast, Ulster Museum.

Scott, D. A., and Eggert, G. 2009. *Iron and Steel in Art*. London, Archetype Publications.

Selkirk, A. 1969. Garton Slack figurines. *Current Archaeology* XVII: 170.

Selwyn, L. 2004. *Metals and Corrosion, A Handbook for the Conservation Professional*. Ottawa, Canadian Conservation Institute.

Simon, F. M. 2008. Images of transition: ways of death in Celtic Hispania. *Proceedings of the Prehistoric Society* 74: 53-68.

Shamir, O. 2004. Coloured textiles found along the spice route joining Petra and Gaza – examples from the first to eighth centuries AD. In L. Cleland and K. Stears (eds.), *Colour in the Ancient Mediterranean World*. British Archaeological Reports International Series 1267: 49-52. Oxford, John and Erica Hedges Limited.

Sharples, N. 2007. Building communities and creating identities. In C. Haselgrove and R. Pope (eds.), *The Earlier Iron Age in Britain and the near Continent*: 174-184. Oxford, Oxbow Books.

Sharples, N. 2008. Comment I; contextualising Iron Age art. In D. Garrow, D. Ch. Gosden and J. D. Hill (eds.), *Rethinking Celtic Art*: 203-213. Oxford, Oxbow Books.

Shennan, S. 1993. Amber and its value in the British Bronze Age. Amber in Archaeology, Proceedings of the Second International Conference of Amber in Archaeology, Liblice 1990: 59-66. Praha, Institute of Archaeology.

Sheridan, A. and Davis, M. 1998. The Welsh jet set in prehistory; a case of keeping up with the Joneses? In A. Gibson and D. Simpson (eds.), *Prehistoric Ritual and Religion*: 148-163. Stroud, Sutton Publishing Limited.

Sievers, S. 1991. Fabrics. In S. Moscati *et al.*, (eds.), *The Celts*: 438-439. Milan, Gruppo Editoriale Fabbri SPA.

Sieveking, G. de. G. (ed.) 1971. *Prehistoric and Roman Studies: Commemorating the Opening of* the *Department of Prehistoric and Romano-British Antiquities*. Oxford, The Trustees of the British Museum.

Siikala, A. L. 1987. *The Rite Technique of the Siberian Shaman*. FF Communications No 220. Helsinki, Suomalainen Tiedakatemia.

Sillitoe, P. 1988. From head-dresses to head messages: the art of self decoration in the Highlands of Papua New Guinea. Man 23: 298-318.

Sinclair, A. 1995. The technique as symbol in late glacial Europe. *World Archaeology*, XXVII: 50-62.

Smith, K. 1977. The excavation of Winklebury Camp, Basingstoke, Hampshire. *Proceedings of the Prehistoric Society* 43: 31-129.

Smith, R. 1907-1909. On a late Celtic mirror found at Desborough, Northants and other mirrors of the period. Archaeologica 61: 329-346.

Smith, R. 1909. A hoard of metal found at Santon Downham, Suffolk. *Proceedings of the Cambridge Antiquarian Society* 13: 146-163.

Smith, R. 1912. On Late Celtic antiquities discovered at Welwyn, Hertfordshire. *Archaeologica* 63: 1-30.

Sopeña, G. 2005. Celtiberian ideologies and religion. E-Keltoi, Journal of Interdisciplinary Celtic Studies. 6. The Celts in the Iberian Peninsula. www.uwm.edu/Dept/celtic/ekeltoi/volumes/vol6/6_7/sopena_6_7.pdf.

Spindler, K. 1994. *The Man in the Ice*. London, Weidenfeld and Nicolson.

Spiro, M. E. 1990. On the Strange and the Familiar in Recent Anthropological Thought. In J. W. Stigler, R. A. Shweder and G. Hendt (eds.), *Cultural Psychology; Essays – Comparative Human Development*: 47-64. Cambridge, Cambridge University Press.

Spratling, M. G. 1970. The late Pre-Roman Iron Age bronze mirror from Old Warden. *Bedfordshire Archaeological Journal* 5: 9-16.

Spratling, M. G. 1972, *Southern British Decorated Bronzes of the Late Pre-Roman Iron Age*. Unpublished PhD thesis, London University.

Spratling, M. G. 1979. The debris of metalworking. In G. J. Wainwright, *Gussage All Saints: An Iron Age Settlement in Dorset*. Department of the Environment Archaeological Reports 10: 125-149. London, Her Majesty's Stationery Office.

Spratling, M. G. 2008. On the aesthetics of the Ancient Britons. In D. Garrow, D. Ch. Gosden and J. D. Hill (eds.), *Rethinking Celtic Art*: 185-202. Oxford, Oxbow Books.

Stacey, R. 2004. Evidence for the use of birch-bark tar from Iron Age Britain. *PAST* 47: 1-2.

Stahl, P. W. 1986. Hallucinatory imagery and origin of early South American figurines. *World Archaeology* XVIII: 135-150.

Stead, I. M. 1965. *The La Tène Cultures of Eastern Yorkshire*. York, The Yorkshire Philosophical Society.

Stead, I. M. 1967. A La Tène III burial at Welwyn Garden City. *Archaeologica* 101: 1-62.

Stead, I. M. 1971. Yorkshire before the Romans. In R. M. Butler (ed.), *Soldier and Civilian in Roman Yorkshire*: 21-43. Leicester, Leicester University Press.

Stead, I. M. 1971a. The reconstruction of Iron Age buckets from Aylesford and Baldock. In G. de. G. Sieveking (ed.) *Prehistoric and Roman Studies: Commemorating the Opening of the Department of Prehistoric and Romano-British Antiquities*: 250-282. Oxford, The Trustees of the British Museum.

Stead, I. M. 1979. *The Arras Culture*. York, The Yorkshire Philosophical Society.

Stead, I. M. 1985. *The Battersea Shield*. London, British Museum Publications Limited.

Stead, I. M. 1988. Chalk figures of the Parisi. *Antiquaries Journal* 68: 9-29.

Stead, I. M. 1991. *Iron Age Cemeteries in East Yorkshire*. London, English Heritage Press.

Stead, I. M. 1991a. The Snettisham treasure: excavations in 1990. *Antiquity* 65: 447-465.

Stead, I. M. 2006. *British Iron Age Swords and Scabbards*. London, British Museum.

Stead, I. M. and Rigby, V. 1986. *Baldock, The Excavation of a Roman and Pre-Roman Settlement, 1968-72*. Britannia Monograph Series No 7. London, Society for the Promotion of Roman Studies.

Stead, I. M. and Rigby, V. 1989. *Verulamium, the King Harry Lane Site*. English Heritage Archaeological Report No 12. Dorchester, English Heritage.

Stead, I. M. and Turner, C. 1985. Lindow Man. *Antiquity* 59: 25-29.

Stead, I. M., Bourke, J. B. and Brothwell, D. (eds.), 1986. *Lindow Man, The Body in the Bog*. London, Trustees of the British Museum.

Steinhoff Smith, R. 1989. Mourning becomes existence : Martin Buber's 'melancholy' ontogoly. *Journal of Religion* 69: 326-343.

Sterckx, C. 1997. Le roi blanc, le roi rouge et le roi bleu. *Zeitschrift fuer Celtische Philology* 49/50 : 837-846.

Stigler, J. W., Shweder, R. A. and Hendt, G. (eds.) 1990. *Cultural Psychology; Essays – Comparative Human Development*. Cambridge, Cambridge University Press.

Stjernquist, B. 1993. Amber in Iron Age finds in Sweden. Amber in Archaeology, Proceedings of the Second International Conference of Amber in Archaeology, Liblice 1990: 88-101. Praha, Institute of Archaeology.

Stratiki, K. 2004. Melas in Greek cultural practices: the case of heroic sacrifices in the Periegesis of Pausanias. In L. Cleland and K. Stears (eds.), *Colour in the Ancient Mediterranean World*. British Archaeological Reports International Series 1267: 106-109. Oxford, John and Erica Hedges Limited.

Straus, A. 2004. The meaning of death in Northern Cheyenne culture. In A. C. G. M. Robben (ed.), *Death, Mourning and Burial, A Cross Cultural Reader*: 71-76. Oxford, Blackwell Publishing.

Stroud, B. 2000. *The Quest for Reality*. New York and Oxford, Oxford University Press.

Sutherland, E. 1994. *In Search of the Picts*. London, Constable.

Svendsen, L. 2006. *Fashion: A Philosophy*. London, Reaktion Books.

Symonds, J. 1999. Songs remembered in exile. In A. Gazin-Schwartz and C. J. Holtorf (eds.), *Archaeology and Folklore*: 106-128. London, Routledge.

Tatton-Brown, V. and Andrews, C. 1991. Before the invention of glassblowing. In H. Tait (ed.), *Glass, Five Thousand years*: 21-61. New York, Harry N Abrams Inc Publishers.

Tait, H. (ed.) 1991. *Glass, Five Thousand years*. New York, Harry N Abrams Inc Publishers.

Tait, H., 1991, Introduction. In H. Tait (ed.), *Glass, Five Thousand years*: 8-20. New York, Harry N Abrams Inc Publishers.

Tilley, C. 1994. *A Phenomenology of Landscape: Places, Paths and Monuments*. Oxford, Berg.

Tilley, C. 1999. *Metaphor and Material Culture*. Oxford, Blackwell.

Tilley, C. 2004. *The Materiality of Stone*. Oxford, Berg.

Timberlake, S. 1990. Excavationas at Parys Mountain and Nantyreira. *Early Mining in the British Isles*. Plas Tan Y Bwlch Occasional Paper No 1: 15-21. Blaenau Festiniog, Plas Tan Y Bwlch, Snowdonia National Park Study Centre.

Timberlake, S. 1990a. Excavations and Fieldword on Copa Hill, Cwmystwyth, *Early Mining in the British Isles*. Plas Tan Y Bwlch Occasional Paper No 1: 22-29. Blaenau Festiniog, Plas Tan Y Bwlch, Snowdonia National Park Study Centre.

Timberlake, S. 1990b. Review of the Historical Evidence for the use of firesetting. *Early Mining in the British Isles*. Plas Tan Y Bwlch Occasional Paper No 1: 49-52. Blaenau Festiniog, Plas Tan Y Bwlch, Snowdonia National Park Study Centre.

Thomas, Ch. 1963. The interpretation of the Pictish symbols. *Archaeological Journal* 120: 31-97.

Topping, P. and Lynott, M. (eds.) 2005. *The Cultural Landscape of Prehistoric Mines*. Oxford, Oxbow Books.

Topping, P. and Lynott, M. 2005. Miners and mines. In P. Topping and M. Lynott (eds.), *The Cultural Landscape of Prehistoric Mines*: 181-191. Oxford, Oxbow Books.

Treherne, P. The warrior's beauty: the masculine body and self-identity in Bronze-Age Europe. *Journal of European Archaeology* 3.1: 105-144.

Turcan, R. 1996. The Cults of the Roman Empire. Oxford, Blackwell Publishers.

Turner, R. C. and Scaife, R. G. (eds.) 1995. *Bog Bodies: New Discoveries and New Perspectives*. London, British Museum Press.

Turner, V. 1967. *The Forest of Symbols: Aspects of Ndembu Ritual*. Ithaca New York, Cornell University Press.

Turner, V. 1969. *The Ritual Process: Structure and Anti-Structure*. New York, Aldine de Gruyter.

Tylecote, R. F. 1986. Fire-dog from burial 1. In I. M. Stead and V. Rigby, *Baldock, The Excavation of a Roman and Pre-Roman Settlement, 1968-72*. Britannia Monograph Series No 7: 387. London, Society for the Promotion of Roman Studies.

Tylecote, R.F. 1986a. *The Prehistory of Metallurgy in the British Isles*. London, Institute of Metals.

Vacano, O. W. v. 1960. *The Etruscans in the Ancient World*. London, Edward Arnold Publishers.

Van der Veen, M., Hall, A. R. and May, J. 1993. Woad and the Britons painted blue. *Oxford Journal of Archaeology* 12: 367-371.

Van der Veen, M. 1996. The plant microfossils from Dragonby. In J. May, *Dragonby: Report on Excavations at an Iron Age and Romano-British Settlement in North Lincolnshire*. Volume 1: 197-211. Oxford, Oxbow Books.

Van Gennep, A. 1969. *Les Rites de Passage: Etude Systematique des Rites*. Paris, Mouton & Co et maison des sciences de l'homme.

Venclova, N. 1991. Glass. In S. Moscati *et al.* (eds.), *The Celts*: 445-446. Milan, Gruppo Editoriale Fabbri SPA.

Verity, E. 1967. *Colour.* London, Leslie Frewin.

Vitebsky, P. 1994. *The Shaman. Voyages of the Soul: Trance, Healing and Ecstast from Siberia to the Amazon*. London, Macmillan.

Wainwright, G. J. 1979. *Gussage All Saints: An Iron Age Settlement in Dorset*. Department of the Environment Archaeological Reports 10. London, Her Majesty's Stationery Office.

Wait, G. A. 1985. *Ritual and Religion*. British Archaeological Reports Series 149. Oxford, British Archaeological Reports.

Wallis, R. J. 2003. *Shamans/Neo-Shamans: Ecstasy, alternative archaeologies and contemporary Pagans*. London, Routledge.

Warburton, D. A. 2004. The terminology of ancient Egyptian colours in context. In L. Cleland and K. Stears (eds.), *Colour in the Ancient Mediterranean World*. British Archaeological Reports International Series 1267: 126-130. Oxford, John and Erica Hedges Limited.

Watson, A. 2001. The sounds of transformation: Acoustics, monuments and ritual in the British Neolithic. In N. Price (ed.), *The Archaeology of Shamanism*: 178-192. London and New York, Routledge.

Watson, J. L. 1988. Funeral specialist in Cantonese Society: Pollution, performance and social hierarchy. In J. L. Watson and E. Rawski (eds.), *Death Ritual in Late imperial and Modern China*: 109-134. Berkeley, University of California Press.

Watson, J. L. and Rawski, E. (eds.) 1988. *Death Ritual in Late imperial and Modern China*. Berkeley, University of California Press.

Wells, P. S. 2001. *Beyond Celts, Germans and Scythians*. London, Duckworth.

Wells, P. S. 2007. Weapons, ritual and communication in Late Iron Age Northern Europe. In C. Haselgrove and T. Moore (eds.), *The Later Iron Age in Britain and Beyond*: 468-477. Oxford, Oxbow Books.

Wertime, T. A. and Muhly, J. D. (eds.) 1980. *The Coming of Age of Iron*. New Haven and London, Yale University Press.

Wertime, T. A. 1980. The pyrotechnical background. In T. A. Wertime and J. D. Muhly (eds.), *The Coming of Age of Iron*: 1-14. New Haven and London, Yale University Press.

Wiessner, P. 1989. Changing relations between the individual and society. In I. Hodder (ed.), *The Meaning of Things: Material Culture and Symbolic Expression*: 56-63. London, Unwin Hyman.

Wilkens, B. 2004. Roman suovitaurilia and its predecessors. In S. Jones O'Day, W. Van Neer and A. Ervynk (eds.), *Behaviour behind Bones: The Zooarchaeology of Ritual, Religion, Status and Identity*: 73-76. Oxford, Oxbow Books.

Willfort, R. 1959. *Gesundheit durch Heilkraeuter*. Linz, Rudolf Trauner Verlag.

Winckelmann, J. J. 1925. *Kleine Schriften zur Geschichte der Kunst des Altertums. Leipzig*, Inselverlag.

Wheeler, R .E. M. 1943. *Maiden Castle, Dorset*. Oxford, Oxford University Press.

Wheeler, T. S. and Maddin, R. 1980. Metallurgy and ancient man. In T. A. Wertime and J. D. Muhly (eds.), *The Coming of Age of Iron*: 99-126. New Haven and London, Yale University Press.

Whimster, R. 1977. Iron Age burial in southern Britain. Proceedings of the Prehistoric Society 43: 317-328.

Whimster, R. 1981. *Burial Practices in Iron Age Britain: A Discussion and Gazetteer of Evidence, Ca 700 BC-AD 43*. British Archaeological Reports Series 90. Oxford, British Archaeological Reports.

Whitehead, N. L. 2001. Kanaimà: Shamanism and ritual death in the Pakaraima Mountains, Guyana. In L. Rival and N. L. Whitehead (eds.), *Beyond the Visible and the Material: The Amerindianization of Society in the Work of Peter Rivière*: 235-246. Oxford, Oxford University Press.

Wood, J. 1997. The horse in Welsh folklore. In S. Davies and N. A. James (eds.), *The Horse in Celtic Culture*: 162-182. Cardiff, University of Wales Press.

Woodward, J. 1997. *The Theatre of Death*. Woodbridge, The Boydell Press.

Wuensche, R. 2004. Die Farbe kehrt zurueck. In V. Brinkmann and R. Wuensche (eds.), *Bunte Goetter: Die Farbigkeit Antiker Skulptur*: 10-23. Munich, Glyptothek.

Wuensche, R. 2004a. Zur Farbigkeit des Muenchner Bronzekopfes mit der Siegerbinde. In V. Brinkmann and R. Wuensche (eds.), *Bunte Goetter: Die Farbigkeit Antiker Skulptur*: 133-147. Munich, Glyptothek.

Young, S. M. M., Pollard, A. M., Budd, P. and Ixer, R. A. (eds.) 1999. *Metals in Antiquity*, British Archaeological Reports 792. Oxford, Archaeopress.

Ziderman, I. 2004. Purple dying in the Mediterranean world: characterisation of biblical Tekhelet. In L. Cleland and K. Stears (eds.), *Colour in the Ancient Mediterranean World*. British Archaeological Reports International Series 1267: 40-45. Oxford, John and Erica Hedges Limited.

Zimmer, S. 1997. Archaismen in Culhwch ac Olwen. *Zeitschrift fuer Celtische Philology* 49/50: 1033-1053.

http://www.hippy.com/albion/woad_and_modern_tribal_bodyart_i.htm

Appendix 1

Sites

Site	Description of site, site spots or findings	Colours	OS number	Reference	Discussed in Chapter
Danebury Hill Fort, Hampshire	Pits burials dug into white chalk and filled with human and/or animal remains, quern stones, iron implements worked bone or antler, charred grain and plant remains, timber, charcoal, burnished pottery shards. Infill in sequential materials and colours. Evidence of violent deaths.	Black, white and sometimes red as main colours	SU323376	Cunliffe and Poole 1991a; Cunliffe 1984; Cunliffe 2003; Hill 1995	9
Dragonby Iron Age Settlement, North Lincolnshire	Blue green stained bone needle possible evidence for tattooing 18 woad fragments together with other seed remains in waterlogged pit	Blue and green	SE907139	Greep, 1996, May 1996, Van der Veen, 1993;1996	10
Gussage All Saints Iron Age Settlement, Dorset	Pit burials, similar to Danebury Hill Fort, cut into white chalk landscape; infill consists of human and/or animal remains, quern stones, bone or antler, iron and pottery. Inverted gender related depositions, high percentage of violent deaths or anomalies on bodies, high percentage of neonatal	Black, white and red as main colours	SU001129	Wainwright 1979; Keepax 1979	9
Uffington White Horse, Oxfordshire	A 110 m long stylised representation of a white horse cut into the chalk landscape of a hill and filled with white chalk puddle	White against seasonally changing colour of landscape	SU301866	Miles, Palmer et. al. 2003	5
Winklebury Hill Fort, Hampshire	One of six pits on hill fort site contained remains of red deer and twelve foxes, possibly alive at deposition	Red	SU6152	Wait 1985, Green 1992, Smith 1977	9

Appendix 2

Artefacts

Artefact	Discovered	Description	Colours	Reference	Discussed in Chapter
Mirrors					
Arras, Yorkshire	1875	Undecorated iron mirror, with bronze mount inhumation burial context	Black, shimmering	Stead 1979	6, 9
Arras, Yorkshire	1815-17	Undecorated iron mirror, now lost, inhumation burial context	Black, shimmering	Stead 1979	6, 9
Aston Hertfordshire	1979	Bronze mirror, decorated; burial context; grave goods included fragments of burnt red clay, burnt charcoal and two re-burnt pots	Red, black, shimmering effects	Rook *et al.* 1982, British Museum	9
Balmaclellan, Galloway	1861	Bronze, decorated, found together with other objects in bog, wrapped in cloth	Red, shimmering effects	Smith 1907, MacGregor 1976, Edinburgh National Museum	9
Billericay I Essex	1860	Bronze, decorated, burial context	Red, shimmering effects	Smith 1907 – 1909 Colchester Museum	9
Billericay II Essex	1860	Bronze, decorated, burial context	Red, shimmering effects	Joy 2007 Colchester Museum	9
Billericay III Essex	1860	Bronze, decorated, burial context	Red, shimmering effects	Joy 2007 Colchester Museum	9
Birdlip Gloucester	1879	Bronze, decorated, discs of red glass, female grave context (although not certain); grave goods included allegedly a gold plated silver brooch and beads of amber, jet and grey marble	Red, shimmering effects	Smith 1907; Jope 2000; Joy 2008 Gloucester Museum	6, 7, 9
Brecon Beacon, Powys	?	Iron plate with decorated bronze handle, burial context	Black, red, shimmering	Joy 2007	9
Bridport West Bay, Dorset	1930 – 1934	Undecorated bronze mirror handle, burial context	red	Joy 2007	9
Bryher, Isle of Scilly	1999	Decorated bronze mirror, cist burial context, with sword	Red, shimmering	Johns 2002	9
Bulbury, Dorset	1881	Decorated bronze mirror, burial context	Red, shimmering, amber coloured glass beads	Cunnington 1884	9
Chilham Castle, Kent	1993	Bronze, decorated, female grave context, placed beneath human remains, undecorated side facing up; brooch on top may indicate wrapping	Red, possibly wrapping (extinction of colour)	Parfitt 1998; Canterbury Museum	9

Artefact	Discovered	Description	Colours	Reference	Discussed in Chapter
Colchester, Essex	1904	Bronze, intricate basket weave decoration, handle with red glass stud; burial context; grave goods included bronze cup with a handle bearing a red glass boss and two red ware mica coated flagons	Red, shimmering effects	Fox 1948; Fox 1958; Jope 2000 Colchester Museum	6, 9
Desborough, Northants	1908	Bronze, very articulated basket weave design, possibly grave context	Red, shimmering effects	Smith 1907 - 1909, London British Museum	6, 9
Dorton, Buckinghamshire	1976-77	Bronze, cross hatched areas, void forms background, cremation burial context, placed beneath human remains, undecorated side facing up	Red, shimmering	Farley 1983 Aylesbury Buckinghamshire County Museum	6, 9
Garton Slack, Yorkshire	After 1968	Iron, undecorated, female inhumation burial context	Black, shimmering	Stead 1979 Hull and East Riding Museum	9
Great Chesterford, Essex	1959	Bronze, cross hatched areas, red opaque glass studs, void form the background, possibly female grave context.	Red, shimmering effects	Fox 1960, Cambridge Museum	6
Holcombe Devon	1970	Bronze, detailed basket weave decoration, handle with red glass stud, placed upside down in a pit within an Iron Age enclosure underlying a Roman villa, possibly wrapped in organic material such as cloth or leather	Red, shimmering effect, wrapped (extinction of light)	Fox and Pollard 1973 British Museum	6, 9
Latchmere Green Hampshire	1964	Bronze, irregular oblong blocks of cross hatching; cremation burial context, cremated remains were deposited in pale red pottery jar, which was possibly re-burnt	Red, shimmering effect, red and black context colours	Fulford and Creighton 1998 Andover Museum	6, 9
Llanwnda, Pembrokeshire	?	Bronze mirror handle with red glass stud	red	Boon 1979 Cardiff National Museum	6, 9
Llechwedd-Du Bach Mirror, Merioneth	1860	plain bronze plate and back, found with tinned plate, burial context	No shimmering effect, reddish bronze	Jope 2000; Fox 1925 Cardiff National Museum of Wales	6, 9
Mount Batton, Stamford Hill, Plymouth, Devon	1864-5	Bronze, crude cross hatching, burial context	Red, shimmering effect, red grave goods	Cunliffe 1988	6, 9
Nijmegen, Holland	1928	Bronze decorated, red enamel, burial context	Red, shimmering, blue, glass vessels ?	Dunning 1928 Valkhoff Museum Nijmegen	6, 9
Old Warden I Bedforshire	1950	Bronze; decorated with precise regular geometrical basket weave, burial context	Red, shimmering effect	Spratling 1970 Bedford Museum	6, 9
Old Warden II, Bedfordshire	1950s	Bronze mirror handle, possibly found with amphora, burial context	red	Joy 2007	9

Artefact	Discovered	Description	Colours	Reference	Discussed in Chapter
Pegsdon, Shillington, Bedfordshire	2000	Copper alloy, decorated, burial context,	Red, shimmering effect,	Burleigh and Megaw 2007, Luton Museum	9
Portesham Dorset	1994	Bronze , decorated, burial context	Red shimmering effect,	Joy 2007 Dorset County Museum	9
Portland Dorset	1878	Plain bronze, burial context	Red	Fox 1949; Joy 2007	9
Trelan Bahow (St Keverne), Cornwall	1833	Bronze, decorated, cist burial context, blue grey and black glass beads	Red, shimmering effect, blue and grey black	Smith 1907, Jope Rogers 1873, British Museum	9
Wetwang Yorkshire	2001	Iron mirror, cart burial context, tassel of horse hair decorated with blue beads and coral,	Red, black, some blue	Hill 2001 British Museum	6, 9
Wetwang Slack Yorkshire	1985	Iron mirror, cart burial context, some coral and bronze grave goods	Black, some red	Dent 1985 British Museum	6, 9
Verne Portland Dorchester, Dorset	1878	Fragment decorated bronze mirror, burial context	red	Joy 2007	9
Terrets					
Auchendolly, Kirkcudbright	Before 1885	Crecentic bronze terret, formal symmetrical design	Red and yellow	MacGregor 1976, Edinburgh National Museum	7
Balmuildy, Lanarkshire	1922	Platform terret, decorated square cells	Red and turquoise	MacGregor 1976, Hunterian Museum Glasgow	7
Bapchild , Kent	Before 1860	Crescentic bronze terret with symmetrical curvilinear design, decoration	Red with blue spots	Henry 1933, British Museum	7
Birrens, Dumfriesshire	1936	Platform terret with straight bar, decoration three cushion like rectangles	Red and blue	Macgregor 1976, Dumfries Museum	7
Bolton, Lancashire	?	Crescentic, flowing scrolls, set off against red enamel field, spots of blue glass	Red, blue spots	MacGregor 1976, unknown site, Bolton Museum	7
Colchester, Essex	?	Sequence of plain bronze diamonds set off against enamel round an inverted crescent	red	Jope 2000, Colchester Museum	7
Ditchley, Oxfordshire	1935	Lipped terret, lipped,	red	Radford 1936, Ashmolean Museum	7
Fremington Hagg I, North Yorkshire	Before 1833	Platform terret with series of spots	red	MacGregor 1976, Yorkshire Museum	7
Fremington Hagg, II, North Yorkshire	Before 1833	Platform terret with three oblong platforms each having four geometrical insets	Blue and red	Macgregor 1976 Yorkshire Museum	7
Great Chesters, Northumberland	?	Platform terret, swastika like cells	red	Macgregor 1976, University Museum Newcastle Upon Tyne	7
High Rochester, Northumberland	1852-55	Platform terret, simple rectangular panels	red	MacGregor 1976, Alnwick Castle Museum	7
Lakenheath, Suffolk	Before 1933	Crescentic bronze terret with symmetrical curvilinear design	Red with blue spots	Henry 1933, Ashmolean Museum	7

Artefact	Discovered	Description	Colours	Reference	Discussed in Chapter
Middlebie, Dumfiresshire	1737	Platform Terret bronze with one projection on each side, two over top,	Blue central glass spot in ring of opaque red	MacGregor 1976, Edinburgh National Museum	7
Owmby, Lincolnshire	?	Crescentic flange terret, curvilinear decoration, tails flowing	red	May 1976, Scunthorpe Museum	7
Polden Hill, Somerset	1800	Lipped Bronze terrets with curvilinear design	red	Brailsford 1975, British Museum	7
Richborough, Kent Terret	Before 1926	Crescentic terret, bronze symmetrical curvilinear design	Red with blue spots	Henry 1933 Richborough Site Museum	7
Runnymede, Berkshire	?	Crescentic bronze terret,wave crests against glass background	red	Henry 1933, London British Museum	7
Saham Toney, Norfolk	1838	Petal like cells on bronze (possibly brass?)	Red, some yellow and blue	MacGregor 1976, Norwich Castle Museum	7
Snettisham Norfolk	?	Bronze lipped terret, spots	red	Green 1972, Norwich Museum	7
Staines, Middlesex	?	Bronze crescentic terret, curvilinear design over crescent face	red	Unpublished, Jope 2000	7
Traprain Law, East Lothian	1921	fragmentary platform terret, ring adorned with three rectangles and geometrical cells,	Red and yellow	MacGregor 1976, Edinburgh Museum	7
Westhall, Suffolk	1855	Crescentic flange terrets, curvilinear	red	Henry 1933, London British Museum	7
Weybread Suffolk	1978	Bronze terret crescentic e, design worked out over coloured background, zigzag bordering	red	Martin 1978, Ipswich Museum	7
Whaplode, Lincolnshire	Between 1958 - 1964	Red enamel ornament	red	Moore 1973, Lincoln Museum	7
Whitton Vale of Glamorgan	1965	Bronze Terret, hot glass in large drilled holes, set off by drilled dot borderings and patterns of decorated areas	red	Savory 1966, Cardiff National Museum of Wales	7
Other Horse Fittings					
Polden Hill Harness Fittings, Somerset	1803	Part of the Polden Hill hoard, eared mounts of bronze with curvilinear red hot glass decoration	Red	Brailsford 1975a, Jope 2000 British Museum	7
Santon Eared Mounts, Norfolk	1897	Eared bronze mounts with curvilinear design, red glass decoration	red	Smith 1909 Cambridge Museum	7
Seven Sisters Hoard, Glamorgan	1905	Bronze strap joiner curvilinear design with red glass decoration, strap junction with triangular red and yellow enamel decoration on brass	Red and bronze, equally proportions of red and yellow on brass (possibly combinations of yellow, red, white and blue)	Davies and Spratling 1976; Davis and Gwilt 2008, National Museum of Wales	7
Westhall Mount, Suffolk	1855	Bronze mount with curvilinear red glass decoration, blue spots	Red and some blue	Henry 1933, British Museum	7

Artefact	Discovered	Description	Colours	Reference	Discussed in Chapter
Weapons					
Battersea Shield London	1857	Complete shield cover made out of bronze with decorated panels, swastika motif against red hot glass	Red against reddish gold	Stead 1985 London British Museum	6, 7
Bugthorpe Sword and Scabbard, Yorkshire	1850	Bronze scabbard with flowing curvilinear design and cross hatching the chape frames of the Meare Sword or the Cambridge chape	Play on light	Stead, 1979; Jope 2000 British Museum	6
Cambridge Chape	?	Bronze chape with basket weave decoration around four pointed star.	Play on light	Jope 2000 Cambridge Museum of Archaeology	6
Isleworth Sword	?	Iron sword blade with brass foil stamps, depicting an animal, perhaps a horse or a dragon	Gold colour on black	Craddock *et al* 2004; Stead 2006 British Museum	4, 8
Kirkburn Sword and Scabbard, Yorkshire	1987	Iron sword, hilt and pommel made of horn covered with iron sheets, iron back of the scabbard, front part of scabbard and the chape of bronze, all decorated with red glass	Red, black, bronze, white	Stead 2006; Gosden and Hill 2008 British Museum	7, 9
Llyn Cerrig Bach Mount, Anglesey	1942	Repoussé bronze mount, ambiguous design, use unclear.	Reddish bronze, play on light	Megaw and Megaw 1989; Macdonald 2007; Jope 2000 National Museum of Wales	6, 8
Meare Chape	?	Bronze chape frame with cross hatching as part of curvilinear design	Reddish bronze, play on light	Jope 2000 Taunton Somerset Museum	5
Tal–y–llyn Hoard, Merionethshire	1963	Reddish bronze shield mounts and boss, showing triskeles, mounts with regular cross hatching forming background to triskeles, tinned bronze plaques, mount with figurative decoration, brass key plate	Reddish to golden, play on light through cross hatching, golden coloured brass	Savory 1964 National Museum of Wales	4, 6
Thames Spear	Before 1931	Iron spear with highly polished bronze cross hatched decoration found in the river Thames, cross hatching forms background	Black, reddish, play on light	Jope 2000 British Museum	5
Witham Shield, Lincoln	1826	Bronze shield cover featuring a central domed umbo with red coral inlays	Red on reddish bronze	Jope 2000 British Museum	7

Artefact	Discovered	Description	Colours	Reference	Discussed in Chapter
Vessels and discs					
Aylesford Bucket	1886	Bucket made out of yew, bound with one iron and two bronze bands, repoussé decoration, found in cremation burial in Aylesford	red	Stead 1971a British Museum	9
Baldock Bucket, Herts	1911	Bucket made out of yew, feet covered with bronze sheets, bronze swing handles, found in cremation burial in Baldock	red	Stead 1971a Letchworth Museum	9
Great Chesterford Bucket, Essex	?	Wooden bucket (species uncertain) with bronze handles and bronze bands, decorated with red hot glass, found in burial	red	Stead 1971a Cambridge Museum	9
Monasterevin Bronze Disc, Kildare, Ireland	?	One of a number of cupped bronze discs or dishes found in County Kildare in Ireland. The surface features curvilinear decoration with fine cross hatching and deliberate slashes	Shimmering effect through cross hatching, disturbed by slashing	Armstrong 1923 British Museum	6
Snowdon Feline Head Caernarvonshire	1974	Feline head, part of a tube handled bronze patera found in Snowdon, decorated with red hot glass	Red on bronze	Savory 1976 Jope 2000 National Museum of Wales	7
Tankard Handles from Seven Sisters, Neath	1975	Tankard handle made out of bronze. Cross hatching as part of an elaborate design which utilizes both void and decorated areas	Cross hatched shimmering effect	Grimes 1939 Jope 2000 National Museum of Wales	6
Welwyn Cremation Burial Vessels	1912	Red pottery amphorae and cordoned pottery tazza found in the two main Welwyn cremation burial vaults together with black coated urns containing cremated bones	Red black and white	Smith 1912, 3 British Museum	9
Torcs					
Snettisham Torcs Norfolk	1948 - 1990	Number of gold and electrum torcs found as part of a dry hoard. The ring terminals of some of the torcs show fine chasing and repoussé work, main body of the torcs is made out of twisted, cabled or braided strands of gold	Shimmering and dazzling effects	Brailsford and Stapley 1972, British Museum	6
Ipswich Torcs, Suffolk	1968	Six gold torcs found as a dry hoard	Twisted design creates dazzling effect	Brailsford and Stapley 1972; Stead 1991a , British Museum	6

Artefact	Discovered	Description	Colours	Reference	Discussed in Chapter
Figurines					
Ballachulish Woman, Scottish Highlands	1880	Wooden figurine carved out of oak, nearly five foot in height, quartz pebbles in eye sockets, asymmetric face, left side damaged, found in bog weighted down.	Reddish dark wood , brilliant quite quartz pebble, shiny surface through crisp and sharp carving	Coles 1990 National Museum of Scotland	6, 8
Battersea London	1993	Little chalk head found in the Thames carved from a small chalk nodule.	White chalk, luminosity enhanced in water	Cotton 1996 Museum of London.	5
Caerwent Monmouthshire	1971	Sandstone head containing a high quantity of quartz found in a shrine in house VIII in Caerwent.	Yellowish white, quartz provides higher luminosity	Boone 1976 Newport Museum, Gwent	6
Kingsteignton Idol, Devon	1867	Wooden figurine carved out of alder, asymmetric face,	Pinkish wood, shiny surface facets	Coles 1990 Newton Abbot Museum	6, 8
Mill Hill, Deal Kent	1987	Chalk figurine, 18cm in height, found at bottom of a shaft, perhaps initially deposited in a niche in the all above.	White against black background	Parfitt and Green, 1987 Dover Museum	5
Roos Carr Figurines, Yorkshire	1836	Five (initially possibly eight) anthropomorphic figures, a boat with an animal head and some shields carved out of yew. Some figures have quartz pebbles as eyes and in pubic area, perhaps representing semen.	Red wood, white shiny quartz, shiny surface, luminosity enhanced through insertion in water	Coles 1990 Hull and East Riding Museum	6, 8
Yorkshire Chalk Figurines, Yorkshire	various	Fifty to sixty white chalk figurines ranging in height from 70mm to 170 mm, some decapitated, some with belts, some hooded, some with swords, some show deliberate defacing and scratching	White against black, scratched effects on luminosity	Stead 1988; Stead 1971; Dent 1978; Mortimer 1905; Jope 2000 Hull and East Riding Museum	5
Other					
Baldock Fire Dog, Herts.	1911	One of a number of iron fire dogs found in Welwyn rite cremation burials	Black, but also red through association with fire	Tylecote 1986 British Museum	9

Appendix 3

Human Remains

Body or Burial	Discovered	Description	Colours	Reference	Discussed in Chapter
Lindow Man II, Cheshire	1984	Iron Age bog body found in Lindow Moss; killed in a violent ritual involving bludgeoning, garrotting and slashing his throat; red fox fur armband.	Black, white and red by association with bog, bones and blood ;	Pyatt et al. 1991, Pyatt et al. 1995 Stead and Turner 1985, Stead et al. 1986 British Museum	9, 10
Lindow Man III, Cheshire	1987	Iron Age bog body found in Lindow Moss; may have had copper based body decoration.	Possibly red, black, green or blue body decoration	Pyatt et al. 1991, Pyatt et al. 1995	10
Queens Barrow, Arras Yorkshire	1815-17	female inhumation burial, orientated North South, necklace of over one hundred glass beads; beads are blue with varying patterns of white or yellow, apart from a small number which are a translucent green decorated with white or yellow scrolls; grave also contained an amber ring, a decorated bronze brooch with red coral inlay, a bronze pendant, two bracelets, a toilet set consisting of a bronze nail cleaner and bronze tweezers and a gold finger ring	Blue and yellow, also some gold, bronze and red	Stead 1979; Whimster 1981	9
Welwyn Cremation Burials	1912	Two main cremation burials, both contained red amphorae and cordoned pottery tazza, urns containing cremated bones probably coated with black varnish, burial A contained copper alloy face masks and studs, burial B two silver cups,	Red, black and white, some silver	Smith 1912; Whimster 1981	9
Welwyn Garden City Burial Site, Herts.	1965	La Tène III burial shows evidence that body had been wrapped in a bear skin prior to cremation, part of the floor covered by mat made probably from oak bark, fragment of animal skin, possibly belonging to a black stoat was found in a corner of the grave	Wrapping, concealment, black	Stead 1967; Whimster 1981	9
Welwyn Garden City Burial Site, Herts.	1965	Cremation burial of adult male with numerous amber beads, translucent brown and yellow glass beads with opaque yellow on the surface, dark blue glass beads with eye fragments, segments of glass bracelets made out of brown glass with meandering tails of opaque yellow glass; set of twenty four gaming pieces in four groups of six pieces, coloured opaque blue, opaque yellow, opaque white and translucent green respectively. The pieces were decorated with spirals of opaque white glass in a translucent green or wine coloured ground. All pieces feature five eyes, apart from one blue piece which has seven eyes. Colours possibly relating to reversal of gender.	Blue and yellow	Stead 1967; Whimster 1981	9

Body or Burial	Discovered	Description	Colours	Reference	Discussed in Chapter
Wetwang Chariot Woman, Wetwang, Yorkshire	2001	Inhumation burial of older female, showing evidence of childbirth, dislocated shoulder and haemangioma; torso covered with pig bones, a single bronze strap union decorated with coral placed underneath her knees and an iron mirror with horse hair tassel and blue beads placed across her lower legs; the body of a cart was placed over her body, though wheels were found separately at the north end of the grave; horse bits with red glass or enamel inlays, terrets and trap unions decorated with coral studs; each terret has five red coral studs held in place by bronze pins; one red glass stud replaced or substituted a coral stud; adhesive used for the harness fittings was made out of black birch bark tar mixed with another resin or tar from a coniferous plant, possibly pine.	Red, against bronze and black, some blue, contrast to white chalk landscape	Hill 2001; Giles 2008; Stacey 2004	9

Appendix 4

Classical Sources for Body Decoration

Author and text	Date	Original	Translation
Strabo Geography 4.5.2	1st century BC	οι δε ανδρες ευμηκεσετεροι των κελτων εισι και ησσον ξανθοτριχες χαυνοτεροι δε τοις σωμασι.	The men of Britain are taller than the Celts, and not so yellow-haired.
Diodorus Siculus Library of History, 5.27-32	1st century BC	Οι δε Γαλαται τοις μεν σωμασιν εισιν ευμηκεις, ταις δε σαρξι καθψγροι και λευκοι, ταις δε κομαις ου μονον εχ φυσεωσ ξανθοι, αλλα και δια της κατασκευης επιτηδευουσιν αυξειν την φυσικην της χροας ιδιοτητα. Τιτανου γαρ αποπλυματι σμωντες τας τριξας συνεχως και απο των μετωπων επι την χορυφην και τους τενοντας ανασπωσιν ωστε την προσοψιν αυτων φαινεσθαι Σατυροις και Πασιν εοικυιαν. Παχυνονται γαρ αι τριχες απο της κατεργασιασ, ωστε μηδεν της των ιππων χαιτης διαφερειν.	(…) and their hair is blond, but they also make it their practice by artificial means to increase the distinguishing colour which nature has given it. For they are always washing their hair in lime-water, and they pull it back from the forehead to the top of the head and back to the nape of the neck, with the result that their appearance is like that of Satyrs and Pans, since the treatment of their hair makes is so heavy and coarse that it differs in no respect from the mane of horses.
Caesar De Bello Gallico 5.14	1st century BC	Omnes vero se Britanni vitro inficiunt, quod caeruleum efficit colorem, atque hoc horridiores sunt in pugna aspectu	All the Britons stain themselves with Vitrum which produces a blue colour, and this gives them a more terrifying appearance in battle
Ovid Amores 2.16, 39	1st century BC	Non ego Paelignos videor celebrare salubres, non ego natalem, rura paterna, locum – sed Scythiam Ciliciasque feros viridesque (or vitreosque) Britannos, quaeque Prometheo saxa cruore rubent.	I seem to dwell not in the healthful Paelignian land nor in my natal place, my father's acres – but in Scythia, and among the fierce Cilicians, and the woaded Britons, and the rocks ruddy with Promethean gore
Propertius Elegies 2.18D, 1-4	1st century AD	Nunc etiam infectos demens imitare Britannos, ludis et externo tincta nitore caput? Ut natura dedit sic omnis recta figurast: turpis Romano Belgicus ore color. An si caeruleo quaedam sua tempora fuco tinxerit, idcirco caerula forma bonast?	Do you still in your madness imitate the painted Britons and play the wanton with foreign dyes upon your head? All beauty is best as nature made it: Belgic colour is shameful on a Roman face. If some woman has stained her forehead with skyblue dye, is sky blue beauty on that account to be desired?
Pomponius Mela De Chorographia 3. 6,51	1st century AD	tantum pecore ac finibus dites, - incertum ob decorem an quid aliud - vitro corpora infecti.	So much that ; rich only in livestock and their territory – it is uncertain whether as an embellishment or for some other reason – they dye their bodies with vitrum
Martial Epigrams 11.53	1st century AD	Claudia caeruleis cum sit Rufina Britannis edita, quam Latiae pectoral gentis habet!	Claudia Rufina, though she is sprung from the sky blue Britons how she possesses the feelings of the Latin race

Author and text	Date	Original	Translation
Pliny Naturalis Historia 22.2	1st century AD	Similis plantaginis glastum in Gallia vocatur, Brittannorum coniuges nurusque tot corpore oblitae quibusdam in sacris nudae incedunt Aethiopum colorem imitantes	In Gaul, there is a plant like the plantain called glastum; with it the wives of the Britons and their daugthers in law stain all the body and at certain religious ceremonies march along naked, with a colour resembling that of Ethiopians
Tacitus, Agricola 29	1st century AD	Omnis iuventus et quibus cruda ac viridis senectus, clari bello et sua quisque decora gestantes	All the young men and famous warriors whose old age was fresh and green every man wearing the decorations he had earned
Solinus, Collectanea Rerum Memorabilium 22. 12	3rd century AD	Regionem partim tenent barbari, quibus per artifices plagarum figuras iam inde a pueris uariae animalium effigies incorporantur, inscriptisque uisceribus hominis incremento pigmenti notae crescunt; nec quicquam mage patientiae loco nationes ferae ducunt, quam ut per memores cicatrices plurimum fuci artus bibant	The area is partly occupied by barbarians on whose bodies, from their childhood upwards, various forms of living creatures are represented by means of cunningly wrought marks; and when the flesh of the person has been deeply branded, then the marks of the pigment get larger as the man grows, and the barbaric nations regard it as the highest pitch of endurance to allow their limbs to drink in as much of the dye as possible through the scars which record this
Herodian, Roman History 3.14,7	3rd century AD	Ta de swmata stizontai grafaiV PoikilaiV Kai zwon pantodapwn eikosin. oqten oude amfiennuntai, ina mh skepwsitou swmatoV taV grafaV	They also tattoo their bodies with various patterns and pictures of all sorts of animals. Hence the reason why they do not wear clothes, so as not to cover the pictures of their bodies
Claudian II, Poem on Stilicho's Consulship 2.247	4th century AD	Inde Caledonio velata Britannia monstro, ferro picta genas, cuius vestigia verrit caerulus Oceanique aestum mentitur amictus	Next spoke Britain, clad in the skin of some Caledonian beast, her cheeks marked with iron, while a sea green mantle giving the illusion of the swell of the ocean rippled over her foot-prints
Claudian II, De Bello Gothico, 416-18	Early fifth century AD	Venit et extremis legio praetenta Britannis, quae Scotto dat frena truci ferroque notatas perlegit exanimes Picto moriente figuras	Next came the legion that had been stationed in remote Britain, that had bridled the wild Irish and, as the Pict lay dying, had gazed upon the lifeless forms, marked by Iron

Author and text	Date	Original	Translation
Bede Ecclesiastical History of the English Nation 1.1	8th century AD	Et cum plurimam insulae partem, incipientes ab Austro, ossedissent, contigit gentem Pictorum de Scythia, ut perhibent, longis nauibus non multis Oceanum ngressam, circumagente flatu uentorum, extra fines omnes Brittaniae Hiberniam peruenisse, eiusque septentrionales oras intrasse, atque inuenta ibi gente Scottorum, sibi quoque in partibus illius sedes petisse, nec inpetrare potuisse. Est autem Hibernia insula omnium post Brittaniam maxima, ad occidentem quidem Brittaniae sita; sed sicut contra Aquilonem ea breuior, ita in meridiem se trans illius fines plurimum protendens, usque contra Hispaniae septentrionalia, quamuis magno aequore interiacente peruenit. Ad hanc ergo usque peruenientes nauigio Picti, ut diximus, petierunt in ea sibi quoque sedes et habitationem donari.	When they, beginning at the south, had made themselves masters of the greatest part of the island, it happened, that the nation of the Picts, from Scythia, as is reported, putting to sea, in a few long ships, were driven by the winds beyond the shores of Britain, and arrived on the northern coast of Ireland, where, finding the nation of the Scots, they begged to be allowed to settle among them, but could not succeed in obtaining their request. Ireland is the greatest island next to Britain, and lies to the west of it; but as it is shorter than Britain to the north, so, on the other hand, it runs out far beyond it to the south, opposite to the northern parts of Spain, though a spacious sea lies between them. The Picts, as has been said, arriving in this island by sea, desired to have a place granted them in which they might settle.